Lecture Notes of the Institute for Computer Sciences, Social Informatics and Telecommunications Engineering   92

Radu Popescu-Zeletin   Karl Jonas
Idris A. Rai   Roch Glitho
Adolfo Villafiorita (Eds.)

e-Infrastructure
and e-Services
for Developing Countries

Third International ICST Conference, AFRICOMM 2011
Zanzibar, Tanzania, November 23-24, 2011
Revised Selected Papers

 Springer

Volume Editors

Radu Popescu-Zeletin
Fraunhofer FOKUS
Kaiserin-Augusta Allee 31, 10589 Berlin, Germany
E-mail: radu.popescu-zeletin@fokus.fraunhofer.de

Karl Jonas
Fraunhofer FOKUS
Schloss Birlinghoven, 53754 Sankt Augustin, Germany
E-mail: karl.jonas@fokus.fraunhofer.de

Idris A. Rai
The State University of Zanzibar
Zanzibar City, Tanzania
E-mail: rai@suza.ac.tz

Roch Glitho
Concordia University
Montreal, Quebec, H3G 2W1, Canada
E-mail: glitho@ece.concordia.ca

Adolfo Villafiorita
FBK Center for Information Technology
38122 Trento, Italy
E-mail: adolfo.villafiorita@fbk.eu

ISSN 1867-8211   e-ISSN 1867-822X
ISBN 978-3-642-29092-3   e-ISBN 978-3-642-29093-0
DOI 10.1007/978-3-642-29093-0
Springer Heidelberg Dordrecht London New York

Library of Congress Control Number: 2012933853

CR Subject Classification (1998): K.4, C.2, K.3, K.6, K.5, J.1

Typesetting: Camera-ready by author, data conversion by Scientific Publishing Services, Chennai, India

Printed on acid-free paper

Springer is part of Springer Science+Business Media (www.springer.com)

Preface

Africa is a continent of diversity that is facing dramatic changes in its social, political, and economical environments. Its population is reaching for the billion, and in particular young Africans demand their share of social inclusion, educational opportunities, and prosperity.

Information and communication infrastructures provide the basis to access knowledge worldwide, blurring social and economic differences while opening opportunities that never existed before. E-services enable or enhance healthcare, agro-business, higher education, and social participation.

Its history, its geography, its (low) population density, and its culture make Africa different from regions in the world where ICT provides ubiquitous access. Technologies as well as services need to be adapted to local challenges. An example are the submarine cables that are becoming available, providing huge capacities at the landing spots but that now need to be connected to the inland population. There is no time to waste, because young Africans will not accept the digital divide. The Internet must come to every household, or the young population will leave their home environment in search for a better future.

The challenge is to reduce operational and capital cost to provide affordable connectivity to all. Services must be adapted to local needs, and business concepts must meet local requirements. New ideas must be tested and prove their superiority; they need to be evaluated, discussed, and challenged.

This is where the AFRICOMM conference comes in. For several years now it provides an open forum where researchers and politicians can discuss new ideas and new challenges. While some of us see the M-services as the logical next step in ICT evolution (which takes place in Africa first), others see them as an intermediate step based on the fact that low-bandwidth services are required because low-bandwidth networks need to be used. Should applications adapt to frequent network failures, or should networks be improved and become more reliable? Probably both, and small steps toward the all-inclusive ICT future were made at this year's AFRICOMM.

Energy efficiency has been a challenge in Africa for many years and is now becoming a hype in Europe as well. And, finally, is the (ICT) situation for rural communities in Europe, the USA or Australia so much different from the situation in rural Africa? While Europeans took advantage of the fact that a monopoly of operators installed copper networks all over the countries, these networks do not meet the requirements of high bandwidth for all. New ideas are required but not only for Africa; perhaps the technological future starts in Africa. Above all, developing countries need relevant content in computing disciplines to spur development. Does it suffice to teach in Africa the same computing programs that are taught in developed worlds? AFRICOMM 2011 provided answers to these questions.

The African continent is, more than ever, in need of cutting-edge and relevant e-infrastructures, e-services, and enabling policies. AFRICOMM was established in 2009 in Mozambique and continued 2010 in Cape Town as a series of annual conferences. Its contributions have been published in the Springer's *Lecture Notes on ICST*.

This book contains the proceedings of AFRICOMM 2011, which was held in Zanzibar. The book contains high-quality papers thanks to the effective and highly specialized Technical Program Committee, which also diligently selected the best paper that was awarded at AFRICOMM 2011. The best paper is entitled "Relevant Computing Curricula in Sub-Saharan Africa," written by Anthony Rodrigues, Isabella Venter, Godfrey Mills, Hussein Suleman, John Edumadze and Idris Rai from universities in Kenya, Uganda, South Africa, and Ghana.

November 2011

Radu Popescu-Zeletin
Karl Jonas
Idris A. Rai
Adolfo Villafiorita

Organization

Conference Committee

Honorary Chair
Radu Popescu-Zeletin   Fraunhofer FOKUS, Germany

General Chair
Karl Jonas   Fraunhofer FOKUS, Germany

TPC Chair
Idris A. Rai   Makerere University, Uganda

TPC Chair - Communication Infrastructures in Developing Countries
Roch Glitho   Concordia University, Canada

TPC Chair - Track on Electronic Service, ICT Policy, and Regulatory Issues for Developing Countries
Adolfo Villafiorita   FBK Center for Information Technology, Italy
Darelle Van Greunen   NMMU, South Africa

Sponsorship Chair
Alessandro Zorer   CREATE-NET, Italy

Local Chair
Omar Fakih Hamad   University of Dar-es-salam, Tanzania
Adnan Ali   State University of Zanzibar, Tanzania

Publicity Chairs
Henning Köhler   Fraunhofer, Germany
Wolf Konrad   Fraunhofer, Germany

Workshops and Demos Chair

Dirk Elias   Fraunhofer, Portugal

Posters and Panels Chair

Hans Schotten   University of Kaiserslautern, Germany

Technical Program Committee

Hisham Abdelsalam	Cairo University, Egypt
Max Agueh	ECE Paris, France
Rui Aguiar	Aveiro University, Portugal
Abdelfettah Belghith	National School of Computer Sciences (ENSI), Tunisia
Dennis Bjiwaard	Inertia Technology, The Netherlands
Tony Bulega	Makerere University, Uganda
Patrick Chikumba	University of Malawi, The Polytechnic, Malawi
Andy Dearden	Sheffield Hallam University, UK
Kevin Doolin	Waterford Institute of Technology, Waterford, Ireland
Dirk Elias	Fraunhofer Portugal Research Center, Portugal
Babak Farshchian	SINTEF ICT, Norway
George Ghinea	Brunel University, UK
Roch Glitho	Concordia University, Canada
Darelle Van Greunen	NMMU, South Africa
Omar Fakih Hamad	University of Dar-es-salam, Tanzania
Ayman Hassan	Orange, France
Janardhan Iyengar	Franklin and Marshal College, USA
Karl Jonas	Franhofer FOKUS, Germany
Matthew Kam	Carnegie Mellon University, USA
Joseph Kizza	University of Tennessee Chattanooga, USA
Santhi Kumaran	Kigali Institute of Science and Technology, Rwanda
Tayeb Lemlouma	Irisa, France
Jude Lubega	Makerere University, Uganda
Tshilidzi Marwala	University of Johannesburg, South Africa
Sougata Mekherjea	IBM Research, India
Edwards Mutafungwa	Helsinki University of Technology, Finland
Faiza Najjar	National School of Computer Sciences (ENSI), Tunisia
Manuel Urueña	Pascual - Universidad Carlos III de Madrid, Spain

Table of Contents

Track II: Electronic Services, ICT Policy, and Regulatory Issues for Developing Countries

Scenario to Serve Remote Areas in Emerging Countries with the Village Internet Service Station

Gaël Fromentoux, Arnaud Braud, and Xavier Marjou

Orange Labs OLNC/RD/CORE/NAS
2 Av . Pierre Marzin France - 22 307 Lannion
{gael.fromentoux,arnaud.braud,
xavier.marjou,nathalie.omnes}@orange-ftgroup.com

Abstract. The provision of Internet to remote areas has raised interests for many years and is particularly tough to address when the expected average revenue per user is low. Providing access to internet services in remote rural areas of emerging countries is a challenge for operators. Actually, the segments addressed may be key to their future market growth given the numerous but un-wealthy end-users. However, we tackle this issue in emerging markets by proposing an incremental scenario which conciliates investors' return on investment and end-users' needs and desire for communication. Actually, we first derive a set of requirements from the market segmentation and then specify the architecture for the low entrant segment. Furthermore, we show that there are possibilities to progressively address new segments in an incremental approach of the architecture first deployed. We also propose design to cost scenarios by combining deployed mobile-phone networks and intermittent data link. In every village an Internet service station is shared among all users in the village.

Keywords: Emerging countries, market segmentation, remote areas, mobile network, design to cost scenario, network architecture, Internet Service Station.

1   Introduction

It is essential for operators to be present in emerging countries given the population needs and the huge expected growth. To address the specific needs of these populations, the context inherent to emerging countries must be carefully considered. Actually, there are huge differences between the different populations, in terms of revenues in terms of needs and challenges to address. We thus start our work by recapitulating, in section 2, the market segmentation, in which are highlighted four different segments: "Low Entrant", "Young and Householder", "Self-employed" and "Premium".

Once these segments have been identified, it clearly appears that each segment is related to a different ecosystem. Thus, we secondly give an insight into the emerging countries ecosystem in section 3. In this section, we focus in particular on the population needs and on its available means in terms of revenue, device, and network coverage. We also briefly describe the potential business model. After having studied the ecosystem for the first 3 segments, we thirdly derive requirements that can be

R. Popescu-Zeletin et al. (Eds.) AFRICOMM 2011, LNICST 92, pp. 1–13, 2012.

applied to one or several of the previous segments. Additional business and technical requirements are stated for remote areas. The 2 most numerous segments with the lowest Average Revenue Per User, ARPU, are found there. These requirements are thus mixed to derive our case.

In section 4, we present our architecture scenarios. We combine the "Low Entrant" architecture scenario with remote areas constraints. The solution first capitalizes on already deployed 2G mobile networks, makes the best possible use of the intermittent data link resources and relies on a "hawker" network for large data clumps. Free services and free contents can be delivered over this low-cost technical solution to a cash-challenged population. By adding features to the already deployed architecture, paying services and contents can then be offered to wealthier but still low income end-users. Increments are thus highlighted to serve the "Young and Householder" segment. In any case, we rely on the 2G mobile network for the signaling and the control of the services. The operators are thus implied in the essential functions of authentication and billing.

We finally conclude our study in section 5, and give some perspectives concerning deployments of the Internet Service Station and future studies.

2   Market Segmentation

It is best addressing the emerging countries ecosystem by taking into account the market segmentation. Mobile content and data services require granular customer segmentation if operators are to meet the needs of a diverse customer base. The majority of users rely on prepayment, thus operators have little information on which to build a decent segmentation model. The analytic capabilities of service, delivery and billing platforms appear quite basic, which hinders an efficient segmentation [1], [2]. The classic pyramid socio-economic segmentation accommodates the split between:

- Urban and rural mobile users: rural users tend to be situated in the lower part of the pyramid and nearly all those at the apex are urban dwellers.
- Smartphone and low-end phone users: the smart-phones users again populate the upper echelons of the pyramid
- Enterprises and consumers: the enterprise users tend to generate higher revenues per user and are accommodated at the top of the pyramid.

2.1   The Entrant or Cash-Challenged Target

Low Entrant customers may either live in rural or in urban areas. They only hold basic telephones allowing voice calls and SMS. They further don't own any credit card and thus prepayment is their privileged payment mechanism [3].

Even though 3G becomes available in big cities, Low Entrant customers' subscription is limited to 2G. They have an intermittent access to a data network (IP), which means they are not permanently under network coverage, moving from 2G areas to white network zone areas. In some countries, they even have smart-phones and access to the data network via hot-spots, for example via some retailer's hotspots. In such a case, the hot-spot must benefit from a link to an ISP, which can be a satellite, a WiMAX or a 3G link. Having numerous retailers is essential to best serve people even in remote areas.

For this segment, the business model is to offer free content to improve the image of the operator in a given country. Revenues can be obtained by advertising. We suggest delivering free on demand content or free services to this segment. The delivered content is limited to on-demand or delinearized content because the data network coverage is not always possible. Low Entrant end-users are mainly interested in content and services related to their everyday concerns, thus we should focus learning, democracy and health, sports and entertainment.

2.2   Young and Householder Target

Most people within this segment are "cash challenged" and earn low incomes and thus typically avoid subscriptions. However, some of them may have some money and will thus be qualified as "low income users". This population holds second-hand mobile-phone, yet some phones may have multimedia capabilities (e.g. J2ME toolkit, Bluetooth…). These users generally have more than one SIM card.

Prepayment should be deployed so that the operator, or a third-party content publisher, can generate revenues. Alternatively, the end-user can pay in cash at a retailer store. Advertising should also be supported to generate alternative revenues. As in the previous segment, the delivered content is limited to free services and on-demand content, because the data network is often not permanently available. Furthermore, we should focus on learning, democracy and health, sports and entertainment.

2.3   Self-employed Target

The "Self-employed" population is technically aware and earns modest means. It lives mostly in urban areas and has access to 2G or 3G networks. Self-employed customers use second-hand mobile-phones having multimedia capabilities (e.g. J2ME toolkit, Bluetooth…). Yet they do not own any credit card. These customers should be delivered both live and on-demand content. As in the previous segments, learning, democracy, health, sports and entertainment services should be privileged. The proposed business model is the same as for the "Young and Householder" target.

2.4   Premium Target

The Premium customers are technically aware and earn important revenues with regards to the average population. They live mostly in urban areas. These customers use a mobile-phone that has multimedia capabilities (e.g. J2ME toolkit, Bluetooth…) and further own a PC, a TV. This segment further subscribes to 2G and 3G data (IP) and each user can have more than one SIM card. Usually Free-To-Air, FTA, satellite is available for TV. The motivation is to re-use the numerous Free-To-Air channels available in satellite distribution and plug into it the possibility to retrieve Content on Demand, CoD.

Table 1. Overview of the four segments

Segment	Low-entrant	Young and Householder	Self-employed	Premium
Population	Young and numerous. Very low income. High illiteracy.		Technically aware. Modest means.	Technically aware. Important revenues.
Geographic area	Urban and rural		Urban	
Language	Mainly vernacular. Mainly oral.			National, international
Device	Single second-hand mobile-phone	Second-hand mobile-phone with multimedia capacities.	3G second-hand mobile-phone with multimedia capacities.	Mobile-phone with multimedia capacities, TV, and PC.
Service	Health, Education, business, on-demand contents and Sports		Live and on-demand. Business, Sports, Education.	
Payment	None	Prepayment		Pre & post paid
Access type	2G only. Possibly intermittent via hot-spot.		2G, and 3G, wifi, wimax, satellite More than one SIM card.	
Business model	Improve operator image, Offer free content, Advertising.	Prepaid content. Advertising.		
Constraint	Strong basis of retailers required.		Raise business interest	Availability of broadcast channels

3   Requirements

3.1   Requirements for the "Low Entrant" Segment

The immense majority of these users have a single device which is the mobile phone. They live in rural and urban areas and are not permanently under data network coverage. They furthermore have no money to "waste". However, access to Internet for health, education and business is demanded by this population. Thus we suggest providing them a free service. For a higher chance of success, we recommend starting with a simple understandable proposition. Then, the transition path towards paying services will be ensured by other segment of populations.

The operator could even try to make a market name with audiovisual delivery to these people. It is difficult to predict whether Digital Rights Management, DRM, will be mandatory or not. Yet DRMs may be required, even if the content is free-of-charge to comply with the regulation. One can manage the distribution of the content by restricting the delivery to authenticated SIM cards owner. In most countries, the problem of limiting the redistribution of content produced locally must be addressed.

For example, in Benin, local content is submitted to DRM while Hollywood blockbusters are not. This would need to be checked specifically per country basis. We thus consider the DRM requirement as optional. Some few people may have a TV set with Free To Air channels. However, we assume that there is fewer opportunity in this content value chain for operators as it would require expensive equipment for the end-user. Eventually, the mobile 2G network coverage is often present when the density of population is high. This is good news for investors which can re-use this infrastructure.

3.2   Requirements for the "Young and Householder" Segment

For this segment of population, the assumptions remain the same as for the "Low Entrant" segment, except we now assume end-users have some limited money they would be ready to spend in services and contents related to entertainment, learning, democracy and health.

3.3   Requirements for the "Self-employed" Segment

For this segment of population, the assumptions are different from the previous ones as it targets rather wealthy users that can afford expensive devices, including second-hand 3G devices. Living in urban areas, these end-users can have access to on-demand and live content. Still, they might not own a TV set.

3.4   Additional Requirements for Remote Areas

The solution must minimize the need for energy. For example, one scenario could ensure that the end-user handset battery will be charged enough for displaying a whole content before having to recharge the battery.

While often covered by 2G mobile networks, the data link is rarely available. Thus the solution must try to make the best of the 2G mobile network large presence in emerging countries and put forward a proposal to overcome the lack of data link. It should be noticed that even for "off the grid" areas solutions have emerged to cope with the lack of energy [4].

Partnerships with various organizations to drive the deployment of these shared-user model initiatives would enhance the success. These can be local or international partners providing micro-loans to local entrepreneurs or charitable and development organizations acting as the sponsors of such projects. This is well-known as in the Village Phone partnerships in Bangladesh and Uganda and the PayPhone Lady joint projects in East Africa.

4   Scenario for the Remote Areas

We consider in the following sub-section 4.1 rural and low income end-users. We thus assume end-users have no smart-phone and have no permanent access to data network nor to 3G network coverage. Most often, people do not own any PC or TV.

The goal of this section is to outline an architecture for delivering internet and contents to the Low Entrant segment. This scenario can be thought as the first step of a two-step scenario, the second step being described in the Section 4.2. The solution though not designed to deliver services for self-employed and premium segments can benefit from the presence of a self-employed person who can play the role of retailer within the remote community.

4.1   Intermittent Data Link - The Village Internet Service Station

This scenario is designed to fit with the lack of network and the low amount of money that the users can afford to get the service. We thus choose to provide a simple and cost-efficient architecture, providing the users with limited but essential functions. In addition, the operator should seek partnerships to benefit from the help of a network of retailers who are connected to a data network. These retailers will motivate the users to try the service and help them to use the services, as for instance downloading Content on Demands, CoD. It is also important to notice that this scenario does not require the user to have a SIM card. When trying to create a "Village Internet" we were faced with 3 major issues:

- The business model
- The network architecture
- Applications that could run on the network architecture

Operators tend to struggle when dealing with big populations with low income as it is not their usual target. To provide data services to African rural population a new approach had then to be found. A strong point with this market segment however was the very strong sense of community and sharing. So instead of trying to address every member of a given community it is easier to address the community as an entity. This was for example the approach taken by MTN when they designed the village phone offer. We decided to extend this approach to internet services and create "village internet", for further reference we design as village a subset of a rural community. A village shares geographical proximity but ultimately is a business entity (i.e. the bigger the business is the smaller the cluster becomes, ultimately becoming a 1 family cluster or 1 person cluster like in Europe but requiring a new approach for the network component). In every village one self-employed person buys and rents an Internet service station that is shared among all users in the village. This corresponds to one user with a higher ARPU that operators can easily address. We call it: the Internet service station owner. He will play the role of retailer.

In addition to a network coverage that does not spread across the whole territory, the population might not easily adopt new telecommunication services. To overcome these issues, we suggest relying on the Internet service station owner who will provide hotspots and help the end-users in having access to the service. The next challenge was to get a data network to our "village internet", for this we derived the concepts of data ferries. As presented in [5], we showed that using hawkers was a cost efficient solution to bring large amounts of data to specific users. We also showed that with 2G mobile networks we could bring some interactivity to services when needed.

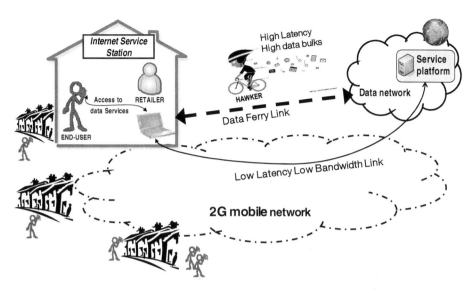

Fig. 1. Intermittent data link - Architecture for areas deprived of data network link

Our "village internet" station would thus use 2 distinct networks: the first one being a 2G+ network for small volume of data and for real time signaling, the second one would be a network of "hawkers" for large data clumps.

A "hawker" is a person travelling the country to ferry data to remote areas deprived of data network access. In our case the "hawker" would not need a high end device since the targeted device is known and should offer USB ports. The hawker network would thus only consist of travelers carrying USB keys. As far as network coverage is concerned, the 2G coverage should be the same as of the already deployed village phones (using Yagi antennas to extend coverage where needed). The hawker network has a virtually infinite coverage range but the higher the range is the more latency in transfer happens (note we are speaking in days here not in milliseconds). Due to the nature of our hawker data link the number of "village internet" station would be however limited also.

An issue with the internet service station we just imagined is that the network connecting it to the rest of the word is congested by design. This is however an issue that African population shares as a whole. Even at a "country" level for example the international peering available for Niger is only 60 Mb/s. This implies that the usual Over The Top, OTT, players are not adapted for African networks as they tend to optimize their services for speed in North America and Europe. So our internet service station would need its own subset of applications designed to operate on our dual network environment.

Those applications should be designed in 2 modes, "online" and "offline". Online mode is almost the typical web applications barring some restrictions on how data is stored and the need to be able to deal with requests coming from the offline application. The application in offline mode is the one dealing with users. As such, the offline application only has access to its own sub-domain (local databases and storage) and some remote fetching methods published by the framework (such as login, short Message and content Ordering). Through the framework (API allowing developers to handle the multiple networks and the intermittent network link), the offline application can request updates or content to be delivered through the data ferries. May the online application be updated (by its developer or due to its nature (for example allowing internet users to post content), the update will automatically be spread to villages by data ferries.

By creating the village internet service station we took the first step in bringing low cost internet to rural populations. As mentioned earlier the next steps would occur when the business grows and more and more users become interested. Possible future work would imply connecting our station to a local wifi mesh bringing new types of high speed local services as described in the next section.

4.2   One Step Forward: Permanent Data Link – Overall Description of the Scenario

The IP connectivity brought to the retailer's premises is obviously the main issue to consider. For the most remote areas this data link is barely available since no one can afford it or by lack of network coverage. Thus, we recommended overcoming this difficulty by relying on an intermittent access through a network of "hawkers" as described in section 4.1.

Now, we consider a case when the retailer devices have access to the open Internet. Any network can be used for this purpose: satellite return-channel, WiMAX, long range Wifi, DSL network and 3G, for example with a 3G router. One possibility is to rely on a satellite-based connection [6]. Another possibility, which should generally make more sense for mobile operators business is to provide it based on a 3G offer.

The end-user owns a mobile phone with any SIM card. Its phone has a Wi-Fi or Bluetooth connectivity.

Full access to the services is possible through the Internet Service Station over this data link. The end-user fetches the data and can begin its service at the retailer's premises. At his convenience, the end-user can also first fetch the data at the retailer premises and begin his service session later. He is authenticated by the 2G mobile network and can pre-order his services (see "services control" in Fig.2).

If there is an additional marketing requirement for it, it may be possible to restrict this service to end-users being the operator's subscriber (e.g. in order to have cheaper SMS, in order to use USSD instead of SMS…). For instance, in case of content delivery, this basic mobile phone will have to embed a light software and have storage capabilities. Its battery capacity should further allow viewing the whole content without access to the electric network. Please note that the device may be shared between several end-users.

The retailer is most often a self-employed person who owns a device connected to the Internet and can thus provide access to a Wi-Fi hot spot. Then, the retailer device may for example be a Home Gateway, a 3G router or a satellite equipment.

The architecture we recommend is depicted in the following figure.

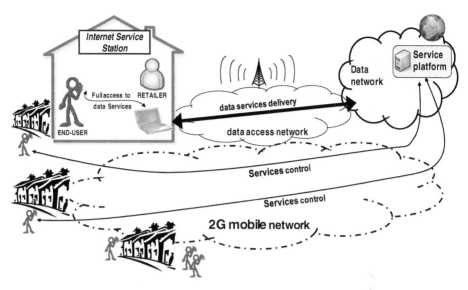

Fig. 2. Permanent data link - Architecture for remote areas

The Strengths, Weaknesses, Opportunities and Threats, SWOT, related to this architecture are depicted in the following table.

Table 2. Low Entrant SWOT

Strengths	− Attract customers and limit churn − Possibly free of charge for the end-user − Rural end-users are eligible to this service − Possible evolution for paying content − Light identification is sufficient
Weaknesses	− Need a permanent data link − Possibly no direct revenue for the operator − Need for advertisement − Specific mobile handsets that must embed multimedia soft − Retailers must be properly trained − Limited to CoD files of small duration
Opportunities	− Improve operators image − Local Contents − Take advantage of mid-range multimedia features phones − Telecom manufacturers are proposing solutions [7]
Threats	− Lack of affordable mobile phone compliant with our requirements − No qualified retailers' network

4.3   Open Issues

The retailers' business model needs to be deeply studied. As a matter of fact, operators often need to have a direct relationship with the end-user. Thus the retailers shall not process the whole transaction on their own.

One noticeable limitation is that the end-user can not benefit from live services. However, CoD can be downloaded at the retailer's premises and will be consumed later. To cope with the storage capacity of the low phone devices, short duration CoDs should be privileged. We propose to deliver free content to these customers. This enables to deliver audiovisual contents even to people that can only afford 2G short subscriptions, which will help in attracting new customers and limiting churn. Local contents either national or regional should be privileged since they are adapted to the people's culture, language and concerns (e.g. FM and wiki-radio). For some services this can be a problem since the low-entrant end users will not necessarily own a device that will have the ability to receive content.

4.4   Two Steps Forward: Increments to Deliver Services to the Young and Householder Segment

This step provides a network solution where the end-user still does not have permanent data network coverage. With respect to the architecture settled in previous section, the main new function needed here is a payment mechanism. Of course this also imposes to include an authentication function of the person who pays for the service. In this scenario, the DRM function is mandatory for the delivery of contents. Like for the previous segment, local content should be privileged. Still, the operator should seek partnerships to benefit from a network of retailers.

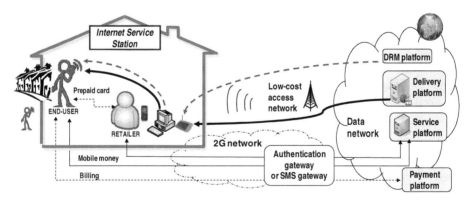

Fig. 3. Permanent data link - Architecture for remote areas

4.5   Additional Elements in the Architecture

We propose an architecture that is very similar to the previous one, with the following additional elements:

- Payment Platform: will be in charge of hosting payment accounts. It may be implemented by Orange Money.
- SMS Gateway: gives the possibility to pre-download CoD at the retailer's shop.

If the user wants to download a big file (e.g. CoD) and the IP network has a really poor bandwidth, it will take a high amount of time to download the file. In order to make it possible to deliver big files, we think that a mechanism authorizing pre-download of the file at the retailer's premise should be possible. The first solution is based on SMS. A possible implementation of such a scenario is the following: when outside the retailer's hotspot, but when under 2G coverage, it should be possible for the application in the end-user device to order a pre-download of the CoD file by sending an SMS with the name of the wanted CoD and the identity of a retailer, which would be its mobile phone number. When the service platform receives this SMS, it should in turn send a SMS to the retailer to ask him to download the file.

This option is particularly interesting in remote areas where the user always visit the same hotspot.

4.6   Payment Mechanism

We recommend the "Pay as you go" mechanism which is a pre-payment technique allowing the end-user to buy short duration content.   Several implementations can be foreseen for this mechanism:

- Scratch prepaid cards: When the end-user wants to buy a specific service, he buys the card to the retailer 1€, 2€ or 3€…
- Mobile money: The end-user transfers money from his account to the service provider account thanks to a transaction done with his mobile phone. This is in the same vein than Orange-Money [8].

Advantage: In both cases, the retailer does not intervene in the monetary transaction when the service is ordered. In the former case, the retailer may be more motivated to sell scratch cards by benefiting from wholesale buying. In the latter case, mobile transfers are cheaper. Drawback: It is not easy to secure the transaction of delivering a service over an unknown network. However it may be possible to re-use the mechanism used by World Food Program in Zambia [9]. Typically, a first payment code and a service identifier is sent in a SMS by the user in order to gets its service. Once the content has been successfully retrieved, the mobile phone software automatically sends another SMS to terminate the transaction.

It may also be questionable whether a cache is needed or not at the retailers' premises [10]. Indeed it may be that some application tricks allow to fill the retailer's cache before the end-user requires the file, for example with a pre-download mechanism as previously described.

Another open issue is about DRM. We believe that a DRM implementation is technically feasible; the major difficulty will first be to know whether right-owners of the content will accept the risk of delivering files with DRM on mobile phones. Indeed, even though DRM provides a certain level of security, one can never be sure it will not be broken. The second difficulty will be to identify an integrator ready to implement and be responsible of DRM for this scenario.

The Strengths, Weaknesses, Opportunities and Threats related to this architecture are depicted in the following table.

Table 3. Young and Householder SWOT

Strengths	− 2G and 3G not needed for the end-user − Attract customers and limit churn − Monetize operator's services − Architecture in delta with previous segment − Authentication via MSISDN is not necessary − Rural end-users are eligible to this service − Incremental scenario with respect to the "low entrant" scenario
Weaknesses	− Specific Mobile handsets must embed multimedia soft − The retailers need to be properly trained − Limited to users that are ready to occasionally buy some CoD. − Limited to CoD files of small duration (depending on the storage)
Opportunities	− Deliver local services & contents − Take advantage of middle-range mobile phones − Value the operator's image (RSE) − Telecom manufacturers are proposing solutions [7]
Threats	− No qualified retailers' network

5   Conclusion

We tackled the provision of data link to remote areas in emerging markets. To overcome the low average revenue per user, we proposed an incremental low cost architecture. The village internet service station takes the first step in bringing low cost internet to rural populations. To comply with the low-cost constraint this solution capitalizes on already deployed 2G mobile networks, makes the best possible use of the intermittent data link resources and relies on a "hawker" network for large data clumps.

Starting with shared enablers and a shared platform allows launching a service while minimizing the related cost. It allows operator to reinforce its position and make a market name while serving a numerous population deprived of internet access. This win-win approach thus conciliates investors' return on investment and end-users' needs and desire for communication. This solution will further allow operators to get feedback from end-users and gather statistics about their real usages.

This study has already led to two different PoC (Proof of Concept) presented in [5] for a Hawker solution which ferries data in white network zones and presented in [6] to bring contents to the low entrant segment.

We identified the wiki-radio service as a good candidate to test the interest and feasibility of this solution. Indeed, this service is of high interest in remote areas – local news, remote communities with own interests and language, voice quality – and gathers the technical and economical challenges since it addresses the least wealthiest segments. We are currently leading a study for a deployment in Mali with local actors. Also, possible future work would imply connecting our station to a local Wifi mesh bringing new types of high speed local services.

References

1. Dawar, N., Chattopadhyay, A.: Rethinking Marketing Programs for Emerging Markets. Long Range Planning 35(5), 457–474 (2002)
2. Mobile contents and applications in emerging markets: operators strategies, Ovum (January 2010)
3. Mobile money in emerging markets, Ovum (June 2009)
4. Johnson, et al.: The Village base station. In: D.L. NSDR 2010 Proceedings of the 4th ACM Workshop on Networked Systems for Developing Regions (2010)
5. Marjou, X., et al.: Using hawkers to ferry Internet data. In: The 14th International Symposium on Wireless Personal Multimedia Communications Symposium, WPMC under review, Brest (2011)
6. Fromentoux, G., et al.: Content Delivery Architectures for Segmented Emerging Markets. In: The First International Conference on e-Technologies and Networks for Development (ICeND 2011), Dar-es-Salaam, Tanzania (2011)
7. Bell Labs India: Mango,
   http://portal.acm.org/citation.cfm?id=1592627
8. By Les Afriques - Lancement d'Orange Money en Côte d'Ivoire (July 10, 2008),
   http://www.lesafriques.com/technologies-et-monetique/
   lancement-d-orange-money-en-cote-d-
   ivoire.html?Itemid=197?article=75670
9. Zambia: New Scratch Card Stramline Flow Of Rations, World Food Program
10. Heimerl, K., Brewer, E.: Internet usage and performance analysis of a rural wireless network in Macha, Zambia. In: NSDR 2010 Proceedings of the 4th ACM Workshop on Networked Systems for Developing Regions (2010)

Enhancing Service Provisioning within Heterogeneous Wireless Networks for Emergency Situations

Christian Lottermann, Andreas Klein,
Hans D. Schotten, and Christian Mannweiler

Chair for Wireless Communications and Navigation
University of Kaiserslautern, Germany
{lottermann,aklein,schotten}@eit.uni-kl.de

Abstract. Emergency situations where lives are at stake, such as natural disasters, accidents, or serious fire, require low reaction times. Especially in sparsely populated areas the distance between the nearest emergency station and its disaster location may be quite large. In order to minimize reaction times, emergency communication is to be prioritized with respect to other network services. For enabling efficient and privileged usage of available network resources for emergency services, we propose to handle diverse service requests, ranging from emergency voice calls to bandwidth-consuming streaming services for emergency news, collaboratively by a Joint Call Admission Control (JCAC) and Dynamic Bandwidth Adaptation (DBA) approach. Therefore, we introduce a novel utility definition of services. It represents a generic measurement of the provided level of importance of the emergency service with respect to the common utility, i.e. the utility of service provisioning for the population. The designed JCAC and DBA algorithms cooperatively manage resources of heterogeneous wireless networks and aim at supporting a maximum number of requested services. Further, system utilization is optimized by improving the QoS characteristics of the already granted, elastic services. Simulation results show an improvement in the overall gained utility for emergency services compared to other research approaches.

Keywords: Joint Call Admission Control, Dynamic Bandwidth Adaptation, Utility, Heterogeneous Wireless Networks.

1 Introduction

Common Radio Resource Management (CRRM) is a key concept for efficiently managing radio resources of co-deployed heterogeneous Radio Access Technologies (RATs), yielding enhanced Quality of Service (QoS) provisioning and system utilization. In the proposed concept, two of the main CRRM functionalities are considered: Joint Call Admission Control (JCAC) and Dynamic Bandwidth Adaptation (DBA). In contrast to Call Admission Control (CAC) in homogeneous RATs, JCAC does not only determine whether an incoming service is

R. Popescu-Zeletin et al. (Eds.) AFRICOMM 2011, LNICST 92, pp. 14–23, 2012.

admitted or not, it is moreover able to decide in which RAT the respective service should be deployed. However, JCAC has to take different service and RAT characteristics into account, while ensuring a minimum level of QoS of the admitted services. JCAC and DBA have been in the focus of many research projects in recent years, e.g. [1], [2]. In [3], a generic approach for admission control is presented that mainly focuses on bandwidth adaptation. QoS parameters are taken into account by the bandwidth usage $b_{service}[\frac{bit}{sec}]$ and the utility function is represented by a mapping of the utility vs. the perceived service performance. In [4], a novel approach for combined JCAC and bandwidth adaptation is proposed which enhances the average system utilization, QoS, and reduces blocking and dropping rates in heterogeneous wireless systems. It is based on a Markov chain model and shows an improvement of up to 20% in terms of system utilization compared to a system without JCAC. However, none of these approaches takes emergency situations into consideration. We propose a novel JCAC and DBA approach that aims to improve the overall common utility increasing the overall system utilization and that takes the different QoS demands of various services, such as elastic, best-effort traffic or non-elastic, voice communication, into consideration. An example for elastic best effort services are streaming services with emergency announcements and an example for fixed bandwidth voice services are conventional emergency calls. The main objectives of the proposed approach are to maximize the common utility of all deployed services and the system utilization of co-deployed RATs by dynamically adjusting the conceded QoS demands of elastic services. Furthermore, our approach aims at achieving a homogeneous traffic load distribution among the deployed RATs and avoiding RAT overload, while ensuring minimum QoS requirements on the connection level for admitted services. This makes it possible to serve a large number of emergency-related services.

The present paper is organized as follows. Section 2 presents the joint JCAC and DBA approach. In section 3, the simulation platform, which has been developed to evaluate the proposed algorithms, is described. The applied simulation parameters are included, and an evaluation of simulation results is given. Finally, the paper concludes with section 4.

2   Joint JCAC and DBA

The following section introduces the designed concepts. It depicts prerequisites and the simulation model, the developed JCAC and DBA algorithms, and their collaboration.

2.1   Prerequisites and System Modeling

In the present work, we assume a scenario in which the cells of 2 heterogeneous RATs, that partly share the same core network entities, such as High Speed Packet Access (HSPA) and Long Term Evolution (LTE), are co-deployed in the same service area. The radio resources of all Radio Access Networks (RANs) are managed commonly by a central entity. Each of the considered RATs uses different radio transmission schemes for service data transmissions, and manages and allocates different types of radio resources. In order to generalize these RAT-specific radio resources and to create a basis for common radio resource management decisions, an *effective bandwidth usage* measure is introduced. Each cell can provide a maximum effective bandwidth that can be allocated to the requested services. Spatially co-deployed cells of different RANs form a group of co-located cells, a so-called *cell area*, that is used as target for new or handover services.

In our model, mobile terminals are characterized by their prioritization class, a randomly chosen dwell time that expresses the duration it is located within one cell, and the number and types of requested services. In the following, we assume that all mobile terminals are multi-mode terminals that are capable of supporting all deployed RATs in the service area. Mobile terminals are able to suuport different services that are required for emergency situations, like conventional cellular phones that are used by first-aid services up to screens that are used to display the latest information of the emergency area.

Further, two kinds of services are considered: *elastic services* and *non-elastic services*. The QoS characteristics of the latter ones are expressed by a range of effective bandwidth values in the range of $b_{min} \leq b_{desired} \leq b_{max}$. The minimum effective bandwidth value b_{min} expresses the minimum value that is required to deploy a service, specified by the minimum QoS demand of the application; whereas b_{max} describes the maximum effective bandwidth value the RAN grants to a service. $b_{desired}$ is defined by the application and describes the level of effective bandwidth that is required to execute the service at a satisfactory Quality of Experience (QoE) level. In contrast, the non-elastic services are fixed with respect to their QoS requirements and, thus, with respect to their required effective bandwidth, i.e. $b_{non-elastic} = b_{min}$. Further, each service class is defined by its service duration and its pause time which expresses the time between two service requests of the same application class.

2.2   Utility Concept

The basic ideas of the utility concept are taken from the field of micro-economics. The term *utility* represents a measure of relative satisfaction and is modeled by the consumption of different goods or services. In the present work, it represents a generic measurement of the overall provided utility of the different services that are required in an emergency situation. In the present case one Mobile Network Operator (MNO) is in charge of the respective RANs. All parameters are related to the Service Level Agreement (SLA) between the devices and the MNO, that also defines services that can be deployed within the network. It is assembled by utility functions that need to take several factors into consideration, which are set by the policies of the MNO and the services requested by the terminal. In general, the utility $u_{i,j}$ for service j deployed in RAN i can be stated as follows:

$$u_{i,j} = U(a_j, \pi_j, \rho_i), \tag{1}$$

where

- a_j: application utility function, that depends on the QoS parameters of the requested service and the current effective bandwidth usage b
- π_j: priority factor, that represents the priority level of the User Equipment (UE) defined by the SLA
- ρ_i: RAN factor that is to be set by the MNO policies; the higher the value the higher the utility for the session in the specific RAN

In the considered scenario, the utility function is assembled by the following utility function

$$u_{i,j} = a_j(b) \cdot \pi_j \cdot r_j, \tag{2}$$

where the utility function of the service depends on the service properties (cf. [3]). Elastic services follow an exponential function (see equation 3), whereas non-elastic services are represented by a step function (see equation 4):

$$u_{elastic}(b) = 1 - e^{-\frac{k \cdot b}{b_{max}}} \tag{3}$$

$$u_{non-elastic}(b) = \begin{cases} 1 & b \geq b_{min} \\ 0 & b < b_{min} \end{cases} \tag{4}$$

2.3   Overall Concept

The handling of all incoming and handover service requests is performed in a bundled manner, i.e. the incoming and handover service requests are queued and the DBA and JCAC algorithms are performed each $TTI_{semipersistent}$ for all cell areas in a central entity. $TTI_{semipersistent}$ denotes the time interval between two runs of the joint DBA and JCAC algorithms. The sequence of algorithm steps is as follows:

1. DBA, *Bandwidth Adaption Arrival:* Check if enough resources are available in the system for the incoming requests (new services and handover services)
2. JCAC, *Serve Handover Services:* Handle the queued handover services first
3. JCAC, *Serve New Services:* Handle the new queued services secondly
4. DBA, *Bandwidth Adaption Departure:* Assign the remaining capacity to the services with elastic traffic in order to increase system utilization

2.4   JCAC Algorithm

The following section introduces the suggested JCAC algorithm that is handled as a General Assignment Problem (GAP).

The GAP belongs to the class of bin packaging problems in which N items (S) need to be assigned to M bins (B) (knapsacks). Each bin i has a certain capacity c_i and each item j has a weight $w_{i,j}$ and utility $u_{i,j}$, respectively, depending on the bin. The objective is to find a subset of $U \subseteq B$ of items that can be placed in the bins B, in a way that the overall utility z is maximized. The mathematical definition of the problem is:

$$z = \max \sum_{i=1}^{m} \sum_{j=1}^{n} u_{i,j} \cdot x_{i,j} \tag{5}$$

$$\text{s.t.} \sum_{j=1}^{n} w_{i,j} \cdot x_{i,j} \leq c_i \quad \forall i \in M = \{1, \ldots, m\} \tag{6}$$

$$\sum_{i=1}^{m} x_{i,j} = 1 \quad \forall j \in N = \{1, \ldots n\} \tag{7}$$

$$x_{i,j} = \{0, 1\} \quad \forall i \in M, j \in N \tag{8}$$

$x_{i,j}$ indicates whether item j is assigned to knapsack i ($x_{i,j} = 1$) or not ($x_{i,j} = 0$).

In the present work, the cells represent the bins, where their capacity c_i is represented by the maximum amount of effective bandwidth. Services are considered as items. The weight of a service is represented by the effective bandwidth usage of the service, which is an input parameter for the utility calculation for the referring service. These relationships allow for reusing existing approximative algorithms with good run-time characteristics. We choose the approach of [5] as a suitable solution. The algorithm itself is split in two main parts: an *outer* and an *inner* algorithm. The first one (see algorithm 1) decomposes the GAP into M 0-1 knapsack problems for which a variety of approximative algorithms exists, see [6] for more information. It requires capacity information of all cells, C, the weight and utility information that depends on the respective RAN for every bearer, W and P, respectively, and returns the assignment vector T which contains the index of the cell in which the respective service is to be deployed. The M 0-1 knapsack problems are solved by the *inner* algorithm that, in principle, can be any algorithm capable of solving 0-1 knapsack problems. It requires the utility and weight vectors of the bearers to be assigned for the considered cell, P_i and W_i, respectively, and the current remaining capacity c_i as input. In turn, the algorithm provides assignment and updated capacity information.

In case the 0-1 knapsack algorithm exhibits an approximation ratio of α, the approximation ratio of the GAP algorithm is $(1 + \alpha)$. In the present work, a simple *Greedy* algorithm is chosen, since it offers the best run-time performance at an eligible approximation ratio, see algorithm 2.

In order to avoid overload situations that occur due to the greedy characteristic of the underlying 0-1 knapsack algorithm, an additional *prioritization* factor is introduced. In case the load of one cell within a cell area is above a certain threshold $\eta_{cell} > \eta_{cell,overload}$, an additional prioritization factor for the respective services is calculated. This factor is accounted for in the utility that is used for the underlying 0-1 knapsack algorithm and decreases with an increasing cell load which in turn leads to a smaller utility value for the knapsack decision. The actual utility value is calculated without this prioritization factor.

Algorithm 1. Outer GAP solver

Input: C, W, P
Output: T, C
  for $i = 1$ to M **do**
    {Create price vector}
    for $j = 1$ to N **do**
      if $T(j) == -1$ **then**
        do $P_i(j) = p(i,j)$
      else
        do $k = T(j)$
        do $P_i(j) = p(i,j) - p(i,k)$
      end if
      KNAPSACK(P_i,W_i,c_i)
    end for
  end for

Algorithm 2. Greedy Knapsack Solver

Input: P, W, C
Output: T, C
  SORT(P, W)
  for $j = 1$ to N **do**
    if $w_j > C$ **then**
      $t_j = -1$
    else
      $t_j = i$
      $c = c - w_{i,j}$
      $z = z + p_{i,j}$
    end if
  end for

2.5 DBA Algorithm

The DBA algorithm is split into two main stages: the *Arrival Algorithm* is performed before and the *Departure Algorithm* after the JCAC.

Arrival Algorithm. First, the *Arrival Algorithm* acquires as much as resources as are required by the queued services in the considered cell area. For that purpose, it degrades already deployed elastic services in order to release sufficient resources. At the beginning of each cycle, the total demand of effective bandwidth of the queued services is calculated $B_{req} = \Sigma_{\forall i} b_i$, whereas b_i holds the bandwidth of service i. The already deployed elastic services are sorted in ascending order according to their *utility slope*

$$u'_j = \frac{\Delta u_j}{\Delta b_j},$$

i.e. $u'_1 < u'_2 < \ldots < u'_n$. In case not enough resources are available in the considered cell area, services could not be served by a single RAN. Hence, the already

deployed services are degraded until all incoming services can be admitted or
until all admitted elastic services have already been degraded to a minimum.
This leads to a minor overall utility loss, since the elastic services, that suffer
the least of utility degradation, are degraded first.

Departure Algorithm. First, elastic services are sorted in descending order
according to their utility slope

$$u_j' = \frac{\Delta u_j}{\Delta b_j},$$

i.e. $u_1' > u_2' \ldots > u_n'$. In case there are resources available, i.e. the system is
not completely utilized in the considered cell area, the already deployed elastic services are assigned more resources in order to increase the overall system
utilization and level of service provisioning. They will be upgraded until their
desired effective bandwidth $b_{desired}$ is reached and in case the bearer is already
served with $b = b_{desired}$, they will be upgraded until $b = b_{max}$. This allows for
improving the gain of bandwidth adaptation, since the services with the steepest
slope will be upgraded first. The services are upgraded until the system reaches
its maximum capacity or all elastic services are upgraded to their maximum
bandwidth.

3   Evaluation

The following section introduces the developed simulation platform that is used
to evaluate the proposed approach, followed by the applied simulation parameters, and obtained simulation results.

3.1   Simulation Parameters

In the following, the parameters that were used for the simulations of all relevant components are presented. All mobile terminals (in the following called
UEs) are characterized both by their *UE class* and their *UE utility factor* π_j,
see table 3. The first one denotes the service types that are requested by a UE of
the respective UE class, whereas π_j represents the utility factor of the randomly
assigned SLA class values. Table 1 states the characteristics of the applications
that are supported by the system. Application 1 and 2 represent non-elastic
services that are fixed with respect to their QoS characteristics, i.e. Voice over
IP (VoIP) and streaming services, respectively. In contrast, application 3 and 4
represent elastic services, that are variable with respect to their QoS characteristics, i.e. best-effort services, such as web applications or file transfers. A cell area
consists of a HSPA and a LTE cell, each characterized by a maximum available
bandwidth and a RAN factor presented in table 2.

Table 1. Service Parameters

App. ID	BW Req. [Mbps]	Active Time [s]	Pause Time [s]
1	$b_{min} = 0.030$	$\mu_{Duration} = 90$	$\mu_{Pause} = 1800$
2	$b_{min} = 0.256$	$\mu_{Duration} = 300$	$\mu_{Pause} = 1800$
3	$b_{min} = 0.0$ $b_{desired} = 0.25$ $b_{max} = 1.00$	$\mu_{Duration} = 50$	$\mu_{Pause} = 420$
4	$b_{min} = 0.0$ $b_{desired} = 1.5$ $b_{max} = 10$	$\mu_{Duration} = 120$	$\mu_{Pause} = 420$

Table 2. Cell Parameters

RAN	B_j [Mbps]	ρ_j
HSPA	14.4	0.6
LTE	80.23	1.0

Table 3. UE Class Parameters

UE Class	A	B	C	D
Applications	{1}	{1,3}	{1,3,4}	{2,3,4}
Distribution	0.2	0.5	0.2	0.1

3.2 Simulation Results

In the following section, performance results of the proposed JCAC and DBA approach with respect to the blocking and dropping rates, the system utilization in the HSPA and LTE cells, and the overall gained utility of all deployed services are given. The proposed approach, which is denoted as *DBAJCAC*, is compared to the *AJCAC* scheme presented in [4] and an approach that does not take JCAC and dynamic bandwidth adaptation into consideration at all.

Blocking and Dropping Probability. The simulation results show that the blocking probabilities of new and the dropping probabilities of handover services are on an acceptable low level for both approaches using JCAC, even at a high number of initial users per cell, see figure 1. In case no JCAC is applied both rates increase in an enormous way at a high number of initial users per cell.

Overall Utility. The overall gained utility, depicted in figure 2, is up to 6% higher using the proposed *DBAJCAC* approach and the distance to the gained overall utility of the *AJCAC* increases for a higher number of initial users per cell. This is due to the greedy characteristic of the underlying GAP solver. In case no JCAC is applied the utility increases too, however at a lower slope.

Cell Load. Figure 3 illustrates the relative cell load statistics both for LTE and HSPA cells, respectively, for all considered algorithms. Apparently, more services are deployed in the LTE cells for both algorithms using an JCAC algorithm up to a number of initial users per cell of $n = 70$. For DBAJCAC, this is due to the utility factor of the RAN, ρ_j, which has a higher value for LTE cells (cf. table

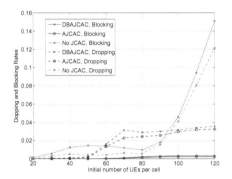

Fig. 1. Dropping and Blocking Probability (mean)

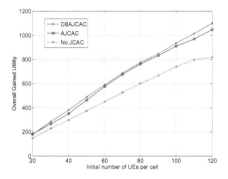

Fig. 2. Overall Gained Utility (mean)

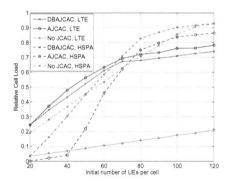

Fig. 3. Cell Load of HSPA and LTE Cells (mean)

2). If the number of initial users per cell increases even further, the cell load of the HSPA cells rises as well. For DBAJCAC, this is due to the load balancing characteristic of the prioritization factor, which is set to $\eta = 0.6$. This leads to a relative increase of the utility used for the underlying 0-1 knapsack algorithm for the HSPA cells. In case no JCAC is applied the LTE cells are only loaded to a minimum whereas the HSPA cells are loaded to a great amount which is a result of not taking JCAC into consideration at all. Thus, all UEs remain in the same RAN during the whole simulation time.

4 Conclusion

The presented work introduces a novel approach for joint JCAC and DBA that enhances resource sharing and service provisioning in emergency situations while taking QoS requirements of services into account. The JCAC task is mapped to a general assignment problem which is well-suited for the resource sharing of different services for emergency use cases. Further, the utility-based definition of services provides a generic measurement of the importance of the service for the community in emergency situations. The performance of the proposed concept is compared to other research approaches and shows an improvement of the achievable utility of approximately 6% with respect to other JCAC approaches, while key performance indicators, such as blocking and dropping rates, are kept at an acceptable level.

Acknowledgment. This work has been funded by the Federal Ministry of Education and Research of the Federal Republic of Germany (Förderkennzeichen 01 BU 1116, SolarMesh - Energieeffizientes, autonomes großflächiges Sprach- und Datenfunknetz mit flacher IP- Architektur). The authors alone are responsible for the content of the paper.

References

1. Niyato, D., Hossain, E.: Connection Admission Control Algorithms for OFDM Wireless Networks. In: Proceedings of the IEEE GLOBECOM, St. Louis, MO, vol. 5, pp. 2455–2459 (2005)
2. Altman, E., Jimenez, T., Koole, G.: On Optimal Call Admission Control in Resource-Sharing System. IEEE Transactions on Communications 49(9), 1659–1668 (2001)
3. Lu, N.: Utility-based Bandwidth Adaptation for QoS Provisioning in Multimedia Wireless Networks, Ph.D. dissertation, Queen Mary University of London, London, United Kingdom (2007)
4. Falowo, O.E., Chan, H.A.: Adaptive Bandwidth Management and Joint Call Admission Control to Enhance System Utilization and QoS in Heterogeneous Wireless Networks. EURASIP Journal on Wireless Communications and Networking 2007 (July 2007)
5. Cohen, R., Katzir, L., Raz, D.: An Efficient Approximation for the Generalized Assignment Problem. Information Processing Letters 100, 162–166 (2006)
6. Martello, S., Toth, P.: Knapsack problems. Wiley, Chichester (1990)

Providing Some Quality of Service for Secondary Users in Cognitive Radios Using Time Slotted Systems

Hudson Okii and Idris A. Rai

Makerere University
P.O. Box 7062
Kampala, Uganda
Okihudsn@yahoo.com
rai@cit.mak.ac.ug

Abstract. The current research in cognitive radio has been considering absolute guarantee for primary users allowing secondary users access to spectrum only if there is no primary users with data to send. At high arrival rate of primary users this might lead to complete starvation of secondary users and yet it is possible to release some spectrum to secondary users by delaying primary users without affecting their quality. We propose a resource allocation scheme that uses delayed time periods of primary users to transmit secondary user's data packets without jeopardizing the quality of primary users. We analytically modeled the scheme using M/G/1 queue. Our numerical experiments demonstrate that secondary users can be offered some quality of service by delaying primary users in the system to a limit that does not degrade their performance.

Keywords: cognitive radio networks, spectrum assignment, quality of service, queueing theory.

1 Introduction

Recent technological advances have led to growth in use of high data rate wireless application and services. The already crowded and congested radio spectrum has become scarce [2]. *Cognitive radio* (CR) which is a smart programmable radio, capable of sensing interference, learning environment, and dynamically accessing the spectrum is a promising technology to alleviate the increasing stress on the fixed and limited radio spectrum. In cognitive radio networks, the *secondary user* (SU) (unlicensed) user can periodically search and identify available channels in the spectrum to communicate among themselves without disturbing communication of the *primary user* (PU) (licensed) users. *Dynamic spectrum access* (DSA) which is the ability of a secondary user to sense and access spectrum opportunistically can resolve this problem by allowing secondary users to transmit in the assigned but under-utilized frequency bands, provided that the primary user are sufficiently protected.

R. Popescu-Zeletin et al. (Eds.) AFRICOMM 2011, LNICST 92, pp. 24–34, 2012.

Literatures by authors in [5], [6] have addressed the area of dynamic spectrum access in time domain, aiming at exploiting idle periods between bursty transmissions of PU using sense-then-transmit spectrum access strategy.

Delay analysis for a cognitive radio network have been studied by authors in [7], [8], [9]. An approach using a finite state markov chain based queueing model to quantitatively analyse the performance metrics in terms of average packet delay, head of line delay and packet drop rate has been done by authors in [9]. It is worth noting that based on the analytical model, tradeoff among the performance metrics was identified and when and where the cost for favouring the secondary user is worthy was also identified.

Our work is different and distinct from past works in spectrum sharing in cognitive radios using time slotted system where secondary users can only access spectrum when primary users channels are idle as done by authors in [4], [1], [3]. Besides, none of the work in those literatures tries to care for secondary users like our proposed scheme does. To the best of our knowledge, our work is the first of its kind on spectrum sharing which proposes a scheme to provide *quality of service* (QoS) to SU without affecting the quality of PUs at all. Quality of service is defined as the guarantees provided on the ability of network to deliver predictable performance like availability (uptime), bandwidth (throughput), latency (delay), and error rate. Our work is an extension of work done by authors in [4]. In particular, we adopt the analytical methodology and our models are derived from an extension of models in that particular paper.

The rest of the paper is organized as follows: in the next section, we discuss the proposed scheme, and we derive its mathematical models in Section 3. We present and discuss numerical results of the proposed scheme in Section 4, and finally we conclude the paper in Section 5.

2   The Proposed Spectrum Allocation Scheme

In this section, we present the proposed spectrum allocation scheme for cognitive radio network. As pointed out earlier, we propose a scheme that in addition to making use of the unused spectrum, it considers delaying primary user's data in order to provide some service guarantees such as to avoid complete starvation to secondary users.

We consider a time slotted cognitive wireless network where a primary user is the owner of the network. We focus on a cognitive network with one primary and many secondary users uplink. In a conventional cognitive radio network, primary users receive full access to the link without any consideration of secondary users at all because they are the ones who pay for the spectrum (the channels). However, because primary users may not be fully utilizing the provided spectrum, secondary users can opportunistically utilize the channel when primary user is idle and also can share it with primary user when another primary user is present. The cognitive radio access network maintains two queues one for each type of users. In both PU and SU queues, requests are served in a first come first served (FCFS) order of service with SU services only if there is no data in

PU queue. The transmission of the packets is implemented by having the secondary user perform spectrum sensing at the beginning of the slot. If there is no primary users signal at the beginning of the slot, the remainder of the slot can be used for secondary transmission. We assume that there is perfect sensing and time synchronization, and that all packets are one slot in time duration and the system time is slotted with a fixed unit time slot. The network is assumed to operate in noise free and error free channel conditions. Transmission of the packet can only begin at the beginning of the slot so that even if a packet arrives at the middle of the slot, it has to wait a half a slot duration, even if the channel is free. Secondary user is assumed to receive acknowledgment indicating a successful packet transmission, the transmission of acknowledgment is assumed to be error free. If SU transmits a packet and fails to receive the acknowledgment, it retransmits the packet when the channel becomes available again. Each time slot is owned distinctly a primary user. In such a system, when the arrival rate of primary users is very high, secondary users are completely starved. To avoid this in situations where secondary users are to be given some consideration, we propose a scheduling scheme shown in figure 1 that delays primary user when they wish to transmit. Instead, the scheduler gives some priority to secondary users to transmit. Note that we assume that secondary users will always be delayed for a number of time slots before they are given such priority. Otherwise, the scheduler will offer absolute priority to secondary users to the expense of primary users extended delay.

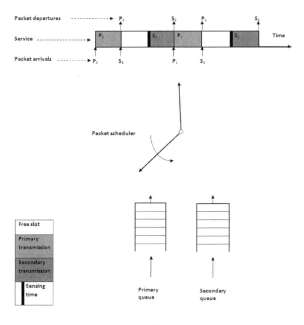

Fig. 1. The model

The number of times primary user's request is delayed in the system before it is allowed to transmit depends on the utilization of the system and the quality requirement of the application. Primary user's requests is not delayed indefinitely, instead primary users application's maximum tolerable delay limit is used to ensure that primary users requests are not starved. The maximum tolerable delay limit depends on the user application. When the number of times primary users request has been delayed approaches maximum tolerable delay limit, the scheme does not delay this requests any longer. It is served immediately so that the quality of its application is not jeopardized. Figure 2 presents the proposed scheduling scheme that schedules primary user's request when $W^P(D = 1)$ and $W^P(D = 2)$ at $t = i$. W^P is the packet delay time for primary users and D is the number of times a single primary users request can be delayed. Let $t = 0, 1, 2...$, index the request service periods, each of 1 time slot. Primary users requests are denoted by P_i and secondary users request are denoted by S_i, let $i = 0, 1, 2, 3...$, index request number. When $D = 1$ at time period $t = i$, primary users packet P_i is delayed by the service of primary users requests P_{i-1} and secondary users request S_i. When $D = 2$ at time period $t = i$, primary users packet P_{i-1} is delayed by the service of primary users request P_{i-2} and secondary users request S_i. When $D = 1$ at time period $t = i$, secondary users packet S_{i+1} is delayed by the service of primary users requests P_{i-1} and secondary users request S_i. When $D = 2$ at time period $t = i$, primary users packet S_{i+1} is delayed by the service of primary users request P_{i-2} and secondary users request S_i.

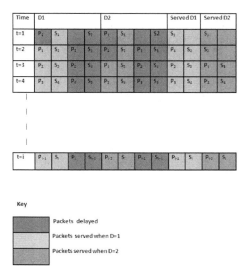

Fig. 2. Request schedule for $W^P(D = 1)$ and $W^P(D = 2)$ at $t = i$

3   Models of the Proposed Scheme

3.1   Mathematical Background

In this section, we derive mathematical expressions of average time that packets of different user types under the proposed scheme spend in the system (aka *response time*). We first derive the expressions under M/G/1 queue which assumes a general packet size distribution G and then consider M/D/1 to derive the expressions for the case when all packets are of the same size.

Let the subscript or superscript r of the following notations represent either primary (P) or secondary (S) users. We denote the mean arrival rate as λ_r, $\overline{X}_r = \frac{1}{\mu_r}$ denotes the average service time of a user, N_Q^r as the average number of users packets in a queue, and W_Q^r as the average waiting time in the queue. We also denote W^r as the total time spent by a packet of any user in the system, TD as mean waiting time until the beginning of the slot, ρ^r as the utilization factor, $W^r(d = i)$ as the average waiting time of one user type after delaying the other user type i times before receiving service.

In what follows, we derive the expressions of response time of packets of different user types under the proposed scheme. We first derive the expressions under M/G/1 queue which assumes a general packet size distribution G and then consider M/D/1 to derive the expressions for the case when all packets are of the same size.

Average Delay of Primary Users. Response time is defined as the total time a packet spends in the system. We model the scheduler to be able to analytically estimate the mean response of packets that belong to different types of users. In this section, we derive the expressions for mean response time of primary user's packet when it is not delayed. We consider a tagged packet that belongs to a primary user. Its mean response time is delayed by primary user's packet it finds in the scheduler's primary queue upon its arrival. The average delay of the tagged primary user's packet is therefore given as

$$W_Q^P = TD + \frac{N_Q^P}{\mu} \tag{1}$$

By using Little's theorem on N_Q^P in the above equation, we obtain the expression for the mean waiting time of the packet as $W_Q^P = \frac{TD}{(1-\rho^P)}$.

Recalling the fact that the average packet delay (time spent in the system) is given by sum of the mean waiting time in the queue and the average service time of the packet, we can express the packet's mean response time for the primary user as follows:

$$W^P = \overline{X}_P + \frac{TD}{(1 - \rho^P)} \tag{2}$$

In the proposed scheme, the priority of the primary users is relaxed by delaying them in the system up to the delay value that does not affect the underlying application's quality. We therefore derive the expressions for primary user's packet mean response time after it has been delayed i times before receiving service. Again, let that packet is tagged. Its average delay is composed of its mean service time and the mean service times of all primary and secondary users it finds in the system upon its arrival. The average waiting time of the tagged primary user's packet is therefore given as

$$W_Q^P(D = i) = TD + \frac{N_Q^P}{\mu} + \frac{i}{\mu_s} \tag{3}$$

By using Little's theorem, we obtain

$$W_Q^P(D = i) = \frac{TD + \frac{i}{\mu_s}}{1 - \rho^P} \tag{4}$$

Adding the mean service time of the packet to Equation (4), we obtain packet's average response time for a primary user as

$$W^P(D = i) = \overline{X}_P + \frac{TD + \frac{i}{\mu_s}}{1 - \rho^P} \tag{5}$$

Next we derive the expression of the mean response time of a secondary user's packets.

Average Delay of Secondary Users. We start with the expression for secondary user's packet mean response time before primary user's packets are delayed to receive service. We again consider a tagged packet that is transmitted by a secondary user. The tagged packet is delayed by primary users packets found in the queue, secondary user's packet found in the queue, and other primary users that finds it in the system. The average delay of the tagged secondary user's packet is therefore given as

$$W_Q^S = TD + \frac{1}{\mu}N_Q^P + \frac{1}{\mu}N_Q^S + \frac{1}{\mu}\lambda_P W_Q^S \tag{6}$$

By using Little's theorem on N_Q^P and N_Q^S, we obtain the expression for the mean waiting time of the packet as

$$W_Q^S = \frac{TD}{(1 - \rho^P)(1 - \rho^P - \rho^S)} \tag{7}$$

and finally the average delay of a packet from secondary user is given by

$$W^S = \overline{X}_S + \frac{TD}{(1 - \rho^P)(1 - \rho^P - \rho^S)} \tag{8}$$

Now let us consider tagged secondary user with data to transmit. We derive the expression for the mean response time of secondary user's packet after primary user's packet has been delayed i times before receiving service which is the essence of the proposed scheme. The average delay of the tagged secondary user is composed of its mean service time and the sum of service times of all primary and secondary users it finds in the system including the packet that is receiving service upon its arrival. The average delay of the tagged secondary user's packet is therefore given as

$$W_Q^S(D = i) = TD + \frac{1}{\mu}N_Q^P + \frac{1}{\mu}N_Q^S \tag{9}$$

By applying Little's theorem on N_Q^P and N_Q^S, we obtain the expression of the mean waiting time of the tagged packet as follows

$$W_Q^S(D = i) = \frac{TD}{(1 - \rho^P)(1 - \rho^S)} \tag{10}$$

Finally, the average delay of the tagged packet is given as

$$W^S(D = i) = \overline{X}_S + \frac{TD}{(1 - \rho^P)(1 - \rho^S)} \tag{11}$$

Average Delay of Primary and Secondary Users Using M/D/1 System. In this section, we address the special case where time is slotted with deterministic service time of one slot (M/D/1) and the fact that packet service can only start at the beginning of the slot. We assume that the service time is one slot and newly arrived packet has to wait for 1/2 slot before the beginning of slot. We can substitute these values in $\overline{X}_P$ and TD in equation (2) to obtain

$$W^P = 1 + \frac{\frac{1}{2}}{(1 - \rho^P)}. \tag{12}$$

We also substitute the service time of 1 slot and the waiting time of 1/2 of a slot in $\overline{X}_P$ and TD in equation (5) to obtain

$$W^P(D = i) = 1 + \frac{\frac{1}{2} + \frac{i}{\mu_s}}{1 - \rho^P}. \tag{13}$$

Substituting the service time of 1 slot and the waiting time of 1/2 of a slot in $\overline{X}_P$ and TD in equation (8) when primary user's packet is delayed before receiving service, we obtain

$$W^S(D = i) = 1 + \frac{\frac{1}{2}}{(1 - \rho^P)(1 - \rho^P - \rho^S)}. \tag{14}$$

And substituting the service time of 1 slot and the waiting time of 1/2 of a slot in $\overline{X}_P$ and TD in equation (11) when primary user's packet has been delayed i times before receiving service to obtain

$$W^S(D = i) = 1 + \frac{\frac{1}{2}}{(1 - \rho^P)(1 - \rho^S)}. \tag{15}$$

4   Performance Evaluation

In this section we discuss numerical results that show the performance of the proposed scheme when secondary users are favoured to access spectrum by delaying primary users, We assume that secondary user's access to spectrun depends on the utilization of the system and the quality requirement of the application, we also evaluate the effect of delaying primary user's packet on varying applications.

4.1   Evaluation of Average Waiting Time for Secondary Users Packet When $W^S(d=0)$ and When $W^S(d=i)$

In this section we analyze the effect of secondary user's arrival rate on its average waiting time when primary user is delayed several times before receiving service and when its arrival rate is fixed and at a service rate equals that of the secondary user.

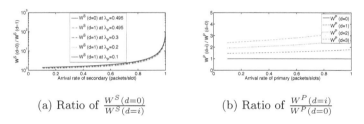

(a) Ratio of $\frac{W^S(d=0)}{W^S(d=i)}$ (b) Ratio of $\frac{W^P(d=i)}{W^P(d=0)}$

Fig. 3. The delay performance for secondary and primary users

Fig 3(a) presents the ratio of $\frac{W^S(d=0)}{W^S(d=i)}$ as a function of its arrival rate for $d = i$ (where i=1) when the primary users arrival rate is varied at $\lambda = 0.495$, $\lambda = 0.3$, $\lambda = 0.2$ and $\lambda = 0.1$ and at equal service rate of $\mu = 1.5$. It can be observed that with high primary user arrival rate fixed at $\lambda = 0.495$, the ratio of $W^S(d=0)$ at secondary users arrival rate of 0.1 is approximately 100/87. This indicates a reduction in average waiting time of secondary users when delayed by 1 time slot at given arrivals rates by approximately 13 percent. With low primary users arrival rate fixed at $\lambda = 0.1$, the ratio of $W^S(d=0)$ at secondary arrival rate of 0.1 is approximately 100/79, which indicates a reduction in secondary users average waiting time by 21 percent. The result shows that the mean response time of secondary user's packets deteriorates when the primary arrival data rate is high.

Evaluation of packet delay time for primary users when $W^P(d = 0)$ and when $W^P(d = i)$. We now analyze the effect of primary user's arrival rate on its average delay time when the primary data is delayed several times before receiving service and when the secondary user's arrival rate is fixed.

Fig 3(b) shows $\frac{W^P(d=i)}{W^P(d=0)}$ as a function of primary users arrival rates for $d = 0, d = 1, d = 2$, and $d = 3$ when the secondary users arrival rate is fixed at $\lambda = 0.4$

and at equal service rate of $\mu = 1.5$. The figure shows that the ratio of $\frac{W^P(d=1)}{W^P(d=0)}$ is approximately 1.5 to 1 and the ratio of $\frac{W^P(d=2)}{W^P(d=0)}$ is approximately 2.1 to 1. It can be seen that at primary users arrival rate of 0.1, for each $d = 0, d = 1, d = 2$, and $d = 3$, there is an increase in the ratio of $\frac{W^P(d=i)}{W^P(d=0)}$ by a factor of approximately 0.5 slots per request delay.

4.2   Evaluation of Packet Delay Time Limit for Data, Audio and Video Applications

In this section we analyze the effect of primary users packet delay as a function of its load on data, audio and video applications. According to International Telecommunication Union (Y.1541 and Y.1221), the maximum tolerable delay limit of audio, video, and data application requests should not be more than 50, 20, and 100 milliseconds respectively. These values will be used in the evaluation and analysis of the results.

Figure 4(a) presents data packet delay in (millisecond) as a function of primary users load ρ when the secondary users arrival rate is fixed at $\lambda = 0.4$ and at equal service rate of $\mu = 1.5$. It can be seen that the maximum tolerable delay limit for data application is 100 milliseconds. Beyond this limit, the quality of the application is degraded.

Figure 4(b) presents audio packet delay in (millisecond) as a function of primary users load ρ when the secondary users arrival rate is fixed at $\lambda = 0.4$ and at equal service rate of $\mu = 1.5$. It can be seen that the maximum tolerable delay limit for audio application is 50 milliseconds, Beyond this limit, the quality of the application is degraded.

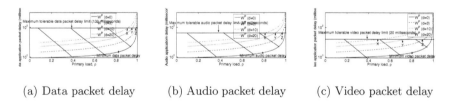

(a) Data packet delay   (b) Audio packet delay   (c) Video packet delay

Fig. 4. The packet delay performance for data, audio and video applications

Figure 4(c) presents video packet delay in (millisecond) as a function of primary users load ρ when the secondary user's arrival rate is fixed at $\lambda = 0.4$ and at equal service rate of $\mu = 1.5$. It can be seen that the maximum tolerable delay limit for video application is 20 milliseconds. Beyond this limit, the quality of the application is degraded.

In this section, our observation and analysis of the figures concludes that data application tolerates higher packet delays at lower load than audio and video applications for a fixed secondary user's arrival rate. It can be observed that primary user's requests can be delayed up to a maximum tolerable limit depending on the application's delay tolerance. The maximum tolerable delay limit for video applications is reached at a load of $\rho = 0.57$ when primary users requests are delayed 20 times. For audio applications, the maximum tolerable delay limit is reached at a load of $\rho = 0.82$ when primary users requests are delayed 20 times. In the case of data applications, the maximum tolerable delay limit is reached at a load of $\rho = 0.92$ when primary users requests are delayed 20 times. Therefore the above results show that video application is less delay tolerant than audio application which in turn is less delay tolerant than data application. Hence video application can be delayed fewer number of times before degrading it's quality of service compared to audio application which can be delayed more number of times. Data application can be delayed more times than video and audio.

4.3 Evaluation of Packet Delay Time Limit for Data, Audio and Video Applications under Varying Time Slot Duration

In this section we analyze the effect of primary users packet delay as a function of its load on data, audio and video applications when primary user's packet are delayed three times under varying time slots of 1, 0.75, and 0.5 time slot duration.

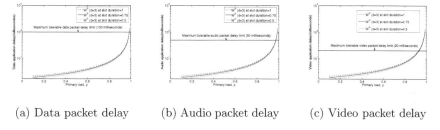

(a) Data packet delay   (b) Audio packet delay   (c) Video packet delay

Fig. 5. The packet delay performance at varying slot durations

Figure 5(a), (b) and (c) present different PU application packet delay in (millisecond) as a function of primary users load ρ when primary user's packet are delayed three times under varying time slot durations of 1, 0.75, and 0.5. It can be observed that the lower the slot duration, the higher the number of times a PU packet can be delayed before it reaches its maximum tolerable limit. The number of times a PU packet is delayed for slot duration 0.5 is higher than for slot duration 0.75 which in turn is higher than for slot duration 1.

5   Conclusion

Unlike conventional spectrum assignment schemes in CR which guarantee absolute priority to PU, we propose an assignment scheme that provides some quality guarantees to SU. Different applications require different quality guarantees, and therefore it is possible to delay some PU data in the system for some time without affecting its quality of service. The novel proposed spectrum assignment approach seems credible for various applications because it directly favors SU so that it is not completely starved in situations when arrival rate of PU is high, unlike other previous schemes [9]and [5].

We extend the models derived from the previous work by authors in [4] to derive analytical expressions of the mean waiting time of SU and PU packets in the proposed systems using queuing theory. We used the models to numerically evaluate the proposed scheme. The results clearly show that it is possible to provide some quality of service to secondary users while preserving the acceptable quality requirements of the PU.

It should be noted that the proposed scheme does not suggest providing absolute guarantees to SU. The models present a general case only. In realistic implementation, PU will be delayed to give room to SU packets only if they SU have been delayed for some time.

References

1. Chen, T., Zhang, H., Katz, M.D., Zhou, Z.: Swarm Intelligence Based Dynamic Control Channel Assignment in CogMesh. In: IEEE International Conference on Communications (2008)
2. FCC, Report of the spectrum efficiency working group, FCC Spectrum Policy Task Force, Tech. Rep. (November 2002)
3. Kang, B., Park, H., Kim, Y., Woo, S., Ban, S.: Out-of-band cooperative spectrum sensing in cognitive radio system of multiple spectrum bands. In: Proceedings of the 3rd WSEAS International Conference on Circuits, Systems, Signal and Telecommunications (2009)
4. Suliman, I., Lehtomäki, J.: Queueing analysis of opportunistic access in cognitive radios. In: First International Conference on Wireless Communication, Vehicular Technology, Information Theory and Aerospace and Electronics Systems Technology, Wireless VITAE 2009 (2009)
5. Xu, Y., Wang, J., Wu, Q.: Interference-Throughput Tradeoff in Dynamic Spectrum Access: Analysis Based on Discrete-Time Queuing Subjected to Bursty Preemption. In: 4th International Conference on Cognitive Radio Oriented Wireless Networks and Communications (2009)
6. Zhao, Q.C., Geirhofer, S., Tong, L., Sadler, B.M.: Optimal dynamic spectrum access via periodic channel sensing. In: Wireless Communications and Networking Conference (2007)
7. Wang, S., Zhang, J., Tong, L.: Delay Analysis for Cognitive Radio Networks with Random Access: A Fluid Queue View. In: The Proceedings of INFOCOM 2010 (2010)
8. Zhang, C., Wang, X., Guan, X.: Quality-of-Service in Cognitive Radio Networks with Collaborative Sensing. In: The Proceedings of GLOBECOM 2009 (2009)
9. Su, H., Zhang, X.: Secondary user friendly TDMA Scheduling for Primary Users in Cognitive Radio Networks. In: The Proceedings of GLOBECOM 2009 (2009)

Fair Usage and Capping for Providing Internet for All in Developing Countries

Yvon Gourhant, Ali Gouta, and Venmani Daniel Philip

Orange Labs, France Telecom R&D, Lannion, France
{yvon.gourhant,ali.gouta,danielphilip.venmani}@orange-ftgroup.com

Abstract. The concept of fair usage is a technique that has existed for years to achieve dynamic network resource allocation when the users do not consume their broadband access continuously all the time. Each user is expected to use his/her Internet access for only a short time or not at full speed all the time. Otherwise they may impair the quality of experience of other users. The purpose of fair usage and capping is to prevent a small range of users from consuming the entire bandwidth allocated by the network operator for all users. In this paper we propose a new fair usage model that aims at satisfying all the actors (OTT providers, network operators, clients on top of the pyramid, mass-market clients). This model is dedicated to developing countries. We implemented it on an open BSD router and measured impact of performances.

Keywords: Developing countries, Fair usage & Capping, Network resources, QoS.

1 Introduction

Fair usage is a technique that was designed and developed to achieve dynamic network resource allocation since research results revealed that the users do not consume their broadband access continuously all the time. Each user is expected to use his/her Internet access for only a short time and/or not at full speed all the time. Otherwise they may impair the quality of experience (QoE) of other users. The idea of fair usage and capping is to prevent a small range of users from consuming the whole bandwidth allocated for all users. Although fair usage was introduced in fixed broadband networks, it is considered to be more relevant with wireless Internet where bandwidth is limited by the scarce radio spectrum. Besides, fair usage is a critical issue for developing countries because it is one important lever of 'Internet For All' which is one of the real challenges for the coming years in the telecom domain. Fair usage is a key issue for building Internet networks based on a design to cost approach. Current Internet offers are mostly targeted to high ARPU (Average Revenue Per User) and the billing is prepaid. This necessitates the need for new solutions comprising both for high and low ARPU customers. The solutions adopted presently in developed countries are not satisfactory because they are based on unlimited offers. This means that the abundance of energy supply, numerous wired access and backhaul resources

R. Popescu-Zeletin et al. (Eds.) AFRICOMM 2011, LNICST 92, pp. 35–48, 2012.
© Institute for Computer Sciences, Social Informatics and Telecommunications Engineering 2012

and the larger spectrum in wireless access leads enables them not be bothered about such issues more likely. However, the current solutions let the door open to heaver users that pay the same as users who underuse their Internet access. A simple counter-measure from operators consists to set arbitrarily low priorities to applications that consume lot of resources, such as P2P (peer-to-peer) because there is no way to distinguish low priority traffic more precisely on other criteria (e.g. contents rather than containers).

Therefore, we advocate for solutions that differentiate content distribution and interactive traffic, and that let the user to deal with a given amount of traffic within given periods of time (peak and low hours). We also aim at distinguishing different offers that fit high and low ARPU clients. Thereby in this paper, we present a new fair usage solution for developing countries that we have validated by a proof of concept integrated to an open source router. The paper is structured as follows. The next section gives an overview of economical drivers in developing countries that require enforcing a solution dedicated to these countries. Section 3 presents current fair usage models, research works that may contribute to define new models and the model that we propose. Section 4 describes the implementation of our solution integrated into an open BSD router and shows the impact on performances. Finally, the last section concludes the paper and gives perspectives on following steps to deploy this solution in real networks.

2   Economical Ecosystem and Problem Statement

In order to define appropriate solution for fair usage and capping models for developing countries, it is necessary to have an idea of the local economical conditions for setting up data networks. We noticed that some specificities that show that providing Internet for all is a real challenge. Addressing this challenge is not only the network operators' responsibility but also a global issue concerning energy suppliers and carriers, OTT (Over The Top) service providers, government and regulatory instances, investors, and even end users that should be aware of limited and costly resources. The major cost investments for setting up and maintaining a data network infrastructure may be distributed on the different network partitions. First, there are cases such as Africa where interconnection costs consist currently a large part of total OPEX (Operational Expenditure) costs; they may raise until 50% of the whole OPEX in some countries; nevertheless they are expected to decrease in the next few years by the arrival of new submarine cables. Countries inside Africa have an additional challenge for setting up a PAN-African backbone based on optical fibers. Second, backhaul and long-haul network partitions may also contribute to increase costs in case of long distance links and of lack of existing wired/optical networks because civil costs are expensive; wireless substitution technologies to fiber and copper are microwaves for short and middle distances (based on multi-hop) or satellites for longer distances in remote areas. Therefore, there may be also bandwidth limitations on this network partition. Third, access network costs represent the highest costs due to the number of sites that replicate costs for site renting, civil engineering for setting up base stations towers (in the case of radio networks that is the most frequent), and energy consumption and maintenance. These factors prevent to deploy too much base stations in a given location (an order of idea about radius is 1 to 1.5km in dense areas, 1 to 5kms in urban and suburban areas, 10 to 15kms in rural and larger distances for remote sites). Moreover, the limited frequency spectrum, especially when there are many operators in the same country is a limitation factor for providing more bandwidth. Therefore building a low cost network infrastructure will not be enough. We will need new mechanisms to use these costly resources optimally in a fairly manner. The cost of present Internet offers is afforded only by a small subset of the population representing the top of the pyramid, including small enterprises. These offers are based on networks that are enabled to provide quality of services (QoS). There is a need to penetrate the Internet access to the rest of the population. This gives an opportunity for telecom operators to reuse their network infrastructures for providing best-effort Internet offers if new offers do not jeopardize existing offers.

3   Fair Usage and Capping Model

3.1   Current Situation in Developed and Developing Countries

In developed countries such as the western European countries, Japan, the U.SA, etc., data mobile rates are falling into unlimited offers drawn by flat rate models in xDSL networks. The inability to create a standard business model that would make every actor to be satisfied is the current situation in such countries. OTT players claim network neutrality whereas network operators declare that network resources consumed by OTT services cost more than final users pay for their traffic consumption. On the user side, we could notice that the resources consumption can be depicted in a Pareto law where 10% of clients are consuming nearly 80% of network resources (see Fig. 1). The users who consume a large amount of the bandwidth claim that they just consume network resources they are allowed to. Some network operators arbitrarily reduce the priority of some applications, such as P2P applications seen as background applications but sometimes erroneously since there is no real standard classification of these applications. Without knowing the end-user point of view while giving such priorities, the impact for the user is not easy to be determined. Therefore, distributing the network resources among clients based on application-level bandwidth management is not well perceived by the end-users. It raises a competition between application-signature recognition in the network by deep packet inspection (DPI) equipments on one hand, and on the other hand, camping new techniques for masking application identity (http masquerading, encryption, dynamic behaviors, changing protocol TCP to UDP, changing ports, etc.).

In developing countries, most offers are based on prepaid, and quotas are set-up to limit the network resource consumption. When a user reaches a quota associated to his/her account then a rate limit is applied or all the associated data traffic is blocked. This is a too simple scheme since the user may be frustrated to

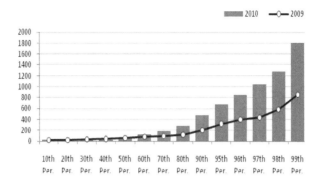

Fig. 1. Distribution of volume among users (sources Cisco)

overtake quota even when the network is not fully loaded. Moreover, quota should not be a single solution because there are some traffic that may be counted in quotas even though they should not be included (e.g., end-user device firmware update, end-to-end retransmission, . . .).

Therefore, this paper aims at presenting new fair usage mechanisms that would make every individual actor satisfied. We assume that the end users are totally aware that the network resources that they are provided with, comes with a cost, as this is the case in developing countries.

3.2   Related Works

In countries like Tunisia, India, etc. quotas are limited according to the periods of time. Network operators distinguish quotas/rates at day time and at night (e.g., unlimited offers limited at night). This is the first step towards the direction that would benefit all but our opinion is that it is not enough. Heavy applications may still grab network resources at peak time until quota thresholds are reached. Applying yield management techniques for providing discount at appropriate time and locations when a cell is not loaded could also be considered as a possible solution. These techniques have succeeded for voice traffic (e.g. traffic-zone, bonus-zone which broadcasts cell-by-cell discounts periodically by Unstructured Supplementary Service Data (USSD) according to the network load of the cell). But these techniques need to be revisited for data which is more complicated. Because, in data networks, network and service may not be provided by the same actor, the network operator does not know service priorities. Different applications have different bandwidth constraints in terms of throughput, delay and packet loss. We consider yield management as a possible solution but we postponed it since it needs first to set up a simpler fair usage and capping model.

Some of the recent works prove that there are already published results on the benefits of using age based scheduling policies on networks to improve user perceived performance [1,2,3,4,5,19]. Priority based scheduling falls in the general framework proposed by Ruschitzka and Fabry [6]. Processor Scheduling (PS) policy has been studied in [7] and compared to round robin. PS is extended to Generalized Processor Sharing (GPS) [8] and Discriminated Processor Sharing (DPS) [9] to support weighted sharing. The LAS/FBPS/FB policy is first studied by Schrage [10] but has received significant recent attention for the case where the task sizes have a large coefficient of variation [11]. Several other blind scheduling policies, such as multi-level feedback-queue scheduling (MLFS) [12], Multi-level Processor-Sharing (MLPS) [13] and its special cases [14] have been also investigated in the context of computers. The scheduling mechanism RuN2C (Running Number 2 Class differentiation mechanism) in [15] gives priority to connections that have small number of packets without penalizing long flows. Its authors suggest setting a threshold that should be well tuned and give two classes of priorities: high and low priority. Scheduling mechanisms defined previously in order to find a compromise between long and short flows suffered from a huge number of parameters that need to be tuned. RuN2C proposes a lighter version in which there is only one threshold to be parameterized and thus distinguish between long and small flows. RuN2C associates the goods of LAS and PS. We had a particular look at [16, 17] because the two different types of age based scheduling policies, LAS and MLPS, are using similar criteria that we looked for. The concept of the Least Attained Service (LAS) scheduling policy is based on size files scheduling. But there is no prior knowledge of a job size, and packets are forwarded according to the amount of processing time that was given to that job. The Multi Level Processor Sharing (MLPS) scheduling policy consists on setting several thresholds; when the number of packets belonging to one job exceeds one threshold this job sees its priority being decreased. So the biggest the size is the more the priority decreases. Finally, authors in [18] quantify benefits and drawbacks related to the deployment of per-flow scheduling (Fair Queuing, Longest Queue First, Shortest Queue First) related to TCP and UDP protocols. Shortest Queue First has an attractive property to implicitly differentiate streaming and interactive traffic, performing as a priority scheduler for applications with low loss rate and delay constraints. In such a way it achieves a similar objective than our solution at a lower cost but further works need to be done to know the impact on heavy flows since it applies to burst periods only. All these works focus on scheduling whereas requirements from the field in developing countries require adapting policies during the day. Our model tries to tackle this.

3.3 Proposed Model

Our proposed solution consists to apply different fair usage policies at given periods of time. We noticed that fair usage is particularly crucial at peak hours because a large proportion of the network resources are dedicated for a short period of time as in fig. 2. If users agree to postpone heavy traffic, especially background applications, after peak periods, then network dimensioning may decrease drastically. The impact on the reduction of the network costs may be seen on the different network partitions, investments for more capacities may be

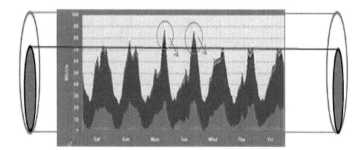

Fig. 2. Evolution of network resource usage during a week (i.e. ratio of traffic load of the aggregation network in y-axis as time is getting on from Saturday to Friday in x-axis). Colors represent different kinds of applications but are not relevant in this context; all applications are cumulated. If some flows (e.g. background applications) can be postponed after peaks, then network operators may reduce Internet prices because they can postpone next investments needed by traffic increase.

postponed by several months. This is really different to the traditional scheduling mechanisms such as shaping which delays some packets in few milliseconds and therefore it appears to be focusing more on dealing with traffic bursts.

One major difficulty is to find a way to set priorities between applications that satisfy the users and the network operator. Although there exist user-network signaling protocols such as Resource Reservation Protocol (RSVP), these protocols are not implemented by Internet applications and not activated in networks for this purpose. So, we can't rely on such a protocol to define user priorities.

Our aims are twofold. On one hand, we suggest to give a better priority to interactive applications during peak hours, and to give better conditions to streaming and download applications at low hours. On the other hand, we consider different user profiles, such as gold/silver/bronze, in order to monetize bandwidth, giving more bandwidth and better rate limit to gold users who pay more. Our solution is based on two criteria: max rate and quotas. Gold users will be granted of a better max rate and a bigger quota than best effort users. Fig. 3 depicts the global schema for our proposed fair usage mechanism.

We allocate a quota and a max throughput rate per user and per period of time taking into account his/her profile. We define two periods of time (peak and low hours) and different bandwidth management policies for each of them. The dissatisfaction that is caused at peak hours will be compensated at low hours, typically upgrading best effort users to gold users at low hours. The impact will consist for instance to reduce the download of a file at a peak hour and to increase it at low hours.

At peak hours, (1) the scheduling policy gives better priority for smaller flows; the priority of more voluminous flows will decrease in two times, respectively by putting them into a best-effort queue, then into a less-than-best-effort queue; we will see in the next section how we pick up these flows and how we have fixed threshold values. (2) We also decrease the rate limit as far as the quota is decreasing for best effort users. There is no impact on gold users clients. More-over, our model gets rid of the need and complexity to display the fare period. Reciprocally, our model includes incentive mechanisms for applications that use protocols which stop transmission whenever they encounter congestion (instead of retransmitting), such as Lower-than-Best-Effort Transport Protocols (LED-BAT). We have included special compensating mechanisms for these applications as well by granting extra-quota at low hours.

At low hours we differentiate gold and best effort users by giving them different rate limits. At the beginning at the low hours, we increase quotas for users that have been quiet at peak time, and we remind the best-effort users that have been impacted at peak hours in order to grant them the same quota than gold users. During low hours, if a quota expires then the user rate limit value is decreased. If order to reduce the impact on interactive applications, there is need to apply a scheduling policy such as SQF (Shortest-Queue-First) that has been discussed in the subsection 3.2.

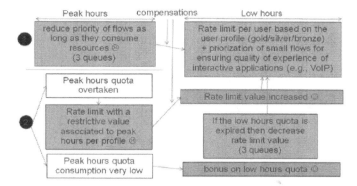

Fig. 3. Schematic diagram for fair usage considering peak and low hours

4   Implementation Issues

4.1   Feasibility Study

As a proof of feasibility, we implemented the schema described above on a real router (OpenBSD). At first we focused on reducing the priority of flows that exceeded a certain volume; the threshold has been set up by trail and error (see subsection 4.3). Then in a second attempt we applied a rate-limit to the traffic of users that exceeded their quotas.

4.2   Reducing Priority of Flows

We classify the flows based on their volume with respect to the consumption of bandwidth at IP level (no need for application-level analysis). We defined a set of queues with different weights (time service) and then according to the volume of a flow through the time we decide to which queue this flow will be forwarded. We maintain a state on the flows that goes through the router. For each incoming packet we look for the state on the flow that is maintained so that we can update the corresponding values (number of packets, volume etc.). We made this choice because OpenBSD uses a strong stateful firewall named Packet Filter (PF). In order to maintain states on connections PF uses Red and Black trees that are typically in-memory structures used to provide fast access to the memory where all states are stored. In this case, R&B trees ensure a fast lookup (if a new packet goes through an interface), insertion (if a new packet of a new connection goes through an interface) and deletion (if a connection is supposed finished, i.e. the packet has got a FIN flag in case of TCP connection). All these operations are about O(log(n)) and this is due to the R&B tree implementation. PF can work in a stateless mode as well as in stateful mode, but its design works in stateful mode by default. We defined filtering rules in the configuration file of the firewall: when a packet matches a rule, then a state is created; all the following packets of the same flow will not check the set of rules; however, they will check the R&B tree to look for the corresponding state entry. Fig. 4. shows these states on flows.

Fig. 4. Description of Packet Filter maintaining the states on flows

OpenBSD uses ALTQ (Alternate Queuing) mechanisms to provide queuing disciplines and other QoS related components required to achieve resource sharing between queues. In the configuration file of the firewall, we defined queues and the scheduling mechanism. Fig. 5. represents the flow diagram for tagging

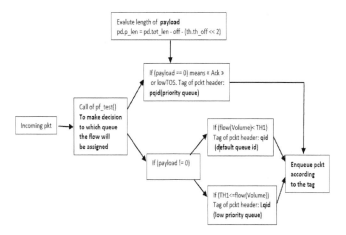

Fig. 5. Flow diagram for tagging packets with the ID of a queue to distinguish the long flow from the small flow according to the threshold TH

packets with the ID of a queue in order to distinguish the long flows from the small flows according to the threshold TH.

We defined queues having different priorities and we queue packets according to the volume of the flow in such a way that we can promote small flows. The issue is that there is no way to re-assign a flow to a different queue. It always gets assigned to one queue which is, the first packet of a flow. So we wrote a process in the firewall that achieves the following behavior: when a new packet comes, after looking for the corresponding state in the R&B tree, the volume of this flow is computed and a tag in the header of that flow is set with the ID of the lower priority queue. All the following packets belonging to that flow will get the same tag. In the next step, we shape the traffic of users that exceeds their quota. In order to avoid to implement a full subscriber management system, we distinguish user profiles (Gold, Best Effort) by referring to their IP addresses in order to simplify the proof of concept. Even addresses represent the Gold profile and odd addresses represent Best Effort profile. The differences between the two profiles are the value of the quota threshold and the value of the rate limit. We implemented two schemes (algorithms)(fig6, fig7) to change the rate-limit associate to IP addresses.

We count the traffic of each IP address and when we find that one IP address exceeded its quota, we add this IP address in a table of exceeders. When a new packet comes, we first check this table to see whether the IP address is listed in this table or not. If it exists then we assign this packet to a Queue which we give the lowest serving time. If it doesn't exist we then check the filtering rules to determine to which queue this packet will be assigned. The following scheme is an example of shaping: assigning traffic according to the profile of the user (Gold or Best Effort), the shaper has 15% of the available bandwidth 10% for Gold profile and 5% for Best Effort profile.

Fig. 6. Create one queue for Gold profile and one queue for Best Effort profile

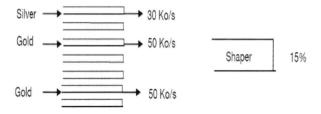

Fig. 7. Create a new queue per IP address and associate its rate limit to the user profile

We make the usual count of traffic per IP address. Then if we detect that a user has exceeded his/her quota, we create a new queue in the configuration file of the firewall and we assign all eventual connections triggered by this IP address to its "own" queue. Then we apply rate limit to the outgoing traffic to a fixed throughput value associate to the user profile. Typically, OpenBSD provides Hierarchical Fair Curve Service (hscf) in order to limit the throughput of a queue with a upper-limit value (e.g. max attained throughput) which the queue will not exceed even if there is a situation when more bandwidth is available. Therefore, if a customer exceeds his/her quota, we first create a new queue on the fly that uses that upper-limit feature of hfsc, then all packets that come from this IP address they will be assigned to that queue. To distinguish the Gold profile from the Best Effort profile we adjust the upper-limit value, respectively 30 and 50 kbytes/s in our proof of concept. Real values will depend on the resources of the operational network dimensioning and the operator strategy. The second scheme is more attractive, but the problem is that the number of filtering rules will become so huge at large scale and this may overload the firewall.

4.3   Performance Issues

In order to evaluate our fair usage model and this implementation, we have captured all the traffic between a DSLAM and a BRAS between 3pm and 4.35pm on a Tuesday on the basis of 2000 clients connected. Then we replayed this captured traffic through the interfaces of the router using 'tcpreplay'.

We dumped the outgoing traffic from the interfaces of the router and compared it with the initial capture using the 'tstat' tool which gives statistics about each flow.

We first used the 'tstat' tool to have a primary idea about the volume, duration and number of connections at that time. We looked at the distribution of flows according to their volume and looked for the duration of flows according to their volume so that we can have an idea about the length of bulky flows and analyze in the mean time the Internet traffic.

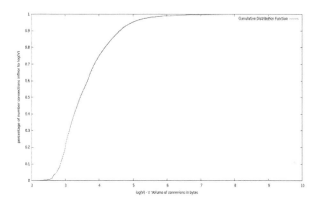

Fig. 8. Repartition of connections according to their volume

Fig. 8. shows the distribution of flows according to their volume within an hour and forty minutes of traffic. Statistics give that there were around 2 millions connections during this duration. We can notice that only 5% of all connections are above 100KB. This is due to basically to the http bursty behavior, e.g. when a client requests a server to open a page. During this time, a lot of connections would be opened just to download some html code. In our case we give interest mostly to bulky and the results underline the assumptions we made for setting up our fair usage scheme.

Fig. 9 shows the duration of flows according to their volume so that we can have an idea about the flows that requires more resources. It is very clear from fig. 7 that the 5% of flows we discussed above are mainly the flows that require most of the resources. Most of them ends in a brief time although they are supposed to be bulky flows.

Then the final test evaluate the impact on performance of reducing the priority of bulky flows so that they either will be dismissed or will be delayed, in order to give more priority to smaller flows. To make this, we replayed the capture of traffic through our OpenBSD router on which we implemented the schemes described in the 4.2. Hence, we observed that the router succeeded to handle more than 10000 connections at the same time without any major decrease in the performance of the router (Fig 10 and Table 1). We also succeeded to set the priority of flows that exceeded our threshold limit and thus redirecting them to less served queues.

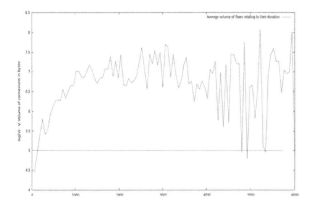

Fig. 9. Distribution of the length of flows according to their volume

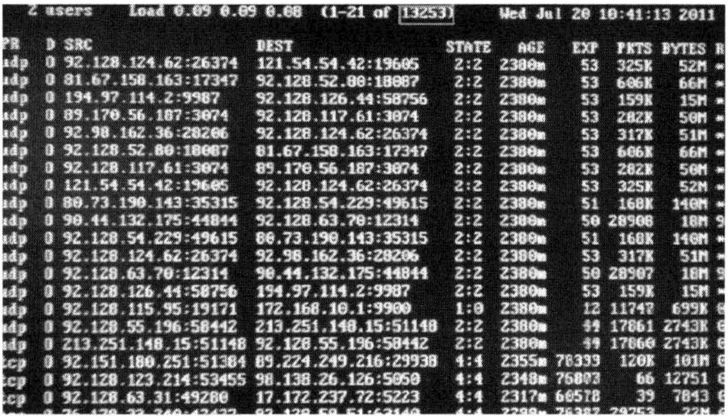

Fig. 10. Capture of the router console showing the impact of the number of connections (in green) on load

Table 1. Impact of changing tcpreplay rate on the router load

Average rate	Number of simultaneous connections	Load(on average every minute)
130Mbps	40000	15%-11%
257Mbps	56000	15%-11%
330Mbps	70000	18%-11%
491Mbps	11000	20%-14%

5   Conclusion

Free access and unrestricted demand for a finite resource ultimately dooms the resource through over-exploitation. This occurs because the benefits of exploitation accrue to individuals or groups, each of whom is motivated to maximize use of the resource to the point in which they become reliant on it, while the costs of the exploitation are borne by all those to whom the resource is available. Before one starts criticizing operators/ISPs for the 'unfair' policy, one needs to understand that bringing a cap to subscriber number per means a direct hit in their revenue and if they need to maintain QoS, they also need to ensure that subscribers too maintain the quality of usage. Through our results, we have proved that it still possible to offer atleast the minimum bandwidth for all the users for certain "given" period of a day that would make every individual actor on the Internet satisfied. However, imposing contention ratio does not help to solve 100% of the problem, but it surely is first step in the right direction. What ISPs need to also ensure is that broadband users are being educated on the usage and repercussions of over-usage and most importantly, quantifying what is fair-usage.

References

1. Massoulie, L., Roberts, J.: Bandwidth sharing: objectives and algorithms. In: IN-FOCOM, vol. 3, pp. 1395–1403 (1999)
2. Guo, L., Matta, I.: Scheduling flows with unknown sizes: Approximate analysis. In: Proceedings of ACM SIGMETRICS (Extended Abstract), pp. 276–277 (2002), extended version available as a Boston University Technical Report BU-CS-2002-009
3. Bonald, T., Proutiere, A.: Insensitive bandwidth sharing in data networks. Queueing Systems 44(1), 69–100 (2003)
4. Yang, S.C., Veciana, G.D.: Enhancing both network and user performance for networks supporting best effort traffic. TON 12, 349–360 (2004)
5. Avrachenkov, K., Ayesta, U., Brown, P., Nyberg, E.: Differentiation between short and long TCP flows: Predictability of the response time. In: Proceedings of INFO-COM (2004)
6. Ruschitzka, M., Fabry, R.: A unified approach to scheduling. Commun. of the ACM 20(7), 469–477 (1977)
7. Coffman, E., Muntz, R., Trotter, H.: Waiting time distribution for processor-sharing systems. Journal of the ACM 17(1), 123–130 (1970)
8. Parekh, A.K., Gallager, R.G.: A generalized processor sharing approach to flow control in integrated services networks: The single-node case. IEEE/ACM Transactions on Networking 1(3), 344–357 (1993)
9. Fayolle, G., Mitrani, L.: Iasnogorodski. R.: Sharing a processor among many job classes. Journal of the ACM 27(3), 519–532 (1980)
10. Schrage, L.: The queue M/G/1 with feedback to lower priority queues. Management Science 13(7), 466–474 (1967)
11. Rai, L.A., Urvoy-Keller, G., Vernon, M.K., Biersack, E.W.: Performance analysis of LAS-based scheduling disciplines in a packet switched network. In: Proc. ACM SIGMETRICS 2004, pp. 106–117 (2004)
12. Silberschatz, A., Galvin, P.B., Gagne, G.: Applied Operating Systems Concepts. John Wiley & Sons (2000)
13. Kleinrock, L.: Queueing Systems, vol. I: Theory, vol. II: Computer Applications. John Wiley&Sons (1975/1976)

14. Aalto, S., Ayesta, U., Nyberg-Oksanen, E.: Two-level processor-sharing scheduling disciplines: Mean delay analysis. In: Proc. ACM SIGMETRICS 2004, pp. 97–105 (2004)
15. Brown, P.: Stability of Networks with Age-Based Scheduling. In: INFOCOM 2007, pp. 901–909 (2007)
16. Ayesta, U., Brown, P., Avratchenkov, K.: Differentiation between Short and Long TCP Flows: Predictability of the Response Time. In: INFOCOM 2004 (2004)
17. Altman, E., Barakat, C., Laborde, E., Brown, P., Collange, D.: Fairness Analysis of TCP/IP. In: Proceedings of IEEE Conference on Decision and Control, Sydney, Australia (December 2000)
18. Carofiglio, G., Muscariello, L.: On the impact of TCP and per-flow scheduling on internet performance. In: Proceeding of 29th Conference on Information Communications, INFOCOM 2010 (2010)
19. Yang, C.-W., Wierman, A., Shakkottai, S., Harchol-Balter, M.: Tail asymptotics for policies favoring short jobs in a many-flows regime. In: SIGMETRICS/Performance, pp. 97–108 (2006)

OpenFlow as an Architecture for e-Node B Virtualization

Venmani Daniel Philip[1], Yvon Gourhant[1], and Djamal Zeghlache[2]

[1] Orange Labs, France Telecom R&D, Lannion, France
[2] TELECOM & Management SudParis, Evry, France
{danielphilip.venmani,yvon.gourhant}@orange-ftgroup.com,
djamal.zeghlache@it-sudparis.eu

Abstract. The ability to enable multiple virtual networks on common infrastructure with different network architectures has been gaining critical importance recently mainly because this kind of sharing does not incur any additional equipment cost for operators. An aim of our ongoing research is to take pragmatic approach towards infrastructure sharing applying operator differentiation and provide a solution to improve traffic prioritization primarily for 4G-LTE mobile networks. We propose a novel solution to the same, based on exploring OpenFlow as an architecture for e-Node B virtualization. By demonstrating the feasibility of adapting the existing OpenFlow mechanism to mobile network architecture, we illustrate the evolution of network sharing via an open network approach, based on OpenFlow. With OpenFlow, we seek to define how far it can be gone within the sharing scenarios based on the architecture of LTE/EPC defined in 3GPP, where the key lock is to open facilities to define flexible and extensible policies.

Keywords: e-Node B Virtualization, Infrastructure Sharing, 4G-LTE, OpenFlow.

1   Introduction

The flexibility to manipulate any hardware device with the ability to program leads to innovation and thus virtualization is one of the key technologies for easy innovation. Virtualization which accounts for and results in resource partitioning are similarly heavily used in network infrastructures. As a result, network virtualization is expected to gain higher interest and be a potential solution to change the way that the communication world exists today. Converging towards this topic, within the context of our research, focusing towards cellular communications, we considered the novel idea of virtualizing e-Node Bs for 4G-LTE mobile networks, thereby enabling operators to share them resulting in enormous cost reduction and take greater advantage of the available resources. The idea emerged from the fact that in recent times, cell site sharing that includes sharing of site locations and masts has been widely adopted as a form of passive sharing especially in rural areas, which was not the case few years before. This is mostly due to the fact that mobile network operators, especially in emerging countries have acknowledged that reducing the cost per bit in their backhaul is now their primary objective. Recent developments show further expansion towards the concept of 'resource sharing' i.e. wider network

R. Popescu-Zeletin et al. (Eds.) AFRICOMM 2011, LNICST 92, pp. 49–63, 2012.
© Institute for Computer Sciences, Social Informatics and Telecommunications Engineering 2012

infrastructure sharing and spectrum sharing. Active sharing (e.g., Radio Access Network (RAN) sharing but not limited to this) has been considered by the operators as a way to reduce cost per bit in the backhaul and has been already set up in different ways which includes 3G RAN sharing between T-Mobile & Hutchison 3 UK, Vodafone & Hutchison 3 Sweden, Orange & Vodafone Spain. It is considered seriously for the rapid deployment of 3G, even in urban areas such as the small towns in Spain with a population range of 1000 and 25000 people, since it achieves approximately 43% saving in Capital Expenditure (CAPEX) and 49% in Operating Expenditure (OPEX), in addition to the passive sharing [28]. Similarly, in Long Term Evolution (LTE), Evolved UMTS Terrestrial Radio Access (E-UTRAN) sharing has already been standardized as an agreement between operators towards active network sharing [27]. Besides, infrastructure sharing has a good impact on energy consumption which is primordial in emerging countries. Africa as a whole is characterized by a very low penetration rate of fixed networks (e.g. 0.7% in Senegal, 3% in Cameroon). By contrast, a significant and rising part of the population owns a mobile phone: 25% on average [1]. Both the rurality of the population and its insolvency acts as a brake upon prospective deployment of fixed infrastructures taking into account the huge investments necessary to install wired solutions. In the sub-Saharan African countries like Kenya, Uganda, Nigeria as well as the Eastern European countries, it is undesirable for each cellular operator to replicate expensive telecom infrastructure to reach the subscribers in remote rural areas even if they were able to afford it. Hence, they go for access network sharing. Digging deeper into the existing network sharing policies [27], it is possible to conclude that operators' consensus on sharing agreement is that a User Equipment (UE) may switch from operator A e-Node B to operator B e-Node B in case of failure in operator A network. This kind of sharing policy can have an impact on the inability of the operators to differentiate themselves over a long duration of time, where every operator becomes unique in terms of QoS. This solution will not be valid when all operators will have enough clients to fill their resource. Additionally, with a high degree of shared resources using today's technologies, the stimulation for competition between the operators is gradually reducing. Hence, from a research perspective, we emphasize the way to evolve infrastructure sharing where the policies could enable "Service Differentiation", ex. service priorities, dynamic sharing policies between operators. Hence, we propose our solution which is based on virtualization of e-Node Bs of operators within the LTE/EPC architecture, where more dynamicity and differentiation in access network sharing could be incorporated by OpenFlow [3], [4] mechanisms, especially when the Telecom regulator imposes it. With OpenFlow, we seek to define how far it can be gone within the sharing scenarios based on the architecture of LTE/EPC defined in 3GPP, where the key lock is to open facilities to define flexible and extensible policies.

Therefore, in this paper, the properties, features, and limitations of OpenFlow enabled devices when illustrated within the context of LTE/EPC architecture are clearly described. The mobile network architecture model was prototypically simplified and simulated by employing the currently available virtualization technique, FlowVisor [5] proposed by the OpenFlow group consortium, since our proposal is based on adapting OpenFlow protocol to the LTE/EPC architecture and the performances were evaluated with comparative results. This paper is a proof of concept experimentation where we pictured two scenarios (but not limited to this) to validate the virtualization behavior of FlowVisor on mobile network architecture. One scenario which evaluates the performance of a network based on OpenFlow protocols compared to the standard virtual local area network (VLAN) slicing techniques [13], since current access network sharing techniques [27] are based on VLANs. The second scenario details about virtualizing the e-Node Bs for different traffic classes and allocating one slice per operator depending upon their traffic needs and evaluates how the available bandwidth is isolated efficiently depending upon the traffic. The most interesting feature of networks based on FlowVisor virtualization technique is that, it gives the operators, the possibility to slice or virtualize bandwidth, traffic, topology of any given network to give each slice its own fraction on a link to the sharing operator. The rest of the paper is structured as follows. Section II describes the various virtualization techniques and gives an overview of the various virtualization projects carried out and its stand in today's communication world. Section III details the adaptation of OpenFlow protocols within LTE/EPC architecture with a brief introduction about LTE/EPC architecture and OpenFlow architecture. This is followed by the last section where we evaluated our results that concludes the paper summarizing our future works.

2   Network Infrastructure Virtualization

Within the context of network infrastructure virtualization, the cellular network architecture can be seen as a physical infrastructure heavily deployed with numerous equipments thus allowing to host multiple virtual networks owned by different mobile network operators. This enables each operator to dynamically adjust in switching resources as well as to maintain independent management control and offer differentiated services in support of the competitive landscape of their geographic region. Taking a brief look on the current state of the art on virtualization techniques, it is already a published result that different operators might manage different virtual networks, all hosted on the Internet, but sharing the same physical infrastructure [6]. Also, virtualization for servers, routers and wire-line links in the internet architecture has already been extensively studied in the literature [7-12].This implies applying the knowledge gained from operating system virtualization experience to network components, leading to virtual network resources like virtual routers, virtual base stations. Vanu MultiRAN [35] is a solution that is available which enables multiple operators to virtually share a single physical network. However, the limitation of this solution is that it is restricted to only 3G and there is no central entity for the each virtual operator to mange all of their virtual networks together. Apart from these, a number of research initiatives and projects all over the globe have started focusing on Network Virtualization, e.g. GENI [15] [16], PLANETLAB [17], VINI [18], CABO [19], Cabernet [20] in the United States; 4WARD [21] [22] in Europe, AKARI [23], AsiaFI [24] in Asia and many others. These show that the current direction in designing the Future Internet is going in favor of having multiple coexisting architectures, where each architecture is designed and customized to fit and satisfy a specific type of network requirements rather than trying to come up with one global architecture that fits all.

3   OpenFlow as an Architecture for e-Node B Virtualization

3.1   LTE/EPC Architecture in Brief

From a technical point of view, Long Term Evolution (LTE) [36] is a radio platform technology that is standardized by 3GPP that allows operators to achieve even higher peak throughputs than other existing mobile technologies in higher spectrum bandwidth. LTE uses Orthogonal Frequency Division Multiple Access (OFDMA) on the downlink which is highly flexible in channelization, achieving peak rates in the range of 100 Mbps in high spectrum bandwidth radio channel sizes ranging from 1.4 to 20 MHz. On the uplink, however, a pure OFDMA approach results in high Peak to Average Ratio (PAR) of the signal, which compromises power efficiency and, ultimately, battery life. Hence, LTE uses an approach for the uplink called Single Carrier FDMA (SC-FDMA). LTE evolution calls for a transition to a "flat," all-IP core network with open interfaces, called the Evolved Packet Core (EPC). The goal of the EPC is higher throughput, lower latency, simplified mobility between 3GPP and non-3GPP networks, enhanced service control and provisioning, and efficient use of network resources. From an investment point of view, it has been revealed the economic reality of LTE migration facing mobile operators around the world and estimated the total CAPEX investment faced by a tier one mobile operator in the first year of roll out [2]. This is listed in Table 1. All these could be envisaged towards infrastructure sharing scenario that would impart savings in equipment costs as well as introduces flexibility in hosting easily configurable virtual networks on a common infrastructure that can be optimized independently by operators to maximize network utility.

Table 1. Cost analysis for LTE investment

Region	Estimated CAPEX investment
US	US $1.78 billion
Europe	US $880 million
Middle East	US $287 million
Asia Pacific	US $227 million

3.2   Choice of Virtualization

Realizing network virtualization technique to the LTE/EPC mobile network architecture means to virtualize the infrastructure of the LTE system. This includes e-Node Bs, routers and even ethernet links and let multiple mobile network operators share a common infrastructure that already exists, by creating their own virtualized network depending on their requirements. From our research prospective, there are primarily two different scopes of virtualization that are foreseen for the LTE/EPC mobile architecture. The first one falls under the scope of virtualization of the air interface between the UE and the e-Node Bs and the second one is to virtualize the physical nodes from the e-Node Bs extending to the backhaul. In [25], the authors carried out virtualization of air interface between the UE and the e-Node Bs by running Hypervisor [44] on the physical e-Node Bs. The simulation results proved that based on the contract configurations and the traffic load of each virtual operator, when the air interface resources are shared among the operators, the overall resource utilization is enhanced and the performance of both network and end-user is better. Although the simulation results are quite specific, the basic findings are representative and show the advantages of applying network virtualization to the LTE/EPC architecture. Their results also demonstrated that the sharing operators benefitted from virtualization mainly by being able to cut costs and providing better performance for the users.

Forecasting such results as the possibility of opening the market to new players especially Greenfield operators that can serve a specific role and have small numbers of users, in this paper, we propose a solution that is based upon virtualization of the physical nodes of the LTE/EPC architecture which particularly includes the e-Node Bs. Each e-Node B is virtually sliced and the resources of physical e-Node Bs owned by an operator are allowed to be controlled remotely by the sharing operator also. Current access network sharing techniques [27] are based on VLANs [13], a common network slicing technique. However, from our research results, we could not be convinced with the advantages that VLANs are offering at the moment. In enterprise and data center networks, VLAN technology is commonplace and continues to evolve. VLANs like IEEE 802.1Q operate mainly on the link layer, subdividing a switched Local Area Network (LAN) into several distinct groups either by assigning the different ports of a switch to different VLANs or by tagging link layer frames with VLAN identifiers and then routing accordingly. When two operators decide to share the same e-Node B with the current VLAN techniques, the operators partition the network by switch port and all traffic is mapped to a VLAN by input port or explicit tag. Nevertheless, these types of partitioning by the VLANs are considered as coarse-grained type of network slicing that complicates IP mobility or wireless handover. On the other hand, in the backbone networks, virtualization in the form of different protocol families utilizing a single Multi Protocol Label Switching (MPLS) core network [34], [35], Virtual Private Networks (VPN) [14] (both layer-2 and layer-3) and tunneling technologies (e.g., IPSec) are widely used and allow some degree of sharing of common physical infrastructures. However, such virtualization approaches are focusing on the virtualization of links and does not allow for traffic differentiation. Accordingly, our solution is based on the idea of having a dedicated OpenFlow network [3], [4] which implements FlowVisor [5] based isolation, which deals with the virtualization of a whole network infrastructure with the ability to control the traffic remotely.

3.3   OpenFlow Architecture in Brief

The fundamental concept behind OpenFlow is that it allows the path of network packets through the network of switches to be determined by software running on a separate server. This separation of the control from the forwarding allows for more sophisticated traffic management than feasible today using Access Control Lists (ACLs) and routing protocols.It works by standardizing the interface between control and data planes and defines atomic behaviors for packet handing within each switching element. The control plane is then moved off-box into a centralized server called the OpenFlow Controller [26], thus enabling users to program their own network behaviors by injecting their own control programs into the controller. FlowVisor is a specialized OpenFlow controller that uses the OpenFlow protocol to control the underlying physical network. It acts as a transparent proxy between OpenFlow-enabled network devices and OpenFlow controllers, using the OpenFlow protocol to communicate with both the controllers and network devices, which are e-Node Bs in our scenario. FlowVisor can logically slice an OpenFlow network and allow multiple controllers to concurrently mange different subsets or different slices of the network resources. Slices can defined by any combination of ten packet header fields [5], including physical layer (switch ports), link layer (src/dst mac addresses, ether type), network layer (src/dst IP address, IP protocol), and transport layer (src/dst UDP/TCP ports or ICMP code). FlowVisor slices can also be defined with negation ("all packets but TCP packets with dst port 80"), unions ("ethertype is ARP or IP dst address is 255.255.255.255"), or intersections ("netblock 192.168.0.0/16 and IP protocol is TCP"). In this way, much like a Hypervisor that acts in a standard machine virtualization, FlowVisor intercepts all control messages to and from the data path and then checks severely and re-writes them to ensure isolation. In an OpenFlow network, when a packet arrives at a switch that does not match any cache flow entries of the switch, the switch generates a message to the controller asking what to do with the packet that has been received of this form. The FlowVisor intercepts this message and makes a policy check to determine which controller is responsible for this packet. This policy check is what we define a slicing definition, i.e. when an OpenFlow switch connects to a FlowVisor, the FlowVisor receives all the slices configured to the OpenFlow switch based on the MAC address. The message is then forwarded to the appropriate controller associated with the slice which makes the forwarding decision. Once the decision is made, the controller sends a corresponding new forwarding rule back down to the switch. The FlowVisor again intercepts the rule and does another policy check, this time, to ensure that the new rule does not infringe on the traffic from other slices. Once the rules are approved by the FlowVisor, it is forwarded onto the switch, cached and then the packet is forwarded on appropriately. Any new packets arriving further, upon matching the cache entry are then forwarded without going through this process again. Thus, all OpenFlow messages, both from switch to the controller and vice versa, are sent through FlowVisor. More explanations about the working of OpenFlow are enumerated in [3-5].

Our scenarios for infrastructure sharing essentially require that typically the e-Node B should have atleast minimal IP support and they must be OpenFlow enabled. With our solution, e-Node Bs are expected to behave as Provider Edge routers or a routing node. With 3GPP's focus on a flat all-IP LTE/EPC architecture, our argument is that, this is realizable. We exploit the capability of FlowVisor based virtualization for virtualizing LTE/EPC architecture because it gives the possibility to slice or

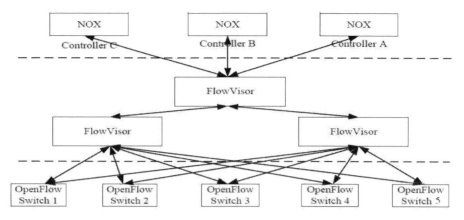

Fig. 1. Block diagram of OpenFlow architecture with FlowVisor and NOX controllers

virtualize bandwidth, traffic, topology of any given network. After virtualization, each operator gets its own portion on a link. As mentioned before, one of the current technologies that is widely used in today's networks as well as a proposed solution for LTE network sharing scenario [27] is based on VLANs. However, VLANs differ from FlowVisor in that rather than virtualizing the network control layer generally, they virtualize a specific forwarding algorithm (L2 learning). FlowVisor, on the other hand, not only supports a much more flexible method of defining networks over set of flows called flow space, it provides a model for virtualizing any forwarding logic which conforms to the basic flow model. Taking advantage of FlowVisor's flexible and fine-grained network slicing technique, with additional capability of hosting multiple OpenFlow controllers with one controller per slice [5], making sure that a controller can observe and control its own slice, while isolating one slice from another, we chose to visualize our proposed solution on network infrastructure sharing based on it.

3.4   Resource Sharing Strategies

Network infrastructure sharing should enable the operators to be able to share the network resources that are already available, without having to invest any further, just by making "slight" modifications to the existing system. This "slight" modification should not result in any additional cost more than it would result in establishing a separate network infrastructure. Our primary solution focuses on the access network sharing extending to the backhaul where the resources from the e-Node Bs until the mobile core network are shared and controlled by operators who have concluded on a sharing agreement. Although, access network sharing has already been standardized in 3GPP [27], there are no solutions proposed to control the resources of e-Node B by another operator other than the one who owns it physically. Now, according to our proposal, each operator will be able to share sufficient amount of its own resource with the other operator(s) who is sharing the infrastructure for the purpose of load sharing as well as to tackle network failure situations of their own network.

As a first step towards this innovative idea, we have elaborated our proposal by considering two scenarios. The first scenario is where the physical equipment, i.e. e-Node B is sliced into two. By this, it is implied that it enforces a policy where there are only two operators who share the same network resources. This is depicted in the Fig. 3. According to this, the entire cellular network resource is divided into two slices by the FlowVisor policy; one for operator A and one for operator B. Each operator operates and controls its own controller(s). Thus, FlowVisor policy slices the network so that operator A's sees traffic from users that have opted-in to his slice. Operators A's slice controller does not know the network has been sliced, so it does not realize it but only sees a subset of only its own traffic. When operator A's controller sends a flow entry to the e-Node Bs, FlowVisor intercepts it, examines operator A's slice policy, and rewrites the entry to include only traffic from the allowed source. Hence the operator A's controller is controlling only the flows it is allowed to, without knowing that the FlowVisor is slicing the network underneath. Similarly, messages that are originating from the e-Node Bs are only forwarded to respective controllers whose flowspace match the message. That is, it will only be forwarded to operator A if the new flow is traffic from a user of operator A that has opted-in to his slice. Thus, FlowVisor enforces transparency and isolation between slices by inspecting, rewriting, and policing OpenFlow messages as they pass. Depending on the resource allocation policy, message type, destination, and content, the FlowVisor will forward a given message unchanged, translate it to a suitable message and forward, or "bounce" the message back to its sender in the form of an OpenFlow error message.

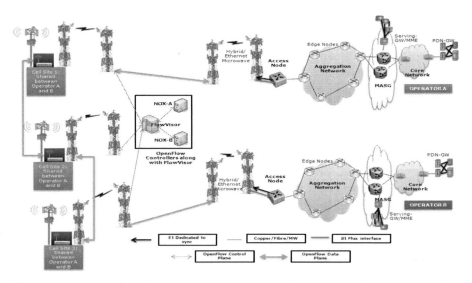

Fig. 2. Access Network sharing between operators using Virtualization (Thanks to OpenFlow FlowVisor)

For a message sent from slice controller to e-Node B, FlowVisor ensures that the message acts only on traffic within the resources assigned to the slice. For a message in the opposite direction (e-Node B to controller), the FlowVisor examines the message content to infer the corresponding slice(s) to which the message should be forwarded. Slice controllers only receive messages that are relevant to their network slice. Thus, from a slice controller's perspective, FlowVisor appears as an e-Node B (or a network of e-Node Bs); from a e-Node B's perspective, FlowVisor appears as a controller. This is one use case by which we trying to elaborate that it is possible to efficiently slice a network according to the needs of the operators.

The second scenario is where the network resources are divided into four different slices. That is each e-Node B is sliced into four for the four different classes of traffic-one optimized for conversational traffic which requires constant bit rate, like voice traffic, one optimized for streaming which is best supported as a variable bit rate service such as audio or video streaming, one optimized for interactive which uses the available bit rate and the last one for background which uses unspecified bit rate like web applications. These four different types of traffic correspond to four different virtual mobile network operators and this is enforced as a policy in the FlowVisor. Fig. 3 shows an example topology that could represent real world OpenFlow mobile network architecture based on our proposal. In Fig. 3, each e-node B in the topology is the connected to a common FlowVisor over a single network path which acts as proxy between the e-node Bs and four different NOX controllers, each operated and controlled by four different operators according to the specified traffic class. Thus, FlowVisor slices every e-Node B of our network and creates multiple logical copies of the same physical network. As explained above, when a controller sends a flow entry to the e-Node B, FlowVisor intercepts it, examines the respective slice policy and rewrites the entry to include only traffic from the allowed source. Thus the bandwidth allocated for each e-Node Bs to carry the traffic towards the core network are isolated virtually and shared among the operators. Thus, operators will be able to control and monitor the resources of a physical e-Node B without really having to take control over it.

The main advantage of this solution are

- Enormous cost reduction: If all the four operators (as in our case) decide to share the cost for deploying the network infrastructure, CAPEX will be greatly reduced for each of them individually.
- Efficient resource utilization: The operators get to optimize their traffic according to the available bandwidth. With our solution we could achieve more optimized use of the available bandwidth according to need of the applications.
- Technically simple solution: Since, the operators do not have to modify the e-Node Bs, it allows for more simplified modification at any time just in the controllers.
- The operators do not have to take care or even pay attention to the traffic of the sharing operator that flows through their own backhaul network infrastructure after the provisioning.
- The operators have the liberty to choose to prioritize the type of traffic that he would want to flow in the sharing backhaul bandwidth. Even better is, the operator can nonetheless care about the traffic priorities and just re-route a part of its own traffic in the shared bandwidth.

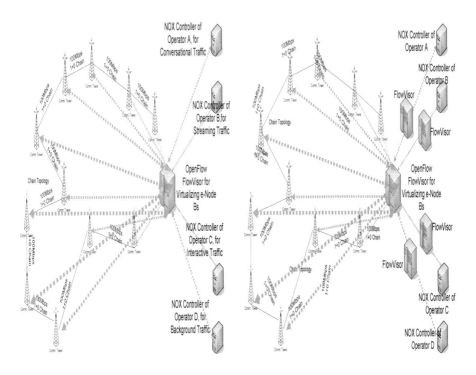

Fig. 3. Access Network sharing between operators using Virtualization based on traffic needs

4   Performance Evaluation

The first part of the simulations was to prove that the efficiency of OpenFlow protocol compared to standard layer 2 switching is better, since a part of our argument also involves proving that the current access network sharing techniques for e-Node B based on VLAN could be replaced by OpenFlow architecture. In order to prove the validity of our proposal, we evaluated the performance of OpenFlow protocol against the standard VLANs. As a result of it, we tried to perform the three tests each separately in linux PC. The first one is use to run TCP friendly tests on the PC which had OpenFlow v1.0 running. The second one is to carry out UDP tests for CBR traffic on another PC which was OpenFlow enabled. In addition, we have to add a simple rule in the flow table to forward input packets with a certain destination or source IP address to the output port interface. The third test is to test the traffic throughput with VLAN switching, which was performed by in Linux machine by using the Bridge-tools to set the layer-2 forwarding of the Kernel. The traffic is generated by iperf [33] in TCP mode for the TCP traffic and UDP mode for CBR traffic at a link speed of 1Gbps. As shown in Table 2 and in the graph below, observing from time 60 seconds in the fig. 4, the results prove that the throughput of any OpenFlow network is almost always slightly higher than the usual switching technology. This is due to the better software implementation of packet forwarding method in OpenFlow technology. But, we also observe that the gain decreases when the packet size increases. This is because, the amount of packet that gets dropped increases when the size of the packet increases.

Table 2. Throughput analysis between openflow and vlans

Packet size (bytes)	64	128	256	512	1024	2056
TCP (Mbps) using OF	462.8	656.2	843.5	921.6	954.7	962.8
UDP (Mbps) using OF	507.4	789.3	887.6	935.5	962.5	970.4
VLAN (Mbps)	402.5	596.5	779.9	916.6	934.4	955.2

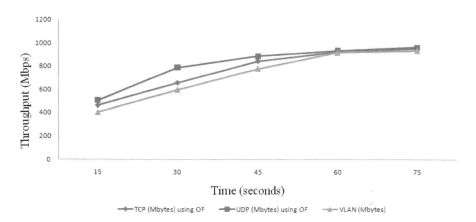

Fig. 4. Throughput analysis between OpenFlow and VLANs for packet size 1024 bytes

The second part of the test is to evaluate the performance gains that could be achieved from virtualizing the LTE/EPC nodes based on OpenFlow implementation exploiting the FlowVisor's bandwidth isolation properties. The fundamental idea is to prove that the network resource that is allocated to a certain physical equipment, which is e-Node B in our case, will be fairly shared among each and every operator who concluded on a sharing agreement based on traffic needs. To demonstrate this, we experimented by considering a simple topology which consists of one OpenFlow Switch connected to four hosts, one FlowVisor Controller and two NOX controllers [26] defining two slices, one is for TCP traffic and the other slice is for UDP traffic. The demonstrated test setup uses two physical machines- one running FlowVisor 0.7.2. configuration [28] the other one runs Mininet simulation tool [30] that helps to populate OpenFlow switches connected to hosts and NOX controllers, running on a virtual LINUX Ubuntu 10.10 [31] as the default OS. Mininet uses the software-based switch type of OpenFlow protocol that use UNIX/Linux systems to implement the entire OpenFlow switch functions. We carried out two sets of experiments. The first one is when the OpenFlow switch is directly connected to the NOX controllers and the second by connecting the switch to FlowVisor, which is inturn connected to the NOX controller. In both the experiments, there are four hosts each connected to two OpenFlow switches on which we carried out TCP and UDP tests using iperf. For the first experiment without FlowVisor connected, when iperf was carried out simultaneously for TCP and UDP traffic on the host machines, we observed that the UDP traffic consumes nearly all the bandwidth and the TCP traffic was only given a part of the bandwidth which averages to 12.28Mbytes of the 1G available link bandwidth. This, in reality means that one operator gets to enjoy more bandwidth than the other when they are sharing a common link. For the second test, where FlowVisor is connected and iperf was carried out simultaneously for TCP and UDP traffic on the host machines, the TCP traffic was able to gain control of the bandwidth ranging to a value of 716Mbytes of the 1G available link bandwidth. This concludes our solution based on FlowVisor isolation where every operator depending upon the contract signed for the specific kind of traffic, will be given a fair share of the network resource. Thus, the FlowVisor does the task of isolating the bandwidth and traffic among the different operators who agreed on sharing. Hence, we could conclude that by adapting FlowVisor based bandwidth isolation features for network infrastructure sharing in LTE/EPC networks, each operator could have its fair share of bandwidth depending upon the traffic needs. Primarily, our emphasis is that with this kind of virtualization technique based on adopting OpenFlow, the configuration of the e-Node B's themselves need not have to be modified in order to change properties of the network infrastructure that is being shared. Also, this scenario allows examination of several aspects of virtualization of e-Node Bs. First, it can be shown that it is possible to migrate one physical network infrastructure entirely into a number of isolated networks just by adding different slice definition in the FlowVisor, without really making many modifications to the existing design of the e-Node Bs. Second, it is possible to share several e-Node Bs in parallel among different operators, sporting different attributes like incorporating different traffic properties for the respective virtually isolated e-Node Bs of the operator. Third, changes within one network can be achieved dynamic during run-time, without any disruption of service in any other virtual e-Node B of another sharing operator. And finally, operators get to control their part of the network without having to be interfered by the sharing operator.

5   Conclusion and Future Works

As the mobile communications sector continues its relentless expansion with more subscribers and more advanced services generating ever-greater volumes of traffic, operators must invest in their infrastructure to provide the bandwidth to meet demand. The LTE/EPC evolution is an evolution towards an all-IP architecture. We believe that OpenFlow opens a door to a new world of virtualization thereby enabling to utilize shared network access. It can be an enabler to network virtualization and service virtualization programmability within the context of mobile network architecture. Network & service virtualization for increasing the ARPU while cutting down CapEx, OpEx can increase revenue opportunities for network service providers. As a part of our proposal towards network infrastructure sharing within the context of LTE/EPC, we have demonstrated in this paper, the adaptability of OpenFlow protocols incorporating the basic additional features to be inculcated into the architecture. With the first phase of results here, we could conclude that network infrastructure sharing by means of virtualization could open new doors not only towards cost reduction but also gives the operators the flexibility they want in terms of traffic prioritization. It allows virtualization of an existing network infrastructure, to start at least between four operators in parallel thus enabling dynamic modification of the properties of one network operator giving fair resource allocation to operators. With such convincing results, our next phase of results would be to extend to prove that with such virtualization technique adapting OpenFlow mechanisms by modifying other parameters to the network infrastructure e.g. adding or removing links, or modifying computing capabilities of virtual e-Node Bs and thus will ease the design of sophisticated network management solutions on top of virtualized networks (e.g. resilient networks).   However, at this level, there are legitimate questions to ask about the performance, reliability and scalability of a controller that dynamically adds and removes flows as the number of e-Nodes could increase for a particular operator: Can such a centralized controller be fast enough to process new flows and program the Flow Switches when it comes to running over an entire cellular architecture? What happens when a controller fails? To some extent these questions were addressed in the context of the Ethane prototype, which used simple flow switches and a central controller [37].   Of course, the rate at which new flows can be processed will depend on the complexity of the processing required by the operator trails. But it gives us confidence that meaningful experiments can be run. Scalability and redundancy are possible by making a controller stateless, allowing simple load-balancing over multiple separate devices. If we are successful in deploying OpenFlow networks in the existing mobile network infrastructure, it will lead to a new generation of control software, allowing operators to re-use controllers.

Acknowledgment. The authors would like to express their gratefulness to the FlowVisor team of Stanford University, U.S.A., especially to Rob SHERWOOD, Deutsch Telecom Labs, Palo Alto, U.S.A., for his ever ending support towards the understanding of FlowVisor.

References

1. Digital World Forum, Low cost broadband access and infrastructure,
   http://digitalworld.ercim.eu/wp3.html
2. http://www.aircominternational.com/
   the-cost-of-lte-demands-innovation-says-aircom.aspx
3. OpenFlow Switch Specification v1.0. Brandon Heller (brandonh@stanford.edu),
   http://www.OpenFlowswitch.org/documents/
   OpenFlow-spec-v1.0.pdf

4. McKeown, N., Anderson, T., Balakrishnan, H., Parulkar, G., Peterson, L., Rexford, J., Shenker, S., Turner, J.: OpenFlow Enabling innovation in campus networks. ACM SIGCOMM Computer Communication Review 38(2), 69–74 (2008)
5. Sherwood, R., Gibb, G., Yap, K.K., Appenzeller, G., McKeown, N., Parulkar, G., Casado, M.: FlowVisor: A Network Virtualization Layer: Technical Report
6. Feamster, N., Gao, L., Rexford, J.: How to lease the Internet in your spare time. SIGCOMM CCR 37(1), 61–64 (2007)
7. Williams, D.E., Garcia, J.: Virtualization with Xen:Including Xenenterprise, Xenserver, and Xenexpress. Syngress Publishing, Inc. (May 2007) ISBN-13: 9781597491679
8. Bhatia, S., Motiwala, M., Muhlbauer, W., Valancius, V., Bavier, A., Feamster, N., Peterson, L., Rexford, J.: Hosting virtual networks on commodity hardware. Georgia Tech. University.Tech. Rep. GT-CS-07-10 (January 2008)
9. Kohler, E., Morris, R., Chen, B., Jahnotti, J., Kasshoek, M.F.: The Click Modular Router. ACM Transaction on Computer Systems 18(3), 263–297 (2000)
10. VROUT, http://nrg.cs.ucl.ac.uk/vrouter
11. VMware Server, http://www.vmware.com/products/server/
12. Cisco VN-Link: Virtualization-Aware Networking, white paper, http://www.cisco.com/en/US/solutions/collateral/ns340/ns517/ns224/ns892/ns894/white_paper_c11-525307_ps9902_Products_White_Paper.html
13. Virtual Bridged Local Area Networks, IEEE Standard 802.1Q (May 2003), http://standards..ieee.org/getieee802/download/802.1Q-2003.pdf (accessed December 17, 2008)
14. Kent, S., Seo, K.: Security Architecture for the Internet Protocol. IETF RFC 430 (December 2005), http://tools.ietf.org/html/rfc4301 (accessed December 17, 2008)
15. GENI Planning Group. GENI: Conceptual Design, Project Execution Plan. GENI Design Document 06-07 (January 2006), http://www.geni.net/GDD/GDD-06-07.pdf
16. GENI: Global Environment for Network Innovations, http://www.geni.net/
17. Bavier, A., Bowman, M., Culler, D., Chun, B., Karlin, S., Muir, S., Peterson, L., Roscoe, T., Spalink, T., Wawrzoniak, T.: Operating System Support for Planetary-Scale Network Services (March 2004)
18. Bavier, A., Feamster, N., Huang, M., Peterson, L., Rexford, J.: VINI Veritas: Realistic and Controlled Network Experimentation. In: ACM SIGCOMM 2006 (September 2006)
19. http://www.OpenFlowswitch.org
20. Zhu, Y., Zhang-Shen, R., Rangarajan, S., Rexford, J.: Cabernet: Connectivity architecture for better network services. In: Workshop on Rearchitecting the Internet (December 2008)
21. Niebert, N., Baucke, S., El-Khayat, I., et al.: The way 4WARD to the creation of a Future Internet. In: ICT Mobile Summit, Stockholm (June 2008)
22. 4WARD project page, http://www.4ward-project.eu
23. AKARI Architecture Conceptual Design for New Generation Network (translatedversion1.1), http://akari-project.nict.go.jp/eng/conceptdesign/AKARI_fulltext_e_translated_version_1_1.pdf
24. Asia Future Internet (AsiaFI), http://www.asiafi.net
25. Zaki, Y., Zhao, L., Goerg, C., Timm-Giel, A.: LTE Wireless Virtualization and Spectrum Management. In: IEEE Wireless and Mobile Networking Conference (WMNC), Third Joint IFIP (2010)
26. http://noxrepo.org/wp/

27. Universal Mobile Telecommunications System (UMTS); LTE; Network sharing; Architecture and functional description (3GPP TS 23.251 version 9.2.0 Release 9)
28. Frisanco, T., Tafertshofer, P., Lurin, P., Ang, R.: Infrastructure Sharing for Mobile Network Operators From a Deployment and Operations View. In: Network IEEE Operations and Management Symposium, NOMS 2008 (2008)
29. http://yuba.stanford.edu/git/
    gitweb.cgi?p=flowvisor.git;a=tags
30. http://yuba.stanford.edu/foswiki/bin/view/OpenFlow/Mininet
31. http://www.ubuntu.com/download/ubuntu/download
32. http://iperf.sourceforge.net/
33. Multiprotocol Label Switching (MPLS) Label Stack Entry: "EXP" Field Renamed to "Traffic Class" Field, RFC 5462
34. Chinni, B.: MR-238, MMBI White Paper on Use of MPLS in LTE (1) (February 2010), info@broadband-forum.org
35. http://www.vanu.com/
36. http://www.3gpp.org/LTE
37. Casado, M., Freedman, M.J., Pettit, J., Luo, J., McKeown, N., Shenker, S.: Ethane:Taking Control of the Enterprise. In: ACM SIGCOMM 2007, Kyoto, Japan (August 2007)

The White Space Opportunity in Southern Africa: Measurements with Meraka Cognitive Radio Platform

Moshe T. Masonta[1,3,*], David Johnson[2], and Mjumo Mzyece[1]

[1] Dept. of Electrical Engineering, Tshwane Univeristy of Technology, Pretoria, South Africa
[2] Univeriry of California, Santa Barbara, Goleta, USA
[3] CSIR– Meraka Institute, P.O. Box 392, Pretoria, South Africa
mmasonta@csir.co.za, davidj@cs.ucsb.edu, mzyecem@tut.ac.za

Abstract. The global migration of television (TV) from analogue to digital broadcasting will result in more spectrum bands (known as TV white space), previously used in analogue broadcasting, becoming available and unoccupied. A question is on how much white space is available and how can it be used opportunistically and dynamically without causing harmful interference to licensed users? In this paper, we present work that is currently ongoing in our research lab with regard to the use of cognitive radio for accessing TV white spaces. We discuss the Meraka Cognitive Radio Platform (MCRP) developed using the second version of the Universal Software Radio Peripheral hardware and the GNU Radio software. We also present early results of the measurements conducted using the MCRP in rural and urban Southern Africa areas. The measurement results indicate that there are substantial white spaces available in both rural and urban areas for digital dividend.

Keywords: cognitive radio, GNU radio, spectrum management, universal software radio peripheral, television, white spaces.

1 Introduction

The demand for broadband access in the modern information society is seen as a driver for rapid growth and development of wireless communication systems. In wireless communication networks, radio frequency (RF) spectrum is the most precious and expensive wireless network resource which needs to be well regulated. Regulators manage the RF spectrum with the aim of minimizing interference between wireless devices. It is therefore crucial to implement effective spectrum management policies to ensure efficient usage and fair sharing of the RF spectrum. With the global digital switchover (DSO) of television (TV) transmission from analogue to digital broadcast, a large portion of the very high frequency (VHF) and ultra high frequency (UHF) bands will be freed and available on a geographical basis for other uses. Such spectrum bands are widely known as TV *"white spaces"* (TVWS). In order to benefit

---

* This work was supported by the Council for Scientific and Industrial Research Council (CSIR) Meraka Institute, Pretoria, South Africa.

R. Popescu-Zeletin et al. (Eds.) AFRICOMM 2011, LNICST 92, pp. 64–73, 2012.

from the digital dividend brought about by the DSO, regulators from the developed countries (such as the United States and United Kingdom) are promoting license-exempt cognitive radio (CR) access to certain licensed TV bands. To enable secondary or opportunistic access to the TVWSs, CR [1] is being intensively investigated by the research community, industry major communication regulators and standardization bodies as a key enabling technology. Cognitive radio is defined by the Federal Communications Commission (FCC) as [2]: *an intelligent wireless communication system capable of changing its transceiver parameters based on interaction with the environment in which it operates.* It allows the implementation of dynamic or opportunistic spectrum access without causing any harmful interference to the licensed or primary users (PUs).

With the decision of the FCC to open up TVWS for unlicensed use [3]-[4], there has been a large amount of interest in producing systems that make use of this new TVWS spectrum using CR technology. Some early experiments have simply attempted to translate the IEEE 802.11 networks into the TV spectrum bands [5]. The same initiative has also been considered by the Office of Communications (Ofcom) in the United Kingdom [6]-[7]. It is believed that regulators, as well as industry and standardization bodies, from other developed countries are also working towards accessing TVWS using CR technology. In South Africa, the Independent Communications Authority of South Africa (ICASA) is also considering different options to ensure a fair and well-balanced reallocation of TVWS in order to benefit from the DSO [8]. However, it is not yet clear whether ICASA will follow the FCC and Ofcom approaches or not.

As research on CR technology develops, and more countries switch over from analogue to digital TV, big questions or challenges arise on the detection techniques to be used and how to protect incumbents. Currently two main techniques are being discussed, and regulators have to decide on the best reliable technique to access the TVWS. The first technique is based on the use of geo-location databases with prediction. And the second technique is based on spectrum sensing using CR technology [9]. Both techniques have their advantages and disadvantages. However, we believe that geo-location databases can be used for the initial set of no-go areas of the spectrum bands and spectrum sensing (with continuous measurements) to be used to avoid unknown and unpredictable sources of interference.

Using TV bands for other communications system can be achieved by understanding the current usage and availability of white spaces. Different techniques, such as spectrum audit, non-real time measurements and real-time measurements (frequency scan) can be used to determine the usage and available spectrum bands. In this paper, we present our initial measurement results showing the actual usage of TV bands transmitted using analogue transmitters in selected urban and rural areas of southern Africa. We scanned TV spectrum in Pretoria, in rural areas of the Northern Cape Province of South Africa, and in Macha, which is in a rural part of Southern Province in Zambia. Measurements were conducted using the Meraka Cognitive Radio Platform (MCRP). In Pretoria, frequency scans were done for more than a week, whereas in the rural areas the scan ran for about twenty four hours. The spectrum scans revealed medium usage of TV spectrum in Pretoria, and very low usage in rural areas.

Even before DSO, large portions of spectrum in the VHF and UHF bands remain constantly unused. We conducted similar measurements in Santa Barbara (US, where one of the authors is based). The results are not included here, due to space limitation, but they show no available bands when compared to Pretoria.

The rest of this paper is organized as follows: Section 2 discusses different cognitive spectrum access techniques for TVWS and some standardization efforts. Section 3 describes the platform used to collect the measurements or frequency scans. The results of our measurements are discussed in Section 4. Section 5 concludes the paper.

2   TV White Spaces Access

The migration of TV stations from analogue to digital or digital switchover (DSO) has already started in some developed countries. In the US, DSO was completed in June 2009 and other countries are also following. Although officially completed in June 2009, DSO in US was not a smooth process. For instance, it was reported that digital TV viewers from many cities in the US could not receive the signal, and FCC officials have held meetings to discuss a potential solution to the reception problems [10]. In some cases, broadcast stations had to increase power levels or add translators to extend the signal to more viewers [10]. Due to the complexity of DSO, several countries decided to extend their DSO completion dates, with UK expected to finish by 2012 and South Africa expected to be complete by December 2013. These countries may learn from the challenges experienced by the US when implementing DSO.

Successful operation of CR for secondary operation in TV bands depends on the successful detection of TVWS and on the ability to avoid harmful interference to the incumbents. In white spaces bands, licensed or primary users (PUs) include digital TVs and wireless microphones. Regulators in most countries are faced with a challenge of deciding the access method for ensuring that CR devises do not cause harmful interference to incumbents. Three methods were considered by the FCC and Ofcom: *geo-location databases*, *spectrum sensing* and *beacons*.

2.1   Geo-location Database Technique

With a geo-location database approach, the PU may be registered in a database and the CR user will have to first determine its location and then interrogate the databases periodically in order to find the free and available channels [9],[11]. It is very important for CR devices to know their geographical location with a prescribed accuracy [11]. Such accuracy may be determined by the regulator. Other data that a CR device is expected to provide to the database may include the device type, model and expected area of operation. In response, a database is expected to reply with the available frequencies, maximum transmission power, and whether the CR device can consult a particular national or regional database.

With this approach, there is a need for either the regulator or operators to build and maintain such databases. Another issue with geo-location databases is the need for an additional connectivity by CR devices in a different band to enable access to the database prior to any actual transmission. A typical TVWS database is shown in Fig. 1. The national regulator can decide to either own or contracts out the supply of a central database, and several secondary or regional databases may be owned by network operators. Geo-location database approach is said to provide a technically feasible and commercially viable solution when compared to the spectrum sensing approach [9].

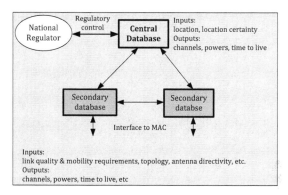

Fig. 1. A Typical White Space Database Structure [9]

2.2   Spectrum Sensing Technique

In the absence of signalling between PUs and CR users, spectrum availability for secondary access may be determined by performing direct spectrum sensing [12]. Spectrum sensing is one of the most challenging, and well explored issues in CR networks (see [12]-[15] and references therein). Two approaches are commonly used for spectrum sensing [16]. The first approach is where a high-performance detection technique is employed at individual radios and a decision on spectrum availability is taken only on one radio's results. However, this method suffers from deep channel fading and the hidden terminal problem [14]. The second approach is where the detection results of multiple radios are combined to combat multipath fading and shadowing, and to mitigate the receiver uncertainty problem [16].

The receiver uncertainty problem, which is a serious challenge for single radio spectrum sensing deployment, is due to lack of knowledge about the PU's location. Cooperation allows independently faded radios to collectively achieve robustness to severe fades while keeping individual sensitivity levels close to the nominal path loss [17]. Though not yet exhausted, research on spectrum sensing has received considerable attention.

2.3   Beacon Technique

The beacon technique allows unlicensed devices to transmit only if they receive a control signal or beacon identifying vacant channels within their service areas [11]. Such signal can be received from a TV transmitter. Without reception of a control signal, the SU will not be permitted to transmit. A challenge with this beacon approach is that it requires a dedicated beacon infrastructure to be in place. Such an infrastructure also needs to be maintained and operated by either the incumbent or a third party. As with single radio spectrum sensing (discussed above), beacon signals can be lost due to the hidden terminal problem.

All the above three techniques have their advantages and disadvantages. It is up to the regulator to decide on the best approach. However, Fitch *et al.* [9] argue that in the future, both database and spectrum sensing techniques will be used together in order to have flexibility and achieve maximum efficiency for secondary or CR users.

2.4   Standardization Efforts

Initial research and development efforts on CR technology for efficient spectrum management have been focused in the US. This was mainly driven by the desire of powerful industry players, such as Microsoft and Google, to get access to the TVWS spectrum [11]. While there are ongoing efforts to standardize the use of CR for efficient spectrum access on TVWS spectrum, the IEEE 802.22 Working Group (WG) [18] is the first wireless air interface standard at an advanced stage. The IEEE 802.22 WG is charged with the development of CR-based wireless regional area network physical and medium access control (MAC) layers for use by license-exempt devices in the TVWS spectrum [19]. A typical use case for the IEEE 802.22 standard would be in sparsely populated rural areas, because TV frequencies offer favourable propagation characteristics [19]. Other CR standardization efforts include IEEE 802.19 [20], IEEE 802.11af and the Cognitive Networking Alliance (CogNea) [21]. The IEEE 802.19 standard is aimed at enabling effective use of TVWS by the family of IEEE 802 wireless standards. IEEE 802.11af working group has been set up to define a standard to implement Wi-Fi technology within the TVWS. CogNea is an open industry association with the intention of commercialising low power personal or portable CR platforms.

3   Cognitive Radio Platform and Measurements

In this section we give a brief description of the Meraka Cognitive Radio Platform (MCRP) and then discuss the setup used for the spectrum scan carried out in both urban and rural areas in Southern Africa.

3.1   Meraka Cognitive Radio Platform (MCRP)

The MCRP is shown in Fig. 2. The platform consists of four CR nodes, and each node is connected to the Internet using the Ethernet cable. A single node is built up of three major hardware components, as shown in Fig. 3: a high speed computer (powered by 2.60GHz Dual Core Intel Pentium Processor, 2 GB memory and 500 GB hard-drive), version two of the Universal Software Radio Peripheral or USRP-2 package (with a single WBX daughter-board) and high gain VHF/UHF antenna (Ellies aerial VHF/UHF Combo with 15 elements). The USRP-2 is a flexible Software Defined Radio (SDR) device developed by Ettus Research LLC [22] which allows the creation of a CR node.

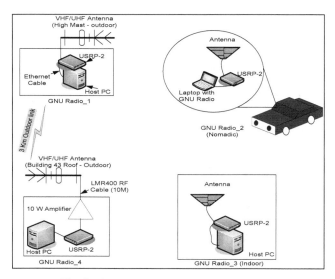

Fig. 2. The Meraka Cognitive Radio Platform

The USRP-2 is composed of a motherboard that performs some baseband processing and of daughter-boards that do the RF front-end part of the radio. Various plug-on daughter-boards allow the USRP to be used on different RF bands. In our lab, WBX daughter-boards with the transceiver of 50 MHz – 2.2 GHz frequency range are used. SDR is a radio communication system where components that would have typically been implemented in hardware are implemented using software.

While traditional hardware based radio devices limit cross-functionality and can only be modified through physical intervention, SDR can receive and transmit widely different radio protocols based solely on the software updates. The CR can be viewed as a SDR which is intelligent and aware of its external operating environment. Each computer hosts the GNU Radio [23] software. GNU Radio is a free software development tool-kit that provides the signal processing runtime and processing blocks to implement software radios using external RF hardware (such as USRP) and commodity processors. GNU Radio has a large and steadily growing worldwide community of developers and users that have contributed to a substantial code base.

In four CR nodes, one node is nomadic, two nodes are located outside the lab, and one is within the lab and the other is located 3 km away. This 3km link allows us to capture typical interference and propagation effects that a production white space system will experience. Depending on the nature of the experiment, a 10 W amplifier can be used to boost the signal during the transmission (at unlicensed bands). An amplifier proved to be important for long distance transmission experiments since the USRP-2 are limited to 100mW output power. Each CR node is connected to the Internet for remote access. This allows remote users to run experiments on the platform from anyway in the world. For our nomadic node, we made sure that the laptop used is also connected to the Internet using the cellular network.

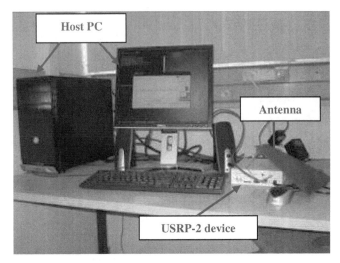

Fig. 3. GNU Radio based SDR Components

3.2   Frequency Measurements

The aim of our measurements was to scan the VHF/UHF spectrum band, from 50 MHz to 1 GHz. We conducted the frequency scan in three different places in Southern Africa. One measurement was carried out in Pretoria at the Council for Scientific and Industrial Research (CSIR) campus, which is the urban area. And the other two were carried out in the rural areas of South Africa and Zambia. In Pretoria, an outdoor CR node was used for the spectrum scan, which ran for more than a week. In the rural areas, a nomadic CR node was used for the spectrum scan, and it ran for less than 24 hours. Multiple consecutive scans were done using 800 kHz bandwidth and Fast Fourier Transform (FFT) size of 2042. The data was post-processed and FFT bins were averaged to 25 kHz buckets.

4   Results

Results of the spectrum scans were plotted from 50 MHz to 1 GHz frequency band. Figures 4-6 show results of our measurements. Fig. 4 shows results from Pretoria (which is urban South Africa). In Pretoria, the CR node antenna was mounted at the high site. Using the national broadcaster's database of TV transmitters around Pretoria, we found that there were at least four TV transmitters. From the plots, it can be seen that even before DSO, there are white spaces available in the urban areas. It is clear that once DSO is completed, there will be even more TVWS available in urban areas.

Fig. 5 shows results of the measurements in Philipstown, which is a rural village in the Northern Cape, in South Africa. As shown on the plot, the majority of the TVWS band is freely available, with some activities at a lower range of the VHF, which appear to be FM radio transmissions. There is only one TV station (SABC 2) available in the area, which appears at 300 MHz. Then other activities are at the 900 MHz, which is occupied by the cellular networks.

Similar trends can be witnessed in the rural Macha area in Zambia, as shown in Fig. 6. However, there are some activities detected between the 200-500 MHz frequency bands.

It can be seen that the spectrum usage in the urban area is much higher than the usage in the rural areas. These results simply mean that rural communities can benefit from the digital dividend using the CR technology. In order to improve broadband connectivity in rural areas, African regulators may either allow license-free operations on TVWS in rural areas or make use of CR technology to access TVWS dynamically.

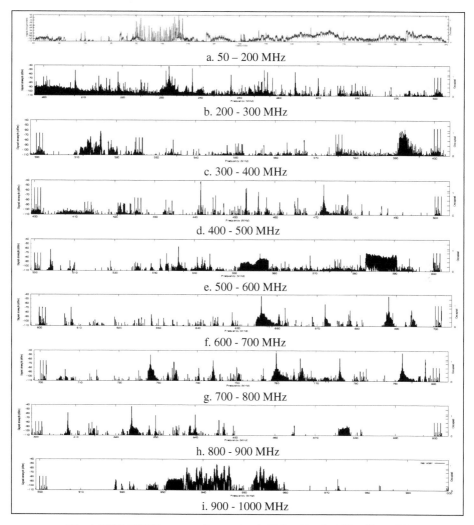

a. 50 – 200 MHz

b. 200 - 300 MHz

c. 300 - 400 MHz

d. 400 - 500 MHz

e. 500 - 600 MHz

f. 600 - 700 MHz

g. 700 - 800 MHz

h. 800 - 900 MHz

i. 900 - 1000 MHz

Fig. 4. VHF-UHF Spectrum Occupation in Urban South Africa (Pretoria)

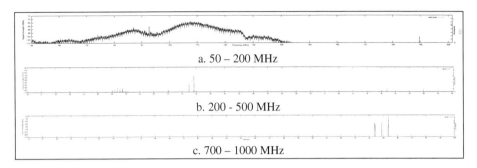

Fig. 5. VHF-UHF Spectrum Occupation in Rural South Africa (Philipstown)

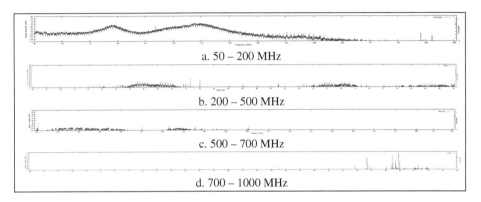

Fig. 6. VHF-UHF Spectrum Occupation in Rural Zambia (Macha rural)

5   Conclusions

The availability of TVWS presents a great opportunity for wider coverage and substantial bandwidth for broadband communications. With the global DSO, there will be even more TVWS available for wireless communications. In this paper we have shown, through active spectrum scans, that there is abundance availability of white spaces in rural areas and urban areas in Southern Africa, as opposed to the results found in Santa Barbara (USA). Our results show that both urban and rural areas will benefit from the digital dividend after the completion of the DSO. Now the question is on how African (or Southern Africa) regulators will regulate the use of TVWS. Will they follow similar approaches to those adopted by the FCC and Ofcom?

This study serves as a starting point towards the development of fully operational white space networks for rural broadband connectivity. Further work will include the development of active spectrum sensing techniques for testing on MCRP. A study on combining both spectrum sensing and geo-location databases for TVWS access will also form part of our future work.

References

1. Mitola III, J., Maguire, G.Q.: Cognitive radio: making software radios more personal. IEEE Personal Communication 6(4) (1999)
2. Federal Communications Commission (FCC): Facilitating opportunities for flexible, efficient and reliable spectrum use employing cognitive radio technologies: Notice of proposed rule making and order. ET Docket 03–108 & 03-322 (2003)
3. FCC: Second memorandum opinion and order in the matter of unlicensed operation in the TV broadcast bands, additional spectrum for unlicesed devices below 900 MHz and in 3 GHz band. ET Docket No. 04-186 & 02-380 (2010)
4. FCC: Second report and order and memorandum. Opinion and order. Technical Report No. 08-260 (2008)
5. Bahl, P., Chandra, R., Moscibroda, T., Murty, R.: White space networking with wi-fi like connectivity. In: Proceedings of ACM SIGCOMM, Barcelona, Spain (2009)
6. Office of Communication.: Statement on cognitive access to interleaved spectrum (2009), http://stakeholders.ofcom.org.uk/binaries/consultations/cognitive/statement/statement.pdf
7. Office of Communication (Ofcom).: Digital dividend review: a statement on our approach towards awarding the digital dividend (2007), http://www.ofcom.org.uk/consult/condocs/ddr/statement/statement.pdf
8. Independent Communication Authority of South Africa (ICASA).: Workshop on the allocation of the digital dividend spectrum (2011), http://www.icasa.org.za/
9. Fitch, M., Nekovee, M., Kawade, S., Briggs, K., Mackenzie, R.: Wireless services provision in TV white space with cognitive radio technology: a telecom operator's perspective and experience. IEEE Comm. Magazine 49(3), 64–73 (2011)
10. Grotticelli, M.: DTV transition not so smooth in some markets (2009), http://broadcastengineering.com/news/dtv-transition-not-smooth-markets-0622/
11. Nekovee, M.: A survey of cognitive radio access to TV white spaces. Hindawi International Journal of Digital Multimedia Braodcasting 2010, article ID: 236568 (2010)
12. Ghasemi, A., Sousa, E.S.: Collaborative spectrum sensing for opportunistic access in fading environments. In: Proc. IEEE DySPAN, Baltimore, USA, pp. 131–136 (2005)
13. Yucek, T., Arslan, H.: A survey of spectrum sensing algorithms for cognitive radio applications. IEEE Tran. on Communications Surveys & Tutorials 11(1) (2009)
14. Ghasemi, A., Sousa, E.S.: Spectrum sensing in cognitive radio networks: requirements, challenges and design trade-offs. IEEE Communications Magazine, 32–39 (2008)
15. Cabric, D., Mishra, S.M., Brodersen, R.B.: Implementation issues in spectrum sensing for cognitive radios. In: Proc. IEEE 38th Asilomar Conference on Signal, Systems and Computers, Pacific Grove, CA, pp. 772–776 (2004)
16. Akyildiz, I.F., Lo, B.F., Balakrishnan, R.: Cooperative spectrum sensing in cognitive radio networks: a survey. To appear in Elsevier Physical Communication Journal (2011)
17. Mishra, S.M., Sahai, A., Brodersen, R.W.:Cooperative sensing among cognitive radios. In: Proc. of IEEE Int. Conference on Communication (2006)
18. IEEE 802.22 Standard, http://www.ieee802.org/22/
19. Cordeiro, C., Challapali, K., Birru, D., Sai, S.N.: IEEE 802.22: an introduction to the first wireless standard based on cr. Jour. of Comm. 1(1), 38–47 (2006)
20. IEEE 802.19: Wireless coexistence working group, http://www.ieee802.org/19/
21. Cognitive Networking Alliance (CogNea), http://www.cognea.org/
22. Ettus Research website, USRP, http://www.ettus.com/ (accessed March 01, 2010)
23. GNU Radio website, http://gnuradio.org/redmine/ (accessed: March 01, 2010)

Strategies for Energy-Efficient Mobile Web Access: An East African Case Study

Le Wang, Edward Mutafungwa, Yeswanth Puvvala, and Jukka Manner

Department of Communications and Networking, Aalto University
P.O. Box 13000, 00076 Aalto, Espoo, Finland
`firstname.lastname@aalto.fi`

Abstract. The limited battery life of mobile handheld devices coupled with the lack of readily or reliable access to electricity is proving to be a major barrier to both adoption and usage of mobile Internet services in most African countries. Therefore, new methods of energy-efficient delivery of mobile web content are essential for prolonging battery life. This paper discusses and evaluates four energy-saving strategies, namely mobile optimization, HTTP compression, caching and proxy. The proposed energy-efficient proxy achieves at most 60% and 74% energy saving in 2G and 3G networks respectively without affecting user experience. As a case study, we consider usage trends and sample web content from three East African countries (Kenya, Tanzania and Uganda).

Keywords: Energy efficiency, Web, Proxy and 2G/3G.

1 Introduction

Mobile computing and communication is quickly becoming a commodity with manufacturers introducing new smart phones almost weekly and operators extending their third generation (3G) and Long-Term Evolution (LTE) network coverage. The development is very welcome for people in developed countries where the society has a state of the art civil infrastructure. In particular, a well-developed power grid is essential for users of modern smart phones because the technological gap between the power consumption of the devices and the current battery technology is increasing [1]. In practice this means that modern smart phones need to be recharged every day because of their increasing demand for energy. Big and bright displays, high-speed mobile connectivity, fancy applications and games all need power from the device battery. For inhabitants of developed countries, charging a phone every day at the office or in the evening at home is not an issue. Yet, in many other countries and geographical locations a stable power grid is not available everywhere [11]. Thus, a mobile device simply has to be very energy-efficient because it can not be charged constantly.

Majority of power consumed by smart phones are attributed to its radio transceiver and modem circuitry [1]. For instance, compared to 848mW power consumption of screen with maximum brightness on a Nokia N900[1], the power consumption of its 3G

---

[1] Nokia N900 specification: http://europe.nokia.com/find-products/devices/nokia-n900.

R. Popescu-Zeletin et al. (Eds.) AFRICOMM 2011, LNICST 92, pp. 74–83, 2012.

radio is around 878mW according to our measurements. As we can see, one of the main factors dominating the energy consumption of web access in the mobile devices is the transmission energy that is proportional to the length of a transmission and the transmit power level. In our earlier work, we have analyzed the power dissipation of 2G, 3G and Wireless Local Access Network (WLAN) radio interfaces [6]. The fixed overhead of transmission is significant when the radio interfaces are in communication state, thus data should be sent in quick bursts (compared to constant small transfers) to enable a longer battery lifetime as interfaces can benefit more efficiently from low power mode. As discussed in [2][3], 2G and 3G links exhibit a residual energy cost after the last packet transmission, before the links switch back to low power state. This is standardized in 3GPP [4], an activity timer triggered when there is no activity still keeps radio modem in high power consumption state for certain period, which can be configured by network operators. Even in WLAN, the radio needs to wait for a predetermined interval to switch from active mode back to power save mode after no frames are received or transmitted.

In the case of web access, energy efficiency is intensively affected by Transmission Control Protocol (TCP) throughput, through the round-trip time (RTT). Based on our measurements, energy consumption per bit significantly increases from 0.536 uJ/bit to 2.103 uJ/bit when RTT rises from 60ms to 1060ms [6]. We can identify different strategies for delivering information and web content more efficiently to the user: the content can be optimized for mobile devices; Hypertext Transfer Protocol (HTTP) compression can be enabled on the server; caching data close to the users help since access times become lower, and we can deploy performance enhancing proxies [5]. The motivation to make use of any of these techniques is that the end users' Quality of Experience (QoE) is improved, which is reflected also back to the network operator and the content provider.

In this paper, we discuss different strategies to help people benefit from mobile web services in areas where stable sources for electric power simply do not exist. As a case study, we consider mobile Internet access and electrification trends from three selected East African countries, namely: Kenya, Tanzania and Uganda. By various measurements we show how much a given enhancement can help the end users and their struggle to extend the lifetime of a modern mobile device.

2   Access to Internet and Electricity

Mobile networks are currently enabling Internet access for millions of previously unconnected users in most emerging markets of Africa. Typically these countries are characterized by miniscule penetration of fixed lines, which implies that Internet access via wireline access infrastructure (e.g. DSL cables) is only possible for a minor segment of the population. On the other hand, mobile networks provide wide-area connectivity with relatively lower upfront costs, thus enabling instant and flexible Internet connectivity for a larger number of users in areas covered with evolved second generation (2.5G) mobile networks, or evolutions thereof.

The subscription data gathered by regulators in the three East African countries of study confirm this trend of exploding mobile Internet service adoption. Statistics from

Kenya's regulator note that the Internet penetration increased from 10% in September 2009 to 22% in September 2010, with mobile Internet access accounting for 99% of the total Internet subscriptions for that period [7]. Similarly, Tanzania's regulator reports that mobile Internet access subscriptions are having the fastest growth rates (42% per year between 2008 and 2010), compared to other fixed wireless and wireline Internet access types [8]. In Uganda, the regulator notes that the mobile Internet subscriptions constituted 94% of all Internet subscriptions by June 2010 [9]. The mobile Internet growth is evident not just in terms of increased subscriptions but also in terms of usage (mobile web traffic). For instance, the mobile web statistics provided by Opera Software (a mobile browser maker) concluded that the number of web page-views and data transferred on mobile handsets in Tanzania grew by 335% and 288%, respectively, in the one year period from December 2009 to December 2010 [10].

However, the continued success in growth of mobile Internet subscriptions is facing a number of barriers, most notably, the lack of a readily available power supply for re-charging of mobile Internet devices. Throughout East Africa, the fraction of the population with mobile Internet access but no access to electricity is growing, particularly in rural areas where less than 3% of the rural population has access to electricity (see Figure 1). Furthermore, with less than 5% of households having computers, mobile handsets are the likeliest Internet access devices. Whilst about half of the urban population has access to electricity (see Figure 1) the supply of electricity can be highly unreliable due to frequent blackouts (see Table 1), because electricity demand exceeds generation capacity in all those countries [11].

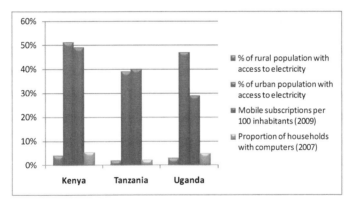

Fig. 1. Comparison of electrification and ICT indicators for three East African countries (Data source: World Bank [11], ITU [12])

Table 1. Electricity blackout data (Data source: World Bank [11])

	Outages (days/year)	Average duration (hours)	Outages (hours/year)	Downtime (% of year)
Kenya	86	8.20	702.6	8.0
Tanzania	67	6.46	435.9	5.0
Uganda	71	6.55	463.8	5.3

It is clear that the very limited access to electricity and unreliable electricity supply presents a significant barrier to continued adoption of mobile Internet services in and sustainability of an acceptable QoE for mobile Internet users in the region. Innovative mobile battery charging methods using solar chargers, used-car batteries or local charging service providers have proved to be very useful for maintaining mobile devices for voice or text messaging services. However, with mobile Internet devices consuming relatively more energy, then energy-efficient methods that prolong the mobile battery life are now very essential.

3   Energy-Saving Solutions

As discussed already, energy-saving solutions become more and more important due to the power constraints. In this section, we discuss four different strategies: mobile web optimization, HTTP compression, caching and performance enhancing proxy.

3.1   Mobile Web Optimization

Mobile web optimization reformats and tailors the web pages to be more accessible and fitted for particular mobile devices. One solution is to tailor any website into a mobile friendly one by concatenating all columns of the pages into a single vertical column, removing the site header, advertisements, resizing or removing all images or even customizing the site with logo adding, and style changing [13][14]. However, the content delivered to mobile devices may not necessarily be the format the site owner intends for mobile users. The other solution is to create the mobile version of websites such that more reliable and optimized content can be directly delivered to mobile users. For example, Facebook offers its mobile web, a lighter version of the actual Facebook.com [15]. Besides, .mobi as a top-level domain name is for mobile devices accessing Internet via mobile web and engaged with the World Wide Web Consortium (W3C) mobile web initiative to formulate practices and publish guidelines for achieving mobile and ubiquitous web [16]. Moreover, a framework for web content and resources adaptation in mobile devices (WRAMD) was proposed in [17]. It adapts web content for specific devices namely standard web content production for desktop machines, which is faster and simpler web content for mobile devices.

Generally, mobile web optimization facilitates web work on mobile devices with speed and less power consumption. However, this strategy, which relies on rather simplified web elements and content, may lead to reduction of QoE for mobile users.

3.2   HTTP Compression

According to RFC 2616 [18], HTTP compression is defined as a way in HTTP 1.1 to transfer HTTP response messages in compressed format from web servers to requesting web browsers. HTTP compression requires both web server and web browser sharing same understanding of compression algorithms (gzip, deflate) so that the web server is capable of encoding the outbound content and the web browser is able to decode the content, which normally are HTML, XML, JavaScript, CSS and other textual files. Nowadays, a majority of network traffic is HTTP traffic and HTTP compression has been widely supported by servers and browsers.

The adoption of HTTP compression in mobile networks are more beneficial because the energy consumed on a single bit transmission over wireless is over 1000 times greater than a single 32-bit CPU computation [19]. The phenomenon indicates that it is energy wise to squeeze bits transmitted over the radio link by spending some CPU cycles in calculations. So, HTTP compression decreases the number of transmitted bits resulting in reduction of the transmission time and leads to reduction in energy consumption as well.

3.3 Web Caching

A further energy-saving technique is web caching which is a mechanism to temporarily store copies of web content on proxy. When subsequent URL requests for the same content are made, the cache responds with either a hit or a miss, indicating the presence of the URL object on the cache. If it is a hit, the web content is transmitted from the cache directly instead of from web server. Caching helps to reduce the traffic on the Internet and server load. On the other hand, it decreases response time and, thus, reduces power consumption of mobile devices when visiting web sites since the devices are able to retrieve web pages faster and be back to idle state quicker.

Normally, there are two types of web caches, namely a browser cache and a proxy cache. A browser cache keeps the copies and returns them to browser locally. By contrast, a proxy cache typically is located in Internet Service Provider (ISP) network and shared by many users. Therefore, a repeat of the download from the original content source can be dramatically decreased. Caching was originally designed for storing static documents. However, dynamic pages, generated dynamically based on request parameters, have been increasing. Thus, dynamic content is also cached on proxy to further reduce download latency and power consumption by increasing hit ratio, as indicated in [20].

3.4 Performance Enhancing Proxy

We have designed an energy-efficient proxy, which applies a simplified data exchange process instead of following standard HTTP to download bundled and compressed web content from web proxy after all the embedded objects are fetched by the web proxy.

By deploying the strategy, the following benefits are offered:

(1) Simplified HTTP message exchange procedure is applied by replacing standard HTTP with bundling between the mobile client and the proxy. Once the proxy receives HTTP request, it is on behalf of the mobile client to fetch all the web content and sends all of the web objects in one bundle to the mobile client. The entire interactive web fetching is offloaded from the mobile device to the web proxy. The

bundling enables the mobile device to enter idle mode and wait in low power consumption state till the proxy sends the bundled objects back instead of keeping its radio on until downloading is finished.

(2) Some studies [20], [21] evaluated the trade-off between transmission and compression, and the results show that compression can be adaptively used to gain energy saving when fulfilling certain conditions, which include considerations of link quality, computation load, file type and compression algorithms. In order to further reduce power consumption, the proxy also compresses the objects selectively based on the compression ratio of compressing the objects and power consumption of mobile devices required for decompressing during the web fetching.

(3) The proxy separates transmission connections between the client and the proxy, and between the proxy and the server. Without the mobile client explicitly requesting all the objects by itself, it improves TCP throughput by reducing delay and enables higher utilization of the wireless network bandwidth between the mobile client and proxy. Ideally, web proxies should be deployed by ISPs or network operators enabling the proxies to be located as close as possible to mobile clients so that the delay between the mobile devices and the web proxy can be minimized.

4   Experimentation and Results

In order to evaluate discussed strategies, we first benchmark our experimental criteria. Then experimental setup is introduced. After that we show our results and discussion.

4.1   Benchmarks

The criteria used for selecting web content samples for use in the experiments are the ranking in terms of being accessed by subscribers in the East Africa region and the origin of the content (local or international content). To that end, the leading website is the international Facebook social media site (which has some localization for local consumptions), while the leading sites from local content providers are the news sites from local publishers [10]. The lack of local content that is optimized for mobile web has been identified as major stumbling block in East Africa [23], this not only reduces accessibility of the content via mobile devices but may also impact on the battery life. Therefore, for the sample websites, we select both regular sites and those that are optimized for the mobile web (see Table 2), so as to further highlight the energy-saving opportunity enabled by optimization of content for the mobile web,

Table 2. Websites selected for the experiment

Note[2]	Facebook	Daily Nation	Daily Monitor
Normal web pages	www.facebook.com	www.nation.co.ke	www.monitor.co.ug
	320978 Bytes	732645 Bytes	820468 Bytes
Mobile optimized web pages	m.facebook.com	mobile.nation.co.ke	mobile.monitor.co.ug
	6458 Bytes	140153 Bytes	87742 Bytes

---

[2] The web pages were obtained the 30th of June, 2011.

4.2   Experimental Setup

In order to obtain quantitative and qualitative understanding of how different strategies affect energy dissipation, we measured the power consumption on the Nokia N900 smartphone and calculated its energy power consumption when mentioned web pages were downloading. To achieve accurate power consumption measurements, the battery of the N900 was replaced by an adapter, which was connected to a 4.1 V DC power supply[3] for stable power source as shown in Figure 3. Then the power supply was serially connected with a 0.1 Ohm resistor. NI cRIO-921[4] was used to collect voltage fluctuations with a rate of 1000 samples per second across the resistor and readings were recorded on a Windows PC with NI-DAQmx software installed. As seen in right upper part of the figure, the readings can be showed in real-time. Based on our measurements, the basic power consumption of the N900 with screen off is around 20mW.

As the benchmarked web sites are located in different countries, RTT between the N900 and each site is variable. Thus, we kept the copies of each web page on our Apache web server for same evaluation criteria and the artificial RTT was 100ms. Besides, the energy-efficient proxy was designed and implemented based on Qt 4.7.3[5], which is the latest SDK of a cross-platform application framework.

4.3   Experimental Results

Considering the electric power is normally accessible in the areas with WLAN coverage, we focus evaluating power dissipation of the cases in 2G and 3G networks. In order to evaluate different strategies, the baseline case for fetching the normal pages was set up by measuring the energy consumption of only using normal HTTP downloading without the help of HTTP compression, cache and proxy. The time spent on fetching the web pages is shown in Figure 3. The relatively higher throughput of 3G networks leads to much less time on downloading the web pages. However, there are no obvious energy consumption differences when the N900 connected to 2G or 3G networks in the cases of downloading normal pages, mobile optimized pages, compressed pages or cached pages, as illustrated in Figure 4. The reason is that the power consumption NI 531.9mW and 878.5mW when the device was operating in 2G and 3G modes respectively. Thus, the product of the time and the power consumption yields basically similar amount of energy consumption, and the average difference is around 10%.

HTTP compression and caching provide almost similar energy-saving according to our measurements. However, as the RTT between proxy and web server increases, caching should provide more energy saving. Mobile optimization as one of the most promising alternatives that offers great energy-saving potential for energy-efficient web access and already has been widely deployed. However, simplified web content affects QoE of mobile users, who have to consider the trade-off between user experience and battery dissipation.

---

[3]   R&S NGMO2 dual-channel analyzer/power supply:
http://www2.rohde-schwarz.com/product/ngmo2.html

[4]   NI 9215 analog input module: http://sine.ni.com/nips/cds/view/p/lang/en/nid/14166

[5]   Qt 4.7.3. http://qt.nokia.com/

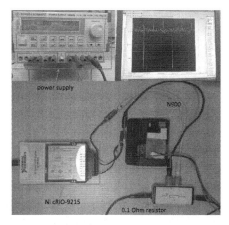

Fig. 2. Experimental setup for measuring power consumption on the Nokia N900

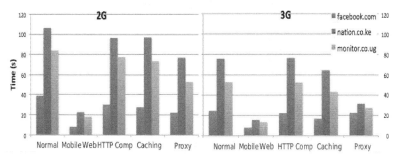

Fig. 3. Time of fetching the three sample web pages using different methods

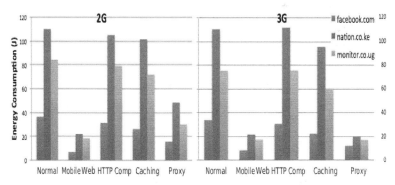

Fig. 4. Energy consumed in fetching the three sample web pages using different methods

Our proposed energy-efficient proxy offers even more energy saving than mobile optimization when the N900 downloaded www.nation.co.ke and www.monitor.co.ug pages in 3G networks. On average, the solution reduces the energy consumption to 41% and 26% of the energy consumption of normal fetching in 2G and 3G networks respectively. Furthermore, it speeds up the downloading speed and decreases the average downloading time to approximately 60% of the time consumed by normal downloading. Since the benefits gained from compression are also depends on the content structure of a web page, the results may be different even through the sizes of two web pages are roughly equal.

As discussed in Section 3.4, the proxy utilizes bundling to simplify message exchange between the mobile device and web server. Based on the measurements, the average power consumption of using the proxy is around 636mW for the 2G connection and 606mW for 3G connection. However, the average power consumption in the other solutions is about 996mW and 1383mW for 2G and 3G networks respectively. The results demonstrate that the simplified web fetching allows radio interfaces to stay in low power consumption state during the web fetching. Besides, the energy consumption is further reduced with the assistance of selective compression and full utilization of link capacity of cellular network.

5   Conclusions

As the growth trend of mobile users and the shift to mobile web access has been accelerating in Africa, the lack of reliable access to electric power for re-charging of mobile devices has become increasingly critical. In this paper, we considered three East African countries as a case study to evaluate different strategies for energy-efficient web access on mobile devices. Our proposed energy-efficient proxy reduced the energy consumption of accessing web content by more than 59% for 2G network and 74% for 3G network. Moreover, it decreased the downloading time to 60% on average compared to normal web content fetching without compromising QoE. The work shows great potential in terms of enhancing energy-efficiency. As future work, thorough analysis of the energy-saving strategies based on the proxy will direct us to even more energy-efficient solution for web access.

Acknowledgement. This work was performed within the ECEWA project, funded by the Finnish National Technology Agency Tekes and industry.

References

1. Silven, O., Jyrkkä, K.: Observations on Power-Efficiency Trends in Mobile Communication Devices. EURASIP J. Embed. Sys., 1–9 (2007)
2. Balasubramanian, N., Balasubramanian, A., Venkataramani, A.: Energy Consumption in Mobile Phones: A Measurement Study and Implications for Network Applications. In: The Proceedings of ACM IMC (2009)
3. Sharma, A., Navda, V., Ramachandran, R., Padmanabhan, V.: Belding, E.: Cool-Tether: Energy Efficient On-the-fly WiFi Hot-spots using Mobile Phones. In: Proceedings of International Conference on Emerging Networking EXperiments and Technologies (2009)
4. 3GPP TR 25.480: Terminal Power Saving features
5. Rosu, M.C., Olsen, C.M., Narayanaswami, C., Luo, L.: PAWP: A Power Aware Web Proxy for Wireless LAN Clients. In: Proceedings of the Sixth IEEE Workshop on Mobile Computing Systems and Applications, December 2-3 (2004)

6. Wang, L., Manner, J.: Energy Consumption Analysis of WLAN, 2G and 3G Interfaces. In: Proceedings of 2010 IEEE/ACM International Conference on Green Computing and Communications, Hangzhou (2010)
7. Communications Commission of Kenya (CCK): Quarterly Sector Statistics Report. 2nd Quarter October-December 2010/2011 (2011)
8. Tanzania Communications Regulatory Authority (TCRA): Report on Internet and Data Services in Tanzania: A Supply-Side Survey (2010)
9. Uganda Communications Commission (UCC): 2009/10 Post and Telecommunications Market Review (2011)
10. Opera Software ASA: State of the Mobile Web, December 2010 (2011)
11. Eberhard, A., Rosnes, O., Shkaratan, M., Vennemo, H.: Africa's Power Infrastructure: Investment, Integration, Efficiency. IBRD/World Bank report, Washington DC (2011)
12. ITU: Information Society Statistical Profiles 2009: Africa. ITU-D report for WTD Conference 2010 (2010)
13. Opera mobile, http://www.opera.com/mobile/
14. Google mobile optimizer, http://www.google.com/gwt/n
15. Facebook mobile web, http://m.facebook.com/
16. goMobi, http://gomobi.info/home.html
17. Guirguis, S.K., Hassan, M.A.: A Smart Framework for Web Content and Resources Adaptation in Mobile Devices. In: Proceedings of 12th International Conference on Advanced Communication Technology, Seoul (2010)
18. Fielding, R., et al.: Hypertext Transfer Protocol – HTTP/1.1. IETF RFC 2616 (1999)
19. Barr, K.C., Asanovic, K.: Energy-Aware Lossless Data Compression. ACM Trans. Comput. Syst., 250–291 (2006)
20. Sailhan, F., Issarny, V.: Energy-Aware Web Caching for Mobile Terminals. In: Proceedings of 22nd International Conference on Distributed Computing Systems, Vienna (2002)
21. Wang, L., Manner, J.: Evaluation of Data Compression for Energy-Aware Communication in Mobile Networks. In: Proceedings of International Conference on Cyber-Enabled Distributed Computing and Knowledge Discovery, Zhang Jiajie (2009)
22. Maddah, R., Sharafeddine, S.: Energy-Aware Adaptive Compression Scheme for Mobile-to-Mobile Communications. In: Proceeds of IEEE 10th International Symposium on Spread Spectrum Techniques and Applications, Bologna (2008)
23. Hersman, E.: The Potential of Mobile Web Content in East Africa. Vodafone Policy Paper Series (2011)

Scalable Scheduling with Burst Mapping in IEEE 802.16e (Mobile) WiMAX Networks

Mukakanya Abel Muwumba and Idris A. Rai

Makerere University
P.O. Box 7062
Kampala, Uganda
abelmuk@gmail.com
rai@cit.mak.ac.ug

Abstract. **O**ne **C**olumn **S**tripping with non-increasing **A**rea first mapping algorithm (OCSA) was proposed by Chakchai So-In et al to schedule bursts on downlinks of base station by giving priority to the largest bursts to OFDMA frame. However, size-based scheduling that favor large items are known to exhibit poor average delay performance especially under workload distributions that are highly skewed (i.e., heavy tailed workloads). In this paper, we first study OCSA and use numerical results to show that it starves short bursts at high loads. We then propose improvement to OCSA (iOCSA) and a new algorithm called **O**ne **C**olumn **S**tripping with **I**ncreasing **A**rea first mapping algorithm (OCSIA). In contrast to OCSA, OCSIA gives priority to short bursts. Our detailed numerical results to compare OCSIA to OCSA under varying workload distributions clearly show iOCSA improves the performance of OCSA, and OCSIA significantly outperforms OCSA under heavy tailed workloads without starving large bursts.

Keywords: bursts, heavy-tailed, scheduling and workloads.

1 Introduction

Scheduling plays a vital role in the QoS provision therefore design of efficient and scalable scheduling algorithms for communication systems is very important. WiMAX or IEEE 802.16e however doesnt specify scheduling leading to concerted efforts by researchers to propose a number of potential scheduling schemes for WiMAX. As such various scheduling algorithms have been proposed for WiMAX [1,2,3,4,5,6] and more other exist. The work in this paper is closely related to bursts *size-based* scheduling schemes that were proposed for mobile WiMAX downlink subframe such as OCSA and eOCSA [1,6].

OCSA is a two dimensional rectangular mapping of bursts on the Orthogonal Frequency Division Multiple Access (OFDMA) downlink subframe in IEEE 802.16e mobile WiMAX. OCSA optimizes frame utilization and maximizes the bursts allocation by giving priority to the largest bursts. However, it is a known fact that scheduling policies that favor large bursts perform very poorly under

R. Popescu-Zeletin et al. (Eds.) AFRICOMM 2011, LNICST 92, pp. 84–95, 2012.

heavy-tailed workload distributions [7]. Such workload distributions, which constitute of a large fraction of very short bursts and a tiny fraction (less than 1%) contributes to about half of the total load, have been shown to be common in Internet files today(see [7] and references therein). By giving priority to the largest bursts under such workloads, OCSA negatively affects scalability of the system at heavy tailed burst sizes.

Chakchai So-In et al also proposed the enhanced (eOCSA) [6], which is similar to OCSA except eOCSA considers only one best mapping-pair either the least width or height of the subframe. Thus eOCSA lowers down the complexity whereas by considering all possible mapping pairs in OCSA, the complexity of OCSA increases with the resource allocation size. The eOCSA however fails to give priority to unscheduled bursts in the future frames and still is based on largest-first-approach. In general, the previous work on OCSA and eOCSA lack investigation on the algorithms' scalability.

In this paper, we first investigate the scalability issues of OCSA by comparing its performance under exponentially and heavy tailed bursts distributions. In particular, we first show that at high load, OCSA offers very poor performance in terms of delay under exponentially distributed workloads. To prevent starvation of small bursts under OCSA, we modify it and get iOCSA which gives priority to bursts that have been delayed up to a delay limit (delay threshold). Finally we propose a novel scheduling scheduling algorithm which we call **O**ne **C**olumn **S**tripping with **I**ncreasing **A**rea first mapping algorithm (OCSIA). As the name implies, OCSIA gives priority to smallest bursts first. Using numerical experiments we show that the proposed algorithm offers good performance even at overload conditions.

The rest of the paper is organized as follows: In the next section, the implementation of OCSA scheduling scheme. In Section 3, we discuss workload distribution and performance metrics, evaluate the performance of the scheduling algorithms and present detailed numerical results. In Section 4, we conclude the paper.

2   OCSA Scheduling Scheme

2.1   Overview of OCSA Algorithm

Under OCSA algorithm, data bursts at WiMAX base stations (BSs) are scheduled and mapped on the OFDMA WiMAX downlink subframe. Each subframe has 360 slots where each is capable of taking one unit of data. At each time unit (aka time slot) a frame can schedule and transmit at once up to 360 units of data. Upon arrival of bursts at the BS, the OCSA scheduler will map them according to the order of decreasing sizes until the frame is full. When the next largest burst doesnt fully fit in the remaining space in a frame, OCSA uses the technique of frame *optimization* which involves computing the unallocated space in the frame and selecting a smaller burst that fits the unallocated space in order to fully maximize system utilization.

Given the natural burst size in data networks, it is possible to have bursts sizes greater than 360 units. These bursts require more than a time slot to complete their service from the scheduler. When such a burst is encountered, OCSA scheduler serves it un-interrupted until it completed its service. Note that while servicing a large bursts greater than 360, similar new large bursts can be generated. Consequently, these are also scheduled first until they are over before any new short bursts receive service. In turn, depending on the workload distribution, the short bursts may experience considerable delays at the expense of favoring large data bursts.

2.2   Improved OCSA Algorithm

OCSA doesnt set any delay limit that a burst can experience. As a result, at very high loads and depending on workload distribution, short bursts may experience very high delays leading to unacceptable QoS performance. To avoid this excessive delays under OCSA, we propose an improved OCSA algorithm (iOCSA). That is, iOCSA sets a delay limit (D) for any burst in the system. This is achieved by giving the highest priority any bursts that have been delayed up to D time slots. They are therefore immediately scheduled before any other burst in the system. The exact value of D to use may be application dependent based on the underlying QoS requirements. That is, applications with stringent requirements require small D values. In summary, iOCSA is similar to the generic OCSA (i.e., it gives priority to large bursts). It additionally employs age based priority such that bursts that have been delayed for exactly delay limit D also have the highest priority regardless their sizes.

2.3   The Proposed Scheduling Algorithm

In this section, we propose a new OCSA based algorithm that we call **One Column Stripping with Increasing Area** first mapping algorithm (OCSIA). OCSIA schedules bursts by giving priority to short bursts, this is analogous to size-based scheduling policy of Shortest Job-First (SJF). At any time slot, OCSIA scheduler maps bursts in the WiMAX frame according to the order of increasing sizes until the frame is full, i.e., starting with the smallest to largest.

The last smallest unmapped burst in OCSIA is likely to be larger that the remaining frame space. In such a case, the OCSIA scheduler splits the burst so that part of its burst is transmitted, and the rest is transmitted in the coming time slots based on OCSIA algorithm. We call the remaining unscheduled part of the burst a *partial burst*. In subsequent time slots, a partial burst is treated the same as any unscheduled burst. The partial burst may therefore be directly scheduled in the immediate slot or any of the future slots. It may also be further split in the subsequent time slots until it is fully scheduled or it may be scheduled in one time slot.

We implemented OCSA, iOCSA and OCSIA in Matlab in order to evaluate their performances and to compare their performances under varying workload distributions and load conditions. In the next section, we define workload distributions and performance metrics used in this paper, and present and discuss our findings.

3   The Performance Evaluation

3.1   Workload Distribution and Performance Metrics

In this paper, we use exponential and bounded Pareto (BP) distributions to generate the workloads (bursts) of varying size behaviors. Exponential distribution is popularly used in practice to model samples and events for practical systems, whereas we use BP distribution to model the highly skewed workload of burst sizes which have recently been observed to model files sizes at various levels of network systems.

We shall represent BP distribution in short form as $BP(k, P, \alpha)$, where k and P are the minimum and the maximum burst sizes respectively and α is the exponent of the power law [7]. The Pareto distributions that emerge in computer system applications typically have $\alpha \in (0.9; 1.3)$. For performance evaluation of the algorithms, we generated exponentially distributed bursts sizes with parameter $\lambda = 0.04$, and heavy-tailed bursts sizes with BP distribution $BP(1, 720, 1.0)$. Both distributions are chosen to have equal mean value of 25. Note that the largest burst size for BP distribution is twice the frame size. Realistically, the largest burst size can be much larger that this but we dont have practical bursts' models based on realistic WiMAX networks. The two distributions are used in this paper to demonstrate the performances of the algorithms at typical distributions with high and low variability.

We draw our performance metrics from queuing theory. For instance, we define the term *delay* as the number of time slots a bursts spends in the queue before it is scheduled. We define *mean delay* as the mean of the number of time slots a burst of a given size remains in the queue before it is serviced. *Backlog* is the sum of the unscheduled bursts and *mean backlog* is the mean of unscheduled bursts. Lastly, as the term vividly implies, *percentage of scheduled bursts* is the percent of scheduled bursts at a given time slot. In the next section, we use these metrics to evaluate the performance of the scheduling algorithms presented in Section 2.3. To study the scalability of the scheduling algorithms we show the results at high load ($\rho = 0.9$) and overloaded ($\rho = 1.5$) conditions.

3.2   Performance of OCSA

Let's first look at the performance of OCSA under both, exponential and BP distributions. Our goal here is to show the weakness of OCSA in terms of penalizing short bursts for workload that have highly varying sizes. Due to limited space, we only show delay performances of OCSA at $\rho = 0.9$. We present more results of OCSA performance in terms of other metrics when we compare it with OSCIA in Section 3.4.

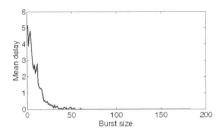 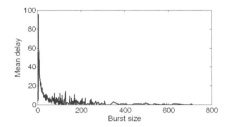

(a) The mean delay as a function of burst size under exponential distribution

(b) The mean delay as a function of burst size under BP distribution

Fig. 1. The delay performances for OCSA at ρ=0.9 under exponential and $BP(1, 720, 1.2)$ distribution

Figures 1(a) and 1(b) show the mean delay as a function of burst size for OCSA under exponential and $BP(1, 720, 1.2)$ at load ρ =0.9 respectively. We can observe from the Figure that the shortest bursts are delayed on average by more than 90 time slots under BP distribution, which is significantly long and much longer compared to the case of exponentially distributed bursts size which exhibits a maximum average delay of only 5 time slots for short bursts. These results clearly show how OCSA penalizes short bursts for heavy tailed workloads. Since under heavy tailed distribution short bursts constitute a very large fraction of bursts this results also clearly demonstrate scalability issues of OCSA scheduler under these workloads.

3.3   Performance of iOCSA

Recall that we propose iOCSA to limit the delay of bursts to avoid significant bursts delays under OCSA regardless of their sizes. In the results we show next, we use a delay limit $D = 5$ for iOCSA just for illustration purposes. Different applications require different practical D values to guarantee their acceptable quality requirements.

Figures 2(a) and 2(b) show mean delay as a function of burst size under exponential and $BP(1, 720, 1.2)$ distributions at $\rho = 0.9$ respectively. Comparing to the OCSA performance depicted in Figure 1 we observe much less mean delay under both workloads. Specifically, we can see from Figure 2(b) that the shortest bursts are now delayed by only 0.4 time slots on average, which is much shorter than 90 time slot as shown in Figure 1(b) for OCSA under BP distribution. Unexpectedly, Figure 2(b) shows that some bursts are delayed 7 time slots (higher than delay limit) on average. This is due to bursts greater than 360 which are generated and given service un-interrupted until all serviced. Compared to the results for OCSA in Figure 1, we can clearly see the performance benefits of iOCSA. It significantly reduces the mean delay of short bursts. In general

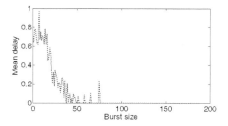

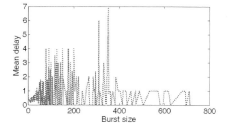

(a) The mean delay as a function of burst size under exponential distribution

(b) The mean delay as a function of time under BP distribution

Fig. 2. The delay performances for iOCSA at ρ=0.9 under exponential and $BP(1, 720, 1.2)$ distribution

however, regardless the distribution of the workload, iOCSA outperforms OCSA with negligible escalation of delay to other bursts.

3.4 Performance of OCSIA

We now compare the performance of OCSIA to OCSA under exponentially and heavy tailed distributed workloads for different values of load ρ. As pointed earlier, for the purpose of studying scalability issues of OCSIA compared to OCSA, we also show the result for overloaded system (load ρ= 1.5) in addition to the results for $\rho = 0.5$ and $\rho = 0.9$. In this section, we present and discuss the performance of the algorithms in terms of all metrics defined in section 3.1.

Exponentially Distributed Workloads. A system is underloaded (Low load system), if utilization or total load of all resources in the system denoted as ρ, is less than 1. We first investigate the performance of OCSIA and OCSA at load ρ=0.5.

Figure 3 shows the delay performance for OCSIA and OCSA. Figure 3.3(a) shows the CDF of delay for OCSIA and OCSA. The results indicate that OCSIA offers delay of zero of all bursts. We note that more than 99% of the bursts experience no delay under OCSIA compared to about 98% of the short bursts with zero delay under OCSA. On the other hand, Figure 3.3(b) shows the mean delay as a function of burst size for OCSIA and OCSA. We can see from the figure that short bursts of less than 40 experience no mean delay and only large bursts above 40 experince low mean delay of less than 1 time slot under OCSIA. In contrast, short bursts under OCSA whereas no large bursts under OCSA experince any delay. This is due to the fact that OCSA favors large bursts and penalizes short ones whereas OCSIA favors short bursts and delays large ones slightly.

Figure 4 shows the delay performance for OCSA and OCSIA under exponentially distributed workloads at ρ=0.9. Figure 4(a) shows the CDF of delay for

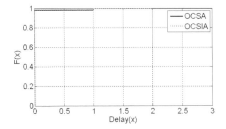

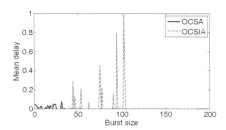

(a) The cumulative distribution function of delay for OCSIA and OCSA

(b) The mean delay as a function of burst size for OCSIA and OCSA

Fig. 3. The delay performance for OCSIA and OCSA at ρ=0.5 under exponentially distributed workloads

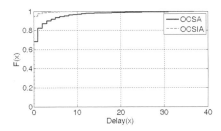

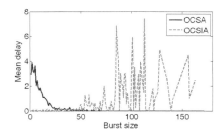

(a) The cumulative distribution function of delay for OCSIA and OCSA

(b) The mean delay as a function of burst size for OCSIA and OCSA

Fig. 4. The delay performance for OCSIA and OCSA at ρ=0.9 under exponentially distributed workloads

OCSIA and OCSA which indicates that OCSIA offers lower delay for most of the bursts. For instance, one can quickly note that about 96% of the short bursts experience no delay under OCSIA compared to 68% of the short bursts with zero delay under OCSA. On the other hand, Figure 4(b) shows the mean delay as a function of burst size for OCSIA and OCSA.

It is evident from the Figure that short bursts experience no or lower mean delay under OCSIA than under OCSA. We also see that, as expected, large bursts experience some delay under OCSIA and no delay under OCSA. This is due to the fact that OCSA favors large bursts and penalizes short ones whereas OCSIA favors short bursts and delays large ones slightly.

Figure 5(a) shows the mean backlog as a function of time for OCSIA and OCSA. We observe that the mean backlog is highly bursty and attains large values for OCSIA and fluctuates around only 10 for OCSA. The mean backlog is computed from the unscheduled large bursts for OCSIA whereas it is from unscheduled short bursts for OCSA. On the other hand, Figure 5(b) shows the

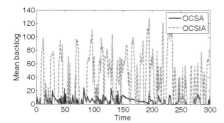 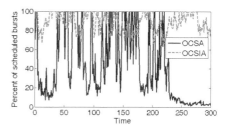

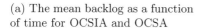

(a) The mean backlog as a function of time for OCSIA and OCSA

(b) The percent of scheduled bursts as a function of time for OCSIA and OCSA

Fig. 5. The backlog performance for the OCSIA and OCSA at load $\rho=0.9$ under exponentially distributed workloads

percentage of scheduled bursts as a function of time for OCSIA and OCSA. As can be seen from the figure, the percentage of scheduled burst is much higher under OCSIA than under OCSA. OCSIA packs many short bursts in the frame. In contrary, when large bursts are serviced under OCSA, very few of these can be parked in the frame.

In real systems, it may happen that bursts arrive to the system at a higher rate than the rate at which they are serviced. This situation is referred to as overload condition where $\rho >1$. Practical systems are often over-provisioned to avoid poor performance at overload conditions, yet in rare cases such as those that lead *flash crowd* phenomena, legitimate requests severely overload systems. Scalable systems should be designed to handle overloaded situations. Therefore, it is useful to study scalability of OCSA and OCSIA at overloaded conditions. Next we compare the performance of OCSA and OCSIA algorithms at overloaded conditions.

Figure 6(a) shows the the CDF of delay for OCSIA and OCSA. We observe that the 95% of the short bursts were scheduled with zero latency for OCSIA compared to 64% of bursts (mostly large bursts) that were scheduled with zero latency for OCSA. This is due to the fact that OCSA gives priority to large bursts and penalizes short ones whereas giving priority to the short bursts, OCSIA delays large ones.

On the other hand, Figures 6(b) shows the mean delay as a function of burst size for OCSA and OCSIA. The figure has two two phases for each algorithm. For OCSIA, phase 1 represents short bursts from 0 to the 50 units which experience zero mean delay. In phase 2, from the 50th burst size to 240, we observe a sharp rise in delay with some large bursts are delayed at most 130 times on average under OCSIA. OCSA exhibits some what opposite pattern from OCSIA algorithm. In phase 1, we can observe from the figure that the shortest bursts are delayed by more than 120 time slots on average, which is significantly long and in phase 2 the large bursts had zero latency for OCSA. We explain this by the fact that OCSA gives priority to large bursts thus the short ones stay longer

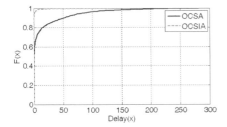
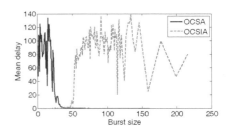

(a) The cumulative distribution function of delay for OCSIA and OCSA

(b) The mean delay as a function of burst size for OCSIA and OCSA

Fig. 6. The delay performance for OCSIA and OCSA at ρ=1.5 under exponentially distributed workloads

in the queue whereas OCSIA gives priority to the short bursts thus the large ones are delayed. Comparing to results for OCSIA and OCSA in Figure 4(b), Figure 6(b) also shows lower mean delays for short bursts for OCSIA.

The results in this section demonstrate that OCSIA indeed favors short bursts whereas OCSA favors large bursts. Even for exponentially distributed bursts, we observe from the figures that more bursts experience shorter latency under OCSIA than under OCSA. However, we also observe higher mean backlog under OCSIA than under OCSA but a larger fraction of scheduled bursts under OCSIA than under OCSA.

Heavy Tailed Workloads. In this section, we compare OCSIA with OCSA under heavy-tailed workloads. Despite lack of measurements to ascertain the exact model for bursts sizes in WiMAX networks, we strongly believe that realistic data burst sizes in WiMAX networks should exhibit similar behaviours as Internet traffic observed today at various levels of networked systems.

Figure 7 shows the delay performance for OCSIA and OCSA for $BP(1, 720, 1.3)$ at ρ=0.5. Figure 7(a) shows the CDF of delay under the BP distribution for OCSIA and OCSA. We observe that OCSIA slightly outperforms OCSA in terms of delay metrics. Firstly, we observe that more bursts experience no latency under OCSIA than under OCSA. Secondly, we also note in Figure 7(b) that mean delay experienced by bursts under OCSIA is shorter than under OCSA.

Figure 8 compares the delay performance of OCSIA with OCSA at load $\rho =$ 0.9. We again observe that OCSIA clearly outperforms OCSA in terms of delay metrics. Observe that more bursts experience no latency under OCSIA than under OCSA. We also see that mean delay experienced by bursts under OCSIA is significantly shorter than under OCSA. Comparing this with the results under exponentially distributed workloads at similar load (Figure 4), we see a very high increase in mean delays for short bursts under OCSA, i.e., shortest bursts experience a mean latency of over 90 time slots under BP distributions compared to only 4 time slots under exponential distribution. This arises especially from

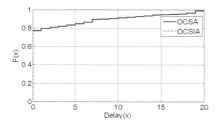
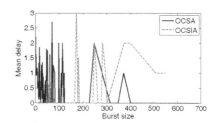

(a) The cumulative distribution function of delay for OCSIA and OCSA

(b) The mean delay as a function of burst size for OCSIA and OCSA

Fig. 7. The delay performance for OCSIA and OCSA at ρ=0.5 under $BP(1, 720, 1.3)$

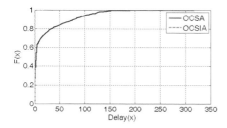
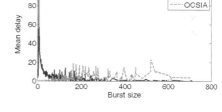

(a) The cumulative distribution function of delay for OCSIA and OCSA

(b) The mean delay as a function of burst size for OCSIA and OCSA

Fig. 8. The delay performance for OCSIA and OCSA at ρ=0.9 under $BP(1, 720, 1.2)$

the fact that heavy tailed distributions like BP have more than 99% of their bursts short and a very tiny fraction of the largest bursts constitute more than 50% of the distributions' weight. Favoring large bursts given workload leads to severe starvation for short bursts under OCSA.

Figure 9b shows that consistently over 95% of bursts are scheduled at each time slot for OCSIA. This is compared to a very small value (negligible percentage) for OCSA. Obviously, the improvement in performance comes with an increase in backlog (due to the tiny fraction of largest bursts constituting more than 50% of the weight of the workload) as shown in Figure 9a. Since this backlog is contributed by a very tiny fraction, we can rightly conclude OCSIA significantly outperforms OCSA under heavy tailed workloads.

Figure 10 shows delay performances of OCSA and OCSIA at overloaded system. Both figures assert the results we observed for load $\rho = 0.9$. It is very intriguing to note that even at overloaded conditions, around 99% of the bursts are scheduled with zero latency under OCSIA compared to only around 35% for OCSA. We also note that short bursts (of sizes up to 50) experience zero or very

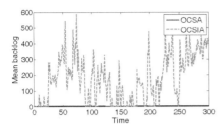
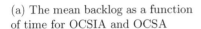

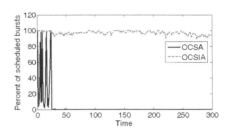

(a) The mean backlog as a function of time for OCSIA and OCSA

(b) The percent of scheduled bursts as a function of time for OCSIA and OCSA

Fig. 9. The backlog performance for OCSIA and OCSA at ρ=0.9 under $BP(1, 720, 1.2)$

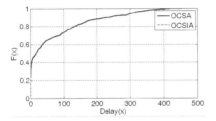

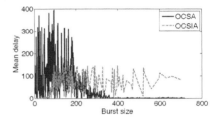

(a) The cumulative distribution function of delay for OCSIA and OCSA

(b) The mean delay as a function of burst size for OCSIA and OCSA

Fig. 10. The delay performance for OCSIA and OCSA at ρ=1.5 under $BP(1, 720, 1.0)$

low latency under OCSIA compared to average latency of close or above 300 for short bursts of sizes up to 200 units for OCSA. The results for backlog and percentage of scheduled bursts for overloaded conditions show a similar trend as for load $\rho = 0.9$ but omitted here due to lack of space.

4   Conclusion

To summarize, we studied OCSA under exponential and heavy tail distributed workloads, proposed a variant of OCSA (iOCSA) that avoids starvation by giving priority to bursts that have been delayed for a given delayed limit, proposed a novel scheduling algorithm (OCSIA). We conducted numerical experiments to study the performance of the algorithms under exponentially and heavy tailed bursts size distributions. We performed our experiments at low, high and overloaded systems in order to investigate and compare scalability performance of the algorithms.

Our findings clearly show that iOCSA provides simple but efficient variant of OCSA that avoids starvation of bursts. The findings also show that the proposed OCSIA algorithm significantly outperforms OCSA algorithm in terms of scheduling more bursts with very low delay at any given time regardless of the workload distribution. We have observed that OCSA offers very poor performance and severely starves short bursts under heavy-tailed workloads, which is known to represent the actual models of realistic transfer sizes in networks and computer systems. It is also very interesting to observe that OCSIA performs very well even at overloaded conditions. It is intriguing that OCSIA successfully serves a significantly large fraction of bursts with zero latency (i.e., more than 99% and about 98% for heavy-tailed and exponentially bursts sizes). This clearly shows that OCSIA is a very scalable scheduling mechanisms for mobile WiMAX networks.

References

1. So-In, C., Jain, R., Al-Tamimi, A.: OCSA: An algorithm for Burst Mapping in IEEE 802.16e Mobile WiMAX Networks. In: Proc. the 15th Asia Pacific Conference on Communications (APCC 2009), Shanghai, China (October 2009)
2. Bacioccola, A., Cicconetti, C., Lenzini, L., Mingozzi, E.A.M.E., Erta, A.A.E.A.: A Downlink Data Region Allocation Algorithm for IEEE 802.16e OFDMA. In: Proc. Int. Conf. on Information, Commun. and Signal Processing (2007)
3. Ben-Shimol, Y., Kitroser, I., Dinitz, Y.: Two-Dimensional Mapping for Wireless OFDMA Systems. Proc. IEEE Transactions on Broadcasting 52, 388–396 (2006)
4. Desset, C., de Lima Filho, E.B., Lenoir, G.: WiMAX Downlink OFDMA Burst Placement for Optimized Receiver Duty-Cycling. In: Proc. Int. Conf. on Commun. 2007, pp. 5149–5154 (June 2007)
5. Ohseki, T., Morita, M., Inoue, T.: Burst Construction and Packet Mapping Scheme for OFDMA Downlinks in IEEE 802.16 Systems. In: Proc. IEEE Global Telecomunications Conf., Washington, DC, USA, pp. 4307–4311 (2007)
6. So-In, C., Jain, R., Al-Tamimi, A.: eOCSA: An algorithm for Burst Mapping with Strict QoS Requirements in IEEE 802.16e Mobile WiMAX Networks. In: Proc. IEEE Wireless Communication and Networking Conference (2009)
7. Rai, I.A.: QoS Support in Edge Routers, Ph.D. dissertation, Ecole nationale superieure des telecommunications, Paris, France (September 2004)

A Pilot of a QoS-Aware Wireless Back-Haul Network for Rural Areas

Philipp Batroff[1], George Ghinea[2], Thorsten Horstmann[1],
Karl Jonas[1], and Jens Moedeker[1]

[1] Fraunhofer FOKUS, Sankt Augustin, Germany
{philipp.batroff,thorsten.horstmann,
karl.jonas,jens.moedeker}@fokus.fraunhofer.de
[2] Brunel University, London, United Kingdom
george.ghinea@brunel.ac.uk

Abstract. Rural areas in emerging regions often lack affordable broadband Internet connectivity, which limits the access to, for example, knowledge, government services or education. The major limiting factors are the Capital Expenditure (CAPEX) and the Operational Expenditure (OPEX) related to traditional wireless carrier equipment, its relatively large energy footprint and the vast but sparsely populated areas to be covered. Since in many rural regions access to a power grid is not available or highly instable, ensuring a 24/7 operation of cell site is a very costly task. To address those issues, we have developed a carrier-grade heterogeneous back-haul architecture in order to complement, extend or even replace traditional operator equipment. Our Wireless Back-Haul (WiBACK) network technology provides wireless back-haul coverage while building on cost-effective and low-power equipment. In this paper we present a pilot scenario in Maseru, Lesotho, where an entrepreneur starts out with three eKiosk/VoIP sites with the goal to cover large parts on the city of Maseru. Using a testbed resembling the initial deployment scenario and identical hardware as planned for Maseru, we validate the self-configuration mechanisms, evaluate their performance in cases of node failures and show that the remaining network can quickly be reorganized.

Keywords: Heterogeneous Wireless Mesh, QoS, MPLS, IEEE 802.21.

1 Introduction

In the last years Wireless Mesh Networks (WMNs) have been a hot topic of interest for commercial operators as well as researchers in the academic world. Their potential to reduce OPEX tremendously by providing a resilient and fault-tolerant network due to Self-configuration and Self-management features, while requiring less deployment cost compared to traditional operator networks is one of the major advantages. This particularly applies if cost-effective network technology is used, e.g. IEEE 802.11[1]. However, in order to be considered as a carrier-grade network which eventually is deployed by an operator to connect customers, WiBACK networks must accomplish the same requirements in terms

R. Popescu-Zeletin et al. (Eds.) AFRICOMM 2011, LNICST 92, pp. 96–105, 2012.

of Quality of Service (QoS), availability and reliability as regular operator net-works. These include the support of triple-play services as nowadays regularly used and expected by todays customers. Given that Voice-over-IP (VoIP) might generate comparatively requirements and load on non-collision free wireless links such as IEEE 802.11 EDCA, the allocation of available link and spectrum re-sources must be strictly managed by the network. Thus, our WiBACK architec-ture provides a Topology Management Function (TMF) as well as a Capacity Management Function (CMF). Whereas the first optimizes the scare radio spec-trum resources by controlling which frequency is used on which link, the latter is in control of allocating the available network capacity to best accommodate user QoS-traffic demands. Additionally, in order to allow for service continuity the CMF quickly reacts on link failures or fluctuations reported by the monitoring component.

The WiBACK architecture itself can be used in manifold use-cases and allows for providing customized solutions which might range from a single-hop long distance wireless link to a region-wide multi-hop back-haul network connecting large urban and rural areas equally. Particularly to address the constraints of rural Africa the WiBACK architecture is designed to maintain a low energy footprint so that WiBACK nodes can be powered with alternative power sources such as solar and wind and hence be easily deployed even in areas without a stable power grid.

Our heterogeneous multi-radio WiBACK is inspired by the work of the EU FP7 CARrier grade wireless MEsh Network (CARMEN) [2] project and adopts its centrally managed cross-layer concept as well as the general concepts of IEEE 802.21 such as command and event services as well as the media abstraction paradigm. Moreover, in order to allow for effective QoS differentiation WiBACK relies on Multi Protocol Label Switching (MPLS)-based Traffic Engineering (TE) and a model to describe wireless channels. For user data transportation between two arbitrary nodes in the network MPLS Label-Switched Paths (LSPs) with dedicated per-hop resource allocation called *Pipes* are established.

The rest of this paper is structured as follows: First we present a prototype deployment scenario for rural areas in Maseru, Lesotho followed by a detailed description of the WiBACK solution. We then show validation and evaluation results regarding the TMF. Concluding, we will summarize our work and an outlook on future work is given.

2   Prototype Deployment Scenario

Larger and rather densely populated areas in developed or emerging countries, can be considered to offer Internet or telephone access to the majority of the population, albeit at highly varying levels regarding the available bandwidth and the cost structure.

In the vast and sparsely populated regions on the other hand, connectivity is often poor or even not available at all. The main reasons for this are the rather high CAPEX and OPEX of traditional operator equipment, unreliable or non-existent connections to a power grid and the lack of trained personnel. Combined with a rather low amount of revenue per customer, larger scale deployments are often not economically feasible.

Hence, to increase the end-user connectivity in rural areas, the CAPEX and mainly the OPEX must be lowered. One option to lower the CAPEX of a deployment scenario is to consider alternative wireless technologies to build the back-haul network. As aforementioned, possible options might be IEEE 802.11 or 802.16 based hardware, which can be adapted to provide high throughput over long distances. It is crucial though, to ensure that requirements such as strict QoS-enforcement and predictable behavior under high load situations can be met.

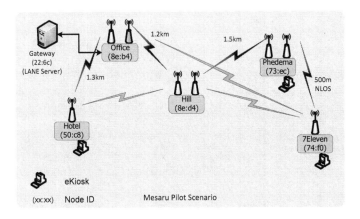

Fig. 1. The initial pilot in Maseru, Lesotho consists of five outdoor WiBACK nodes and one indoor node acting as a WiBACK and eKiosk management node

In this paper we outline a planned prototype deployment scenario in Maseru, Lesotho. A local entrepreneur is planning a small eKiosk businesses with the goal to provide reliable voice and data services. The initial setup, as depicted in figure 1 consists of five wireless nodes and one gateway which will have a connection to a local ISP. The first eKiosk systems are to be deployed at the *7eleven* and *Phedema* as well as at the *Hotel* site. In contrast the *Office* and *Hill* nodes are simple repeater nodes only forwarding traffic. Moreover, the *Gateway* and *Office* nodes will be connected via an Ethernet cable whereas the connections between all other nodes will be realized through Line of Sight (LOS) Wifi links with a range of approximately 1.2 km to 1.5 km. Parallel to the implementation arrangements for Lesotho we setup a smaller testbed with the same topology but smaller distances at our premises in Sankt Augustin for initial testing. All nodes are equipped equally in terms of hardware and number of Wifi devices in order to allow for an easy replacement of nodes in case of a hardware failure and to avoid extensive pre-configuration. A node determines the proper configuration by itself during the initial bootstrap phase. As antennas directional flat panels are used to support the black colored links in figure 1. However, communication via the grey colored links is also possible although with sub-optimal link budget. It should be noted, that the network does not aim at remaining constant in terms of size and nodes but rather to constantly grow, and by establishing more eKiosk systems to cover larger parts of Maseru.

3   WiBACK Approach

The architecture of WiBACK can be divided into the data and the control plane. The control plane is used to setup, manage and maintain the network nodes. Therefore the key concepts of the IEEE 802.21 standard [3] are adapted to support all challenges of wireless network management. While the standard covers seamless handover between heterogeneous technologies the included concepts of media abstraction can be easily extended. As depicted in Figure 2, the Interface Management Function (IMF) is the central messaging component in the control plane at each node. It extends the functionality of the IEEE 802.21 Media Independent Handover Function (MIHF) and supplies an integrative interface to higher level modules. These modules can use a common set of technology agnostic primitives to communicate with each other or with MAC adapters, located logically below the IMF. While the technology specific MAC adapters conduct the management of the radio interfaces, the modules provide all necessary functionalities to setup and manage the network like topology discovery, route calculation or monitoring. For this, the IMF utilizes the messaging services defined by IEEE 802.21. The media independent messaging mechanism can be used by the modules via the MOD_SAP^1 and the AI_SAP^2 for exchanging commands locally and remotely, either between modules or between modules and MAC adaptors.

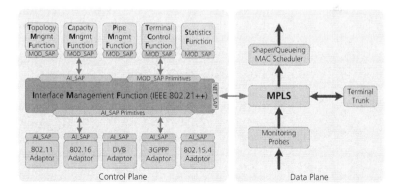

Fig. 2. The WiBACK architecture

---

[1] IMF Module Service Access Point.
[2] IMF Abstract Interface Service Access Point.

The WiBACK network management is based on a centralized approach. Following the concept of a centralized stateful Path Computation Element (PCE) [4], authoritative *Master* nodes controls the resource allocation and routing state of a set of *Slave* nodes in their administrative area. Backup *Master* nodes can be used to keep the network area operational if a primary *Master* node fails. Thereby the discovery and routing setup process can be abbreviated in such a case. In contrast to well known routing protocols such Open Shortest Path First (OSPF) [5] or Optimised Link State Routing (OLSR) [6] a centralized management offers the opportunity to perform network wide optimizations. Requirements like global radio planning or assigning the overall network capacity to best match payload demands can be fulfilled by the *Master* nodes by using monitoring information regarding the link states and resource allocation. In typical distributed link state protocols, like for example Open Shortest Path First - Traffic Engineering (OSPF-TE) [7], these information have to be kept up-to-date and consistent among all nodes locally to make coherent TE routing decisions. Especially wireless links in an unlicensed spectrum often suffer from volatile conditions so that distributed protocols may be inconsistent or not even converge at all, see [8]. In these scenarios a centralized approach addresses the described challenges much better because only the *Master* nodes need to be kept up-to-date and they can calculate resource allocation based on consistent state.

The centralized approach requires a communication path between a *Master* node and each of its *Slaves* to enable the message exchange for the Command, Event and Information service of the IMF. Therefore *Management Pipes* are setup so that the modules and MAC adapters can communicate to each other on the control plane. On the data plane *Data Pipes* can be established between two arbitrary WiBACK nodes. Such *Data Pipes* can be distinguished on their specific QoS demands such as *Best Effort* or *VoIP*. To fulfill the QoS requirements, monitoring the link state is a major task at each node. Thus within the data plane a monitoring component performs fast per-packet link and LSP measurements. Accumulated data will be pushed to the *Statistics Function* where they are further processed, enabling timely reactions to link degradations or failures can be triggered. For example with the MPLS Fast Reroute (FRR) feature WiBACK pipes can be protected against link failure. Furthermore TE processes to ensure QoS assurances are supported by the usage of MPLS.

The WiBACK network management can be divided into two time scales. While the Topology Management Function (TMF) manages nodes, radio interfaces and spectrum resources on a slowly time scale in a range of minutes, the Capacity Management Function (CMF) assigns the available capacity to resource requests and particularly reacting to capacity changes due to link status fluctuations at a faster time scale in the dimension of seconds. The CMF operates on a set of logical links which is a subset of all physical links managed by the TMF. Both modules push pipe state into the network through the Pipe Management Function (PMF) which modifies existing pipe resource allocations or tear down pipes.

3.1   Topology Management Function

For topology discovery the TMF uses a ring-based approach starting at a *Master* node by setting up his own radio interfaces. To achieve an optimal radio configuration, the local capabilities as well as the ambient spectrum are assessed by a passive channel utilization analysis. On successful completion the *Master* starts sending WiBACK beacons on all configured, active interfaces to inform neighbor nodes (*Slaves*) about its availability.

After the bootstrap phase the *Slave* nodes start scanning on all administratively permitted channels for WiBACK beacons sent by a *Master* node or already associates *Slave* nodes. The scanning process is executed periodically to allow the slave node to react on the scan results. If one or multiple WiBACK beacons from other connected nodes are detected, the *Slave* will try to associate with the highest rated neighbor, determined by *Signal Quality* and *hop distance* to the gateway.

The decision making in the association process is based on local knowledge only and might not be an optimal choice considering overall network topology or other TMF optimization criteria. Therefore the TMF *Master* can reject the actual association request and offer alternative nodes or interfaces to associate with.

The currently used optimization criteria is to establish point-to-point links whenever possible as well as choosing the least occupied channel. To minimize channel interference, a separation of at least 60 MHz for IEEE 802.11 radios using 20 MHz channel bandwidth will be ensured.

In the event of a node or link failure the *Master* will be notified, and the affected links/nodes will be marked as *down* in the topology. If other members of the network are afflicted by that, the *Master* will try to reconnect the afflicted nodes according to his optimization criteria. Whenever a *Slave* detects a connection problem to its *Master*, it will stop broadcasting Beacons and jump back into the *beacon scan* mode and attempt a new association.

3.2   Capacity Management Function

Once a new *Slave* is successfully associated with the WiBACK network, the TMF computes the optimal channel configuration out of all available adjacent WiBACK nodes. The set of *ASSIGNED* links is then pushed to the CMF to establish *data pipes* to or in between nodes to manage capacity allocation. The CMF implementation is a central, stateful PCE using Media Independent Handover (MIH)-style primitives for the messaging of the Path Computation Element Protocol (PCEP). For each link the CMF keeps track of the actual allocated resources and the available resources. In order to maintain an up-to-date state of the network wide resource allocation and the link state under his control, the CMF can subscribe to various events like LINK_STATUS_CHANGED or *pipe* related events.

3.3 Pipe Management Function

PMF implements Resource ReSerVation Protocol - Traffic Engineering (RSVP-TE)-style LSP setup and tear down signalling using source-routed IMF messages. Additionally existing LSP resources can be reallocated or altered if needed. Both regular downstream-assigned and upstream-assigned multicast LSPs are supported. PMF uses MIH messages for pipe setup and teardown and allocates resources described via the *TrafficSpecififcations* Type-Length-Value (TLV) at each outgoing interface along the path. This information is used to monitor and enforce the proper QoS-handling of an LSP and Media Access Control (MAC) layer resources by configuring traffic shapers, IEEE 802.16 service flows or IEEE 802.11e queuing parameters.

Classifier Rules are used and maintained to determine which payload from an *Edge Interface* is sent via a specific *Pipe*. These rules can be stateless such as, i.e. a typical IPv4/IPv6 five-tuple rule, or stateful in order to allow a more complex matching. Once a *Pipe* has been set up, the rules can be changed, edited or removed at runtime. A duplex connection between two WiBACK nodes can only be established by configuring a pair of *Pipes*, since each pipe is a unidirectional resource.

3.4 Terminal Control Function

Terminal Control Function (TCF) is an optional component of the WiBACK architecture which provides the functionality required to directly connect User Terminals (UTs) to WiBACK nodes. Depending on the implementation, TCF may provide multiple services such as UT detection and hand-over control as well as local capacity management to match UT traffic demand. The main task is to keep UT/*Pipe* bindings up to date by maintaining proper *Classifier Rules*.

TCF may be implemented to support seamless terminal mobility via for instance, integration with Proxy Mobile IP (PMIP). If mobility is not a major concern, for example, due to rather fixed or nomadic UT usage patterns, less complex approaches such as our QoS-aware LAN Emulation (QLANE)-style mechanism may be implemented.

4 Validation

During the last months the implementation in Maseru has been delayed by unexpected additional costs for waveband licensing. This is still under negotiation with the Lesotho Communication Authority and might break the business case for the local entrepreneur. Therefore we decided to present in this section the obtained results in our outdoor testbed which was build to match the planned Maseru scenario as closely as possible. The main difference is that the distances between nodes are rather in the range of 10...20m instead of 1...2km. In order to provide similar connectivity among the nodes, we have used directional antennas and adopted the transmit power accordingly. Despite those efforts the overall connectivity is higher compared to what we expect for the actual deployment site, but the higher quality links are the same as planned for Maseru.

4.1   TMF Validation

We have evaluated if the TMF properly detects and configures the six-node topology assuming a blackout scenario where all nodes are switched on at the same time. With the current parameterization regarding channel scan and channel analysis timing, it took between three and five minutes for TMF to completely configure the topology and to install the additional *Best Effort* and *VoIP data pipes*. Figure 3 depicts the link and channel configuration after a completed discovery process where TMF has properly detected and configured point-to-point links and assigned channels maintaining a minimum of 60 MHz center frequency separation.

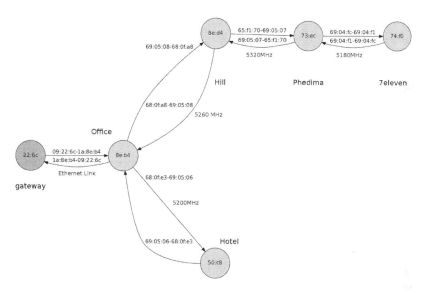

Fig. 3. The TMF Master at node 6c:22 (*Gateway*) has successfully discovered and configured the network by forming point-to-point links

4.2   TMF Evaluation

We have validated the recovery procedure of the Topology Management Function in case of node failures to verify that TMF properly reconnects all remaining nodes. As a second test we've performed an initial evaluation of the recovery functionality to quantify the down times of parts of the network depending on the failing node. For this we disconnected each of the nodes ten times and measured the duration until the complete network was recognized and connected again (Table 1) independently of the discovered topology. Though the network usually finds the same arrangement based on the given environmental circumstances.

The result shows that the network always reconnects whereat the duration varied distinctively. On the one hand this leads back to the periodic scanning behaviour (about 40s, depending on the possible frequencies) of all disconnected nodes, on the other hand the duration mainly depends on the disconnected node and the count of nodes on the path behind. E.g. disconnecting the *Hill* (8e:d4) also cut off the *Phedima* (73:ec) and *7eleven* (74:f0), based on the ring-based algorithm described in section 3.1, the *Hill* get reconnected than *Phedima* and finally *7eleven*.

Table 1. Measured times to complete network recovery after temporary disconnecting a single mesh node

Node	arg/stddev	Samples								
8e:b4	234.5 ± 33.0	246.2	275.3	219.3	245.9	177.3	233.3	284.0	209.3	219.9
8e:d4	213.8 ± 35.0	243.7	193.9	242.4	196.7	208.5	174.4	279.6	175.3	209.4
50:c8	46.1 ± 4.1	41.1	45.4	49.3	51.0	50.5	49.9	41.4	44.6	41.4
73:ec	46.0 ± 6.6	58.0	36.1	42.1	44.6	45.9	43.3	42.8	54.5	46.4
74:f0	60.9 ± 5.5	58.5	63.9	53.4	59.6	59.1	68.2	69.1	61.8	54.2

5 Conclusion and Future Work

We have described the use case of our WiBACK pilot in Maseru, Lesotho, our WiBACK architecture and have shown that it addresses the technical requirements while supporting a rather low cost implementation. Using a testbed resembling the actual deployment scenario, we have verified that our Topology Management Function properly detects and configures the given topology in order to provide collision free wireless links among the involved nodes. The performed measurements exhibit the duration of network reconfiguration periods as a reaction to node failures. With the conservative parameterization it took between 46 seconds and 235 seconds to reconfigure the network.

Future work will focus on tuning the periodical channel scanning mechanism in order to reduce the reconnection times. Further within the framework of the *SolarMesh*[3] project we will exploit how far energy-awareness can lower the overall energy footprint or improve the systems independence from a power grid.

Acknowledgement. This work has been funded by the Federal Ministry of Education and Research of the Federal Republic of Germany (Förderkennzeichen 01 BU 1116, SolarMesh - Energieeffizientes, autonomes großflächiges Sprach- und Datenfunknetz mit flacher IP- Architektur). The authors alone are responsible for the content of this paper.

References

1. IEEE standard for information technology-telecommunications and information exchange between systems-local and metropolitan area networks-specific requirements - part 11: Wireless lan medium access control (mac) and physical layer (phy) specifications, IEEE Std 802.11-2007 (Revision of IEEE Std 802.11-1999), pp. C1–1184 (December 2007)

[3] http://www.solarmesh.de

2. Banchs, A., Bayer, N., Chieng, D., de la Oliva, A., Gloss, B., Kretschmer, M., Murphy, S., Natkaniec, M., Zdarsky, F.: Carmen: Delivering carrier grade services over wireless mesh networks. In: Proc. IEEE 19th International Symposium on Personal, Indoor and Mobile Radio Communications PIMRC 2008, September 15-18, pp. 1–6 (2008)
3. IEEE standard for local and metropolitan area networks- part 21: Media independent handover, IEEE Std 802.21-2008, pp. c1–301 (January 2009)
4. Farrel, A., Vasseur, J.-P., Ash, J.: A Path Computation Element (PCE)-Based Architecture. RFC 4655 (Informational) (August 2006)
5. Moy, J.: OSPF Version 2. RFC 2328 (Standard). Updated by RFC 5709 (April 1998)
6. Clausen, T., Jacquet, P.: Optimized Link State Routing Protocol (OLSR). RFC 3626 (Experimental) (October 2003)
7. Katz, D., Kompella, K., Yeung, D.: Traffic Engineering (TE) Extensions to OSPF Version 2. RFC 3630 (Proposed Standard). Updated by RFC 4203 (September 2003)
8. Bernardos, C.J., Fitzpatrick, J., Kuo, F.-C., Kretschmer, M., Lessmann, J., Niephaus, C., de la Oliva, A., Robitzsch, S., Zdarsky, F.: Carrier-grade wireless mesh networks: D3.4-unicast and multicast routing specification and analysis (December 2009), http://www.ict-carmen.eu/wp-uploads/2009/D3.4.pdf

SolarMesh - Energy-Efficient, Autonomous Wireless Networks for Developing Countries

Christian Mannweiler, Christian Lottermann,
Andreas Klein, and Hans D. Schotten

Chair for Wireless Communications and Navigation
University of Kaiserslautern, Germany
{mannweiler,lottermann,aklein,schotten}@eit.uni-kl.de
http://www.eit.uni-kl.de/wicon

Abstract. This paper presents the research and development activities within "**SolarMesh** - Energy-Efficient, Autonomous, Wide-Area Wireless Voice and Data Network", a R&D project funded by the German Federal Ministry of Education and Research. The project, bringing together expertise from academia and industry in Germany, is specifically dedicated to develop reliable wireless communications infrastructure for rural areas in developing countries, such as in sub-Saharan Africa. Wireless mesh networks based on IEEE 802.11 Wireless LAN technology combined with intelligent functions for self-configuration and self-adaptation can provide affordable ICT infrastructure for access and backhaul operation while at the same time offering carrier-grade QoS for voice and data services. Moreover, the paper outlines how the SolarMesh network operates independently from (potentially unreliable) local energy grids using autarkic energy supply (solar power) and implementing energy-aware routing and handover functions.

Keywords: wireless mesh networks, communications infrastructure for rural areas, autarkic energy supply, situation-aware network management, self-adaptation.

1 Introduction

Today, information and communication technology (ICT) infrastructure (both operator equipment and consumer electronics), besides being very costly, is generally developed according to needs and requirements of urban areas in developed countries. In rural areas and even more so in developing countries (except for the big cities), we encounter completely different conditions and deployment environments and significant financial restrictions. Therefore, the most feasible approach is to conceptually and technically adapt, extend, and improve existing equipment so that it better reflects the needs of thinly populated regions in developing countries. The SolarMesh project, a consortium funded by the German Ministry of Education and Research, consisting of two research institutions and three companies, develops such an autonomous, resource-efficient, easily deployable and maintainable system, as presented in this work. The remainder of the

R. Popescu-Zeletin et al. (Eds.) AFRICOMM 2011, LNICST 92, pp. 106–115, 2012.

paper is structured as follows: The next two subsections briefly describe the motivation and objectives of the SolarMesh project. Section 2 provides an overview of related work, Section 3 outlines the system concept of SolarMesh. According research challenges are presented in Section 4 whereas Section 5 discusses expected results. The paper concludes with a summary and description of future work in Section 6.

1.1   Motivation

From an overall perspective, the SolarMesh project is motivated by a lack of affordable connectivity that at least supplies basic bandwidth and QoS levels for rural areas in both developing and developed countries. More specifically, the project aims at resolving the following problems:

- **Opening Up for New Markets**
  Billions of people in rural areas and developing regions do not have satisfactory access to the Internet or other telecommunication services. Tapping this demand offers a significant market and business potential.
- **Technological Challenges**
  The lack of reliable energy supply, large coverage areas in thinly populated regions, scarce availability of technically trained personnel, as well as extremely harsh climate conditions are some of the difficulties faced when deploying and operating a large-scale wireless mesh network. Hardware and software have to be designed accordingly:

  - **Autarkic energy supply**
    Due to limited or unreliable energy supply, SolarMesh network nodes exploit solar power from panels attached to the nodes. However, this self-reliance comes at the cost of potential outages due to the limited storage capabilities.
  - **Wireless backhaul network**
    Similar to solar energy supply providing independence from the local energy grid, a wireless backhaul network guarantees an autonomous operation of high capacity backbone links, independent from existing wired infrastructure. However, spectrum usage has to be reconciliated with local authorities and organizations in order to avoid interference from other radio systems.

- **Compatability and Future Proofness**
  Accelerating progress in mobile communications technologies will lead to new terminal generations and increasing requirements w.r.t. to QoS. Considerable investments, especially in rural areas, can only be justified if scalable and extensible communications systems support these trends. In Africa, the current majority of GSM terminals will (sooner or later) be replaced by more sophisticated terminals disposing of several air interfaces, e.g. smartphones. Therefore, the SolarMesh architecture incorporates advanced WLAN access points, thus making the system future-proof in an affordable manner.

– **Economic Cooperation and Development Issues**
In many developing countries, communication networks are the only means
for accessing information. Hence, investments into these infrastructures will
have direct consequences on the quality of medical services, education, interaction with governmental agencies, and diversity of opinion.

1.2 Objectives

Based on the motivation described in the previous section, the project has identified five key objectives that will guide the development of the wireless mesh
network:

1. **High-performing, Adaptive and Extensible System Architecture**
The overall architecture will be developed in a way that technologies beyond those considered in the project (WLAN IEEE 802.11 and GSM) can
be integrated easily. This holds particularly true for those alternative radio
technologies reducing costs, energy consumption, or access barriers. Therefore, the integration of GSM as an additional access technology is motivated
by three reasons: GSM terminals are relatively affordable, their energy consumption is comparably low, and, finally, they are very common in (rural)
Africa. Moreover, many services, including governmental services, merely
rely on SMS signalling. However, the termination of the GSM connection
already takes place in the access points in order to avoid expensive GERAN
infrastructure.

2. **Development of a Mesh Network Based on Autarkic Energy Supply**
Energy supply of the mesh nodes is based on regenerative sources (solar
power). Hence, all components (hardware, software, backbone and air interface) and mechanisms (routing, scheduling, handover, radio transmission)
have to be optimized taking into account fluctuating power availability and
limited energy storage capacities. The partners will develop according advanced energy-aware methods for network control.

3. **Advanced Auto-Configuration Capabilities**
Deployment and start up of the mesh network will not necessarily require
technically trained personnel. Individual nodes as well as the network as a
whole will configure mostly autonomously and adapted to their respective
deployment area.

4. **Advanced Self-adaptation Capabilities**
Besides considering energy efficiency as a main factor, network management
and load balancing have to support a large-area mesh network with time-
variant topology and dynamically changing traffic load. Availability of individual nodes will be significantly reduced due to limited energy resources,
extreme weather conditions (high temperatures, strong rain, sand storms),
and maintenance work. The network will have to cope with these characteristics in an autonomous and signalling-efficient manner.

5. **Implementation of Efficient Handover und Routing Mechanisms**
Handover and routing processes will be optimized and executed in a situation-aware manner to facilitate mobility support for the user and multi-KPI (key performance indicator) network management for the operator. For the latter, this allows for both control and prediction of power consumption, radio link availibility, and load distribution in the network. The user will benefit from seamless connectivity, independent of service and radio technology.

2   Related Work

Carrier-grade wireless mesh networks generally have been subject to former research projects. In EU FP7 CARMEN [5], a wireless mesh infrastructure has been developed that abstracts from different link layer technologies by the usage of IEEE 802.21. The design of the infrastructure and the routing mechanisms provides different QoS classes.

Generally, system-level models optimize the overall system performance w.r.t. a chosen set of parameters [2], [8]. When including energy consumption, transmission power is an important factor. Accordingly, current energy models particularly optimize network topology (i.e. the location of BTSs). Energy consumption is modeled based on path loss ($\frac{1}{d^n}$, where d denotes the distance between transmitter and receiver and n depends on the environments of the considered system), with additional consideration of large-scale fading using log-normal distributions as well as small-scale fading using Rayleigh distributions, e.g. [7] and [9].

For wireless ad-hoc networks deploying nodes running with regenerative energy sources (e.g. solar power for countries of sub-Saharan Africa), routing protocols also play an important role in energy consumption [3]. Several energy-aware routing algorithms have been developed that take the characteristics of regenerative energy supplies and the referring outage situations into consideration. In [1], an energy-aware routing within the scope of wireless mesh networks based on a WLAN architecture is mapped to an assignment problem and solved by a generic algorithm. In [6], the general relation between energy consumption and throughput in the scope of WLAN infrastructures is given. Frequently, total energy consumption is modeled in a linear way, using metrics for consumed energy per information unit routed, such as "energy per bit", or "energy per packet". Obviously, these linear models do not properly reflect energy consumed due to unsuccessful attempts to acquire the channel (media contention), messages lost due to collision, bit errors, or loss of wireless connectivity [4].

3   System Concept

The following section describes the main system concept of SolarMesh. It depicts an introduction to the overall system architecture, the auto-configuration and self-adaptation mechanisms and finally to the handover and routing mechanisms that are implemented.

3.1 System Architecture

Several SolarMesh nodes create a wireless, autonomous meshed backhaul network based on IEEE 802.11 wireless technology, as depicted in Fig. 1. The mesh network has three tasks: Providing connectivity to the external core network, offering heterogeneous wireless access to user terminals and, most importantly, serving as a wireless backhaul network within a particular area, thus replacing wired infrastructure. The first one is realized by several gateway connections to the core network and the Internet, whereas the second one is provided by utilizing commonly used Wide Area Network (WAN) technologies, e.g. GSM (in order to take advantage of the cheap off-the-shelf user devices) or Wireless LAN (thus exploiting its affordable network components). Backhaul connectivity is solely based on IEEE 802.11, incorporating mechanisms for carrier-grade QoS; i.e. different services and the accordingly required QoS classes are supported by the overall SolarMesh architecture, namely best-effort and delay-sensitive VoIP services.

The overall system architecture consists of several nodes, disposing of different functionalities:

- **SMN** (SolarMesh Node) holds the SolarMesh capabilities and embodies a basic interface for other nodes within architecture. The main task of the SMNs is to build up the mesh backhaul network and to forward the user- and control-plane traffic w.r.t. the QoS requirements among the SMNs (to the target sink).
- **SMGW** (SolarMesh Gateway) constitutes the gateway of the wireless backhaul network to the external backbone networks via Global Area Networks (GANs), e.g. a satellite link.
- **SMAP** (SolarMesh Access Point) provides the wireless access interface to the user terminals. It is equipped with at least one radio interface dedicated to the user terminal access, which do not carry the backhaul traffic. Available access technologies are IEEE 802.11 and GSM.
- **SMC** (SolarMesh Coordinator) performs cluster-wide, centralized decisions within a cluster of SMNs. The task of the SMCs is to consider both cluster- and network-wide optimization goals for radio planning, energy-aware node and link configuration, capacity management or handover decisions

Besides a comprehensive modeling of the system for simulation purpose, a future testbed will be set up with IEEE 802.11 based *meshnode IV* modules by saxnet GmbH which will be used to deploy the SolarMesh backhaul network. To realize the GSM-based access network, SMAPs will be extended with additional *USRP 2* from Ettus LLC controlled by *openBTS* and an *Asterisk PBX* software.

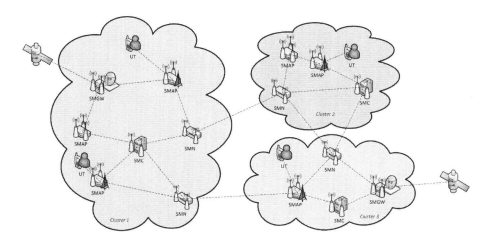

Fig. 1. Overview of System Concept

3.2 Auto-Configuration and Self-adaptation

One of the main characteristics of SolarMesh is the ability of auto-configuration and self-adaptation, as shown in Fig. 2. This is realized by an autonomous topology detection and configuration of the deployed SMNs. They are grouped into clusters in order to decrease the overall singaling effort and to perform local, i.e. cluster-wide, optimization concerning routing and handover decisions. Within a cluster, a SMC is determined that is responsible for the cluster-wide decisions and optimizations. Hence, a SMC can decide to switch off a SMN due to low utilization of the according SMN or its low energy status, e.g. caused by an almost empty buffer battery and, simultaneously, no energy supply by solar panels. As a result, the network topology is reconfigured and the traffic of the considered SMN is dynamically re-routed via other routes. SMNs are able to modify transmission power, modulation and coding schemes, respectively, as well as provided QoS in an autonomous way.

   Target access points for the user terminals are selected depending on the load situation on the target SMAPs, the capabilities of the user terminals and the SMAPs and the QoS that has been requested by the user terminal.

3.3 Efficient Handover and Routing Mechanisms

The handover and routing decisions are primarily based on mobility, load situation, energy situation within the SMNs and the provided and requested QoS parameters. Mobility-based handovers are triggered by the local SMNs whereas the remaining handover decisions are performed by the SMCs in order to allow for a cluster-wide or global optimization. Both horizontal, i.e. within the same radio technology, and vertical, i.e. across different radio networks, handovers

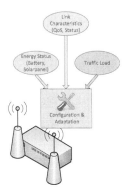

Fig. 2. Auto-Configuration and Self-Adaptation Functionalities of a SMC Node

can be performed. For each end-to-end connection, the most efficient path w.r.t. energy status or load situation is selected.

4   Research Challenges

Within SolarMesh, several research challenges need to be tackled which will be described in the following section.

4.1   Autarkic Energy Supply and Energy Efficiency

SolarMesh components will be designed to work in regions with harsh environmental and climate conditions and will cope with unreliable infrastructures, e.g. w.r.t. energy supply or availability of maintenance resources. In order to guarantee a continuous operation mode, nodes need to be equipped with their own energy supply. Power consumption of the SMNs needs to be kept at a minimum aiming at achiving a long operation time. Therefore, an energy management function is required that is capable of reducing power consumption by shutting down certain capabilities. This is handled by an energy management function that employs a detailed energy model of the SMNs. The model takes as input parameters the power consumption of the supported wireless access networks (e.g. IEEE 802.11 and GSM) depending on different modulation modes, supported states of operation as well as state changes. Additionally, the influence of traffic load on the SMNs is considered, which in turn is dependent on the type of the node: SMCs need to handle more control plane traffic than simple SMNs which in turn leads to a higher power consumption. In general, decisions concerning energy management are taken at different hierarchy levels, as depicted in Fig. 3. As an example, modulation schemes for the terminal link can generally be decided at the local node. In contrast, the decision of shutting down an entire node can only be taken at higher levels (cluster or global) since the individual node is not foreseen to have enough information to take that decisions and to assess the consequences.

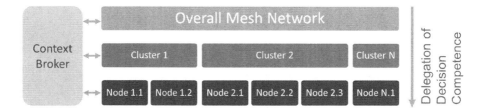

Fig. 3. Network Energy Management Concept

4.2 Network Management

Within the meshed network infrastructure, an advanced network management entity is required in order to perform the required reconfigurations of the constantly changing network topology. This entity has instances at node, cluster, and global level and implements, among others, routing and re-routing mechanisms, handover algorithms, as well as network topology management functionalities. Besides network-side parameters, such as dynamic characteristics of load, traffic situation w.r.t. QoS classes, it takes into consideration mobility and capabilities (such as available air interfaces, display size, or available codecs) of registered UTs.

4.3 Technology Integration

One of the key challenges of SolarMesh is to ensure that the whole infrastructure can be set up and maintained without any or only minimal technical knowledge of the staff (which is a typical situation in rural regions of Africa). This requires sophisticated auto-configuration functionalities of the nodes that guarantee autonomous topology detection and setup of the whole meshed wireless backhaul network over large distances. Another goal is to keep the costs per node at a low level. Finally, the integration of different wireless technologies imposes special requirements on the design of a common network management functionality, i.e. it has to be abstracted from the specific characteristics of indivdual link layer technologies.

5   Expected Results

Within SolarMesh, a wireless mesh infrastructure will be realized that aims to keep the overall deployment and operational costs at a very low level, as required for operation in rural areas of sub-Saharan Africa. The overall system design will be evaluated by a mixed simulation and emulation and will finally be implemented and validated in a testbed environment. Routing and handover decisions will be optimized and accelerated by the usage of context-aware decision functions. Seamless connectivity will be realized by the support of mobility (horizontal and vertical handover) and dynamic routing and re-routing. Due to the usage of the advanced energy management, a significant reduction of the overall power consumption will be realized. Most importantly, the mesh network will rely on and being able to cope with autarkic energy supply solutions, thus gaining independence from locally deployed, potentially unreliable energy grids.

6   Conclusion and Outlook

The paper has outlined the motivation, objectives, research challenges, and the initial system concept of the SolarMesh project. Their relevance for rural regions in developing countries has been demonstrated.

The core **motivation** of the project is the observation of unsatisfying Internet access for rural areas especially in developing countries. Derived from that, the **objective** is to develop a communications infrastructure that considers the special operation requirements of sub-Saharan African countries, thus bringing broadband Internet connectivity to these regions. This includes simple and (semi-)autonomous deployment, operation, and energy supply as well as the use of mesh technology on WLAN basis for cost-efficient access and backhaul network. According **research challenges** hence lie in the areas of autarkic energy supply and energy efficiency, autonomous network management functionalities (including situation-aware routing and handover control), and technology integration (e.g. integration of satellite, GSM, and WLAN).

Future work includes the detailed specification and development of a **system architecture** disposing of hardware and software components that meet the defined requirements. Finally, the system will be validated and evaluated based on simulations and testbed experiments.

Acknowledgment. This work has been funded by the Federal Ministry of Education and Research of the Federal Republic of Germany (Förderkennzeichen 01 BU 1116, SolarMesh - Energieeffizientes, autonomes großflächiges Sprach- und Datenfunknetz mit flacher IP- Architektur). The authors alone are responsible for the content of the paper.

References

1. Badawy, G., Sayegh, A., Todd, T.: Energy aware provisioning in solar powered wlan mesh networks. In: Proceedings of 17th International Conference on Computer Communications and Networks, ICCCN 2008, pp. 1–6 (August 2008)
2. Chan, T.F., Cong, J., Shinnerl, J.R., Sze, K., Xie, M., Zhang, Y.: Multiscale optimization in vlsi physical design automation (2006)
3. Chang, J.-H., Tassiulas, R.: Energy conserving routing in wireless ad-hoc networks. In: IEEE Infocom, pp. 22–31 (2000)
4. Feeney, L.M., Nilsson, M.: Investigating the energy consumption of a wireless network interface in an ad hoc networking environment. In: IEEE Infocom, pp. 1548–1557 (2001)
5. Kretschmer, M., Robitzsch, S.: Wireless Mesh Network Coverage with QoS Differentiation for Rural Areas. In: First International Workshop on Wireless Broadband Access for Communities and Rural Developing Regions (2010)

6. Serrano, P., Hollick, M.: On the Trade-Off between Throughput Maximization and Energy Consumption Minimization in IEEE 802.11 WLANs. Journal of Communications and Networks 12 (2010)
7. Rodoplu, V., Meng, T.H.: Minimum energy mobile wireless networks. IEEE Journal on Selected Areas in Communications 17, 1333–1344 (1999)
8. Schrijver, A.: Theory of Linear and Integer Programming. John Wiley & Sons, Chichester (1986)
9. Wieselthier, J.E., Nguyen, G.D., Ephremides, A.: On the construction of energy-efficient broadcast and multicast trees in wireless networks. In: IEEE Infocom, pp. 585–594 (2000)

Critical Information Infrastructure Protection (CIIP) and Cyber Security in Africa – Has the CIIP and Cyber Security Rubicon Been Crossed?

Basie von Solms[1] and Elmarie Kritzinger[2]

[1] Academy for Computer Science and Software
Universtity of Johannesburg
Johannesburg, South Africa
basievs@uj.ac.za
[2] School of Computing
University of South Africa
kritze@unisa.ac.za

Abstract. This paper reviews some very negative views, made over the last few years, about Critical Information Infrastructure Protection (CIIP) and Cyber Security in Africa. The paper addresses the expressed negative views that Africa can become the vehicle or platform from where cyber-attacks could be launched against the rest of the world. The paper evaluates the reasons for such negative views and then suggests some steps which should be taken in Africa to counter such negative impressions and to protect itself cyber wise.

Keywords: Critical Information Infrastructure Protection, Cyber Security, Africa.

1 Introduction

Over the last few years, several negative comments about Africa's lack of preparedness to combat cybercrime and protect its own CIIP have been made. This creates the impression that Africa has no control over such cyber protection matters and that the continent therefore becomes a risk and a danger to the rest of the world.

Three such comments will be reviewed.

In [1] it is stated:

Africa: The Future Home of the World's Largest Botnet? IT experts estimate an 80% infection rate on all PCs continent — wide (in Africa), including government computers. It is the cyber equivalent of a pandemic. Few can afford to pay for anti-virus software, and for those who can, the download time on a dial-up connection makes the updates out of date by the download is complete. Now, with the arrival of broadband services delivered via undersea cables, ...there will be a massive, target-rich environment of almost 100 million computers available for botnet herders to add infected hosts to their computer armies."

R. Popescu-Zeletin et al. (Eds.) AFRICOMM 2011, LNICST 92, pp. 116–124, 2012.
© Institute for Computer Sciences, Social Informatics and Telecommunications Engineering 2012

This statement was made in 2008, and is therefore about 3 years old. Whether it was a valid statement at that time, can be debated, but have impressions changed over the next few years? Not if the second comment on this matter is reviewed!

In [2] it is seems even worse!

'Think that Russia and China pose the biggest hacking threats of our time? The virus-plagued computers in Africa could take the entire world economy offline. Imagine a network of virus-driven computers so infectious that it could bring down the world's top 10 leading economies with just a few strokes. It would require about 100 million computers working together as one, a "botnet" -- the cyber security world's version of a WMD. But unlike its conventional weapons equivalent, this threat is the subject of no geopolitical row or diplomatic initiative. That's because no one sees it coming -- straight out of Africa. Broadband Internet access will allow Africa's virus and malware problems to go global. With more users able to access the Internet (and faster), larger amounts of data can be transferred both out and inward. More spam messages in your inbox from Africa's email fraudsters will be only the beginning.'

This statement above was made in March 2010, a little more than a year ago, and it continues as follows!

'Unfortunately, in cyberspace, the whole is only as strong as its weakest link -- and the majority of African countries are downright frail. That fact won't be lost on skillful cybercriminals operating out of an unregulated Internet café in the slums of Addis Ababa, Lagos, or Maputo. The biggest botnet the world has ever known could be lurking there.'

Microsoft states:

'As Internet penetration increases across the continent, so does the risk of sophisticated cyber-attacks, threatening African nations' security, infrastructure, economic growth and citizen services. Microsoft detected over 126 million samples of malware worldwide in the second half of 2009 alone, an increase of 8.9% over the first half of the year. Worse still is the association of cybercrime with Africa, where such countries as Nigeria have become synonymous with advance fee fraud or "419" scams. The cybercriminals who pose as government "officials" requesting assistance in exchange for advance payments undermine the trust as well as the freedom of a healthy Internet economy'. [3]

For Africa, it is important to evaluate these comments, and investigate whether such situations do exist or whether they will exist in future, and if so, what should be done about it from an African level.

In the next paragraph these comments will be briefly commented on, and in paragraph 3 possible reasons for such pessimism will be investigated. Paragraph 4 will discuss some solutions, while paragraph 5 will elaborate on one specific proposal. Paragraph 6 provides a brief summary.

2   Evaluating the Comments above

An immediate knee-jerk reaction is probably to reject these comments as wrong and unscientific. However, the author of this paper, coming from Africa, would hesitate to do so! Surely the comments are 'overstated' and maybe a little too much 'over the top', but they do contain aspects which should be evaluated. They do contain certain truths which may indicate that Africa has not yet crossed the CIIP and Cyber Security Rubicon.

These truths will be investigated in the next paragraph.

3   Why Is Africa at Risk Cyber Security-Wise?

Developing countries, such as those in Africa, are particularly vulnerable to cyber-attacks due to a combination of factors, including increasing Internet penetration rates, high levels of computer illiteracy, and ineffective legislation. These factors all introduce a higher level of cyber security risks and expose the critical infrastructures in such countries to higher levels of risk.

Some factors driving such increased risks, as discussed in [4], are briefly discussed below.

3.1   Increasing Bandwidth

Traditionally bandwidth available to Africa has been limited. However, this is no longer the situation. In recent years, Sub- Saharan Africa has experienced a growth in the number of fiber-optic cables that have made landfall. This has had a dramatic effect on how governments, companies, and individuals interact with Internet-based technologies.

With the increasing bandwidth, there is a drive for governments and businesses to adopt and implement e-services and citizen e-participation. Governments are specifically moving towards e-Government and e-Governance environments.

[5] States :

'E-governance and e-participation are therefore crucial phases in the development of government processes. However, despite the opportunities they offer, they also introduce new challenges, particularly for the countries targeted by this study and, more broadly, West African countries: limited and unequal access to ICTs, lack of infrastructure, electronic fraud, and the absence of or inadequate legal frameworks. The initiatives studied illustrate that citizen participation through the use of ICTs is developing effectively in Africa. Governments have demonstrated a real willingness to transform relationships between government services and their users, particularly by strengthening the use of ICTs and by offering information services online.'

All such systems use the Internet. This has the promise of allowing these bodies to interact with their customers in a more efficient manner. Along with adopting Internet-based technologies for the provision of services, there is also a drive to utilize these technologies to provide interconnection for a number of critical systems. The development of these interconnecting systems allows developing nations to compete more effectively in an increasing interconnected world.

In [6] the following is stated

"With a new decade beginning, the continent of Africa which was regarded as "backwards" has been able to get a leap into the world of ICT. This leap has not come without a heavy price. The rapid rate of diffusion of cybercrime in Africa has been a call for concern. This concern even gets more sickening when literature indicate that, out of the top ten countries in the world with a high level of cybercrime prevalence, Sub Sahara Africa is host to four of these countries (Nigeria, Cameroon, Ghana and South Africa)."

However, this wider access to the Internet creates new risks to Critical Information Infrastructure systems.

3.2   Increasing Use of Wireless Technologies and Infrastructure

Developing nations have long experienced problems in providing services to far-flung regions within their borders. The prospect of providing a physical link to a remote region is not feasible in many cases. However, the growing use of wireless technologies allows vast areas to be connected by investing in a number of wireless transmitters. Cellular networks, wireless mesh networks, and similar technologies are connecting communities at a much greater pace than what would have been possible using traditional means. Wireless technologies often present an attractive alternative for developing countries.

Statistics of mobile telephone users support these observations. As outlined in a report published by Cisco Systems, of the 4 billion cellular telephone users worldwide, 75 percent of those are in developing countries. The use of these new technologies creates a wider user base; however, these new users often do not have the computer security skills that in turn increase the overall risk in developing countries.

Again, such infrastructures essentially use the Internet, and provide access to the Internet, again creating cyber risks. This cyber risks are not only related to PCs n Africa but also to new and intrusive technologies for example smartphones.

"In the rapidly evolving mobile landscape in Africa, the growth has been fuelled in large part by the liberalization effort resulting in the formation of independent regulatory bodies and increased competition in the market. The total African mobile subscriber base is roughly 280.7 million people (30% of the total). With at least 15 mobile operators already announced plans of introducing 3G and data services (including Tanzania, Kenya and Nigeria)". [7]

The realization of above mentioned is that smartphones and Africa is not as impossible combination as one imagined. [8]

Result of increase in Smartphone use [9]:

"In a major shift in cybercrime trends, scammers are now moving their focus from Microsoft's Windows-based computers to other operating systems and platforms including smart phones, tablet computers and mobile platforms."

It is therefore vital that cyber risks connected to smartphones must be realized and taken into account within the Critical Information Infrastructure. It is also vital that independent regulatory bodies as mentioned above are involved within improving and protecting the Critical Information Infrastructure (see section 3.5).

3.3   Lack of Cyber Security Awareness

Developing nations are often seen has having poor literacy rates. Consequently, there is a severe lack of computer literacy and computer security awareness. In order to access eServices, new users must utilise the Internet without being equipped with the necessary skills to identify well-known threats (such as phishing). Attackers are now able to reuse old techniques, as users in developing nations have not experienced this type of attack before.

It is well known that banks in Africa are 'aggressively' rolling out internet-based banking services. Many such new users have maybe never used a desk top computer, and are not cyber security aware.

The situation in Africa is summarized in the quote from [10]:

'Millions of Africans are using mobile phones to pay bills, move cash and buy basic everyday items. It has been estimated that there are a billion people around the world who lack a bank account but own a mobile. Africa has the fastest-growing mobile phone market in the world and most of the operators are local firms. In countries like South Africa, for example, mobile phones outnumber fixed lines by eight to one. In Kenya there were just 15,000 handsets in use a decade ago. Now that number tops 15 million'.

In [11] some consequences of this growth are highlighted.

.'as more individuals worldwide gain Internet access through mobile phones, Cyber criminals will have millions of inexperienced users to dupe with unsophisticated or well-worn scamming techniques that more savvy users grew wise to (or fell victim to) ages ago.'

This surely increases the cyber security risks in Africa.

3.4   Ineffective Legislation and Policies

Legislation and policy in developing countries often do not adequately address Internet-based technologies. This often prevents cyber security measures and CIIP structure from having the required legal backing to operate effectively. The development of effective legislation and policies is essential to create effective cyber security and CIIP infrastructures.

Many African countries, including leaders like South Africa, do not yet have a proper national Cyber Security Policy or a national Computer Security Incident Response Team (CSIRT).

Without proper legislation and policies, very often well intended cyber security measures are not effective.

3.5   Technical Cyber Security Measures

The whole world is struggling with attacks using malicious software, and often the best and up to date anti-virus protection measures do not prevent infections. This problem is even more acute in Africa, as the cost to just keep up to date on anti-virus software updates, and patches for operating systems may be financially not reachable.

To approach this problem, Africa needs some new models for technical cyber security protection. One such example, placing more responsibilities in Internet Service Providers (ISPs) is described in [12] and [13].

3.6   Summary

Taking all the aspects discussed above, and some others not even mentioned, into account, it seems clear that Africa is still on the wrong side of the Cyber Security Rubicon! (The idiom "Crossing the Rubicon" means to pass a point of no return, and refers to Julius Caesar's crossing of the river in 49 BC).

4   What Must Africa Do to Cross the CIIP and Cyber Security Rubicon?

Surely there are a multitude of actions which can and should be taken to make Africa more Cyber secure. Maybe that is the reason why progress is slow and the cyber risks remain worryingly high.

However, international experiences and best practices in this area highlight one core issue, and that is **collaboration.** Before African states do not really start cooperating on CIIP and Cyber Security, progress will remain disjointed and incomplete.

It is well known that expertise in CIIP and Cyber Security is at a premium internationally, and so much more so in Africa.

Internationally there are regional bodies in the area of CIIP and cyber Security which are very active. In Europe ENISA is such an example, while CLARA plays a similar role in Latin America.

ENISA is the EU's response to these cyber security issues of the European Union. As such, it is the 'pace-setter' for Information Security in Europe, and a centre of expertise. [14]

The development of cooperation among CERTs in the region of South America and the Caribbean took a path similar to that in European. CLARA (Cooperation of Advanced Networks in Latin America) has established a working group to address security issues The group is focusing on two main areas:

- The protection of the critical infrastructure of REDClara – the network connecting Latin America National Research and Education Networked (NRENs) with each other and Europe
- The creation of security working groups in the NRENs [15].

At an ITU conference in 2008 it was stated:

'Africa is in dire need of such a regional facility which will really deliver value. Very often initiatives are taken in Africa, but never really implemented. In Africa, he said, the ICT revolution might fail to bring the desired and much needed results if countries do not adopt a sound regional approach to establishing national cyber security policies and legislation. In this respect he noted that constant developments in ICT make up an ever-changing environment which is too complicated for any one country to understand and handle alone. Therefore, countries in the region need external expertise to effectively meet the challenges posed by ICTs. Over time, the region as a whole must develop collective expertise and establish public-private partnerships to help each other in their respective approaches in building cyber security capacity.' [16]

The first, and most important step for Africa to cross the CIIP and Cyber Security Rubicon, is to build a bridge over this Rubicon river. The form of this bridge will be a Regional (or continental) CIIP and Cyber Security Alliance between African States. This Alliance establishes and fund a Centre to address CIIP and Cyber Security in Africa.

For discussion purposes, let this Alliance be called the African Cyber Security Agency (ACSA), and the Centre the African Cyber Security Centre (ACSC).

5   ACSA – The Bridge over Africa's Cyber Security Rubicon

ACSA will have African countries as members, and one of its main priorities will be to establish and fund the African Cyber Security Centre (ACSC).

ACSC could perform a wide range of services, of which the most obvious are briefly discussed below.

5.1   Cyber Security Awareness

A comprehensive set of Cyber Security Awareness material should be made available to all member countries of ACSA. Cyber Security Awareness courses are very much standardized internationally, and it is unnecessary for everyone to develop new material. Internationally the ITU has material which can be adapted and used. The National Cyber Security Alliance in the US also has a wide range of material available.

The challenge is not to create such material, but rather to consolidate and 'package' it for Africa – That is what ENISA and Clara do.

ACSC must be the central place in Africa where all member countries can get their material.

5.2   Provide Capacity Development and Skills Development

There is a dire need for such courses in Africa. In May 2011 the author chaired a session during a recent ITU event in Genève – The Fourth Parliamentary Forum on

Shaping the Information Society: The Triple Challenge of Cyber-Security, Information, Citizens and Infrastructure. The Forum was attended by a number of Parliamentarians form Africa, and all of them desired to attend some course to bring them up to date on their oversight role as far as CIIP and Cyber Security in their countries are concerned. Hap hazard ad hoc courses do not work – it must be centralized in one body – ACSC.

Such course for a wide range of other industrial and specifically Government officials are sorely needed.

ACSC must be the central place in Africa where all member countries van be exposed to such courses.

5.3   Legislative and Policy Aspects

Many countries in Africa are struggling to create national policies and relevant regulations. Again, redeveloping the wheels in such cases only delays or completely stalls the issue. ACSC could provide help and support in drafting such documents and even present short courses on how to create such policies and related problems.

ACSC must be the central place in Africa where all member countries could get advice on these aspects – even draft policy templates.

5.4   National Computer Security Incident Response Teams (CSIRTs)

CSIRTs are essential for CIIP and proper Cyber Security, but few countries in Africa already have such institutions. Only two countries in Africa belong to FIRST, the international Forum of Incident Response and Security Teams [17]. The single most benefit of a CSIRT is its international connections.

ACSC could play a central role in providing expertize to member countries to create CSIRTs and to cooperate and coordinate between them. It should be a contact body for CSIRTs in Africa and for CSIRTs from outside Africa.

ACSC must be the central place in Africa where all member countries could get expertize to create CSIRTs and to cooperate and coordinate between them.

5.5   Research in Cyber Security and CIIP

ACSA should also have a research and development facility of which all member states can make use of.

5.6   Many Other Functions

ACSC must be the central place and contact point in Africa where all aspects related to CIIP and Cyber Security are coordinated and where expertize and skills in these areas are available.

It should be the starting point in any search or problems related to CIIP and Cyber Security.

5.7   The Structure of ACSC

Although it seems the best way to start ACSC as a geographically centralized facility, it seems logical that in time it should have distributed facilities in member countries to make it easier for stakeholders to use the facilities provided by ACSC.

6   Summary

Surely Africa has not yet crossed the CIIP and Cyber Security Rubicon, but with political will, and starting platforms like ACSA and ACSC, it will do so. It will be Africa's best interest to do so very soon.

References

1. Carr, J.: Inside Cyber Warfare. O'Reilly (2009)
2. http://www.foreignpolicy.com/articles/2010/03/24/africas_cyber_wmd
3. http://blogs.technet.com/b/microsoft_on_the_issues_africa/archive/2010/07/01/laying-the-foundation-for-cybersecurity-in-africa.aspx
4. Ellefsen, D., von Solms, S.H.: A Community-Oriented Approach to CIIP in Developing Countries, CIP Report, Center for Infrastructure Protection and Homeland Security, vol. 9(12). George Mason University, USA (2011)
5. http://ictdegov.org/e-gov/WA-epart.html
6. Akuta, E.A.M., Ong'oa, I.M., Jones, C.R.: Combating cyber crime in Sub-Sahara Africa; A Discourse on Law, Policy and Pricatice. Journal of Peace, Gender and Development Studies 1(4), 129–137
7. http://news.bbc.co.uk/2/hi/business/8194241.stm
8. http://allafrica.com/stories/201102150340.html
9. http://www.mikekujawski.ca/2009/03/16/latest-mobile-phone-statistics-from-africa-and-what-this-means/
10. http://internationaldigitalmarketing.com/2010/10/29/mobile-marketing-trends-smartphones-conquering-africa/
11. http://www.cisco.com/en/US/.../annual_security_report.html
12. Kritzinger, E., von Solms, S.H.: A New Role for Information Service Providers (ISPs) as Part of Critical Information Infrastructure Protection in Africa, CIP Report, Center for Infrastructure Protection and Homeland Security, USA, vol. 9(12) (2011)
13. Kritzinger, E., von Solms, S.H.: Cyber security for home users: A new way of protection through awareness enforcement. Computers & Security 29, 840–847 (2010)
14. http://www.enisa.europa.eu/about-enisa
15. http://www.enisa.europa.eu/
16. http://www.itu.int/ITU-D/cyb/events/2009/tunis/index.htm
17. http://www.first.org/members

Geographic Information System as a Tool for Integration of District Health Information System and Drug Logistics Management Information System in Malawi

Patrick Albert Chikumba[1] and Auxilia Nyaukaya Kaunda[2]

[1] Department of Computing and Information Technology,
University of Malawi-The Polytechnic, Private Bag 303, Blantyre 3, Malawi
[2] Concern Universal, 21 Link Road, Namiwawa, P.O. Box 1535, Blantyre, Malawi
patrick_chikumba@yahoo.com

Abstract. While the Health Management Information Systems (HMIS) at the national level in Malawi is integrated, separate health information subsystems operate independently at the district level. For instance computerized Information Systems, such as District Health Information System that stores health data and Drug Logistics Management Information System that stores drug logistics data, operate as separate independent systems at the district level. Evidence however shows that information derived from fragmented systems is characterized by poor quality, irrelevancy, unreliability, untimely reporting and therefore inadequacy for management requirements. As one way of addressing problems associated with disintegrated HMIS, organizations worldwide are making collaborative efforts to integrate disparate information systems into one. Hence, this paper discusses possibilities of using Geographic Information System (GIS) to integrate District Health Information System and Drug Logistics Management Information System at district level in Malawi.

Keywords: Drug Logistics MIS, GIS, HIS, Integration.

1 Introduction

Health Information Systems (HIS) are widely recognized as technology enablers, improving patient care coordination, enhancing provider productivity, as well as facilitating knowledge management activities. A multitude of stand-alone administrative and clinical management systems exist, but their true value is realized when they become an integrated electronic health record solution that can address information requirements across multiple functions and sites. HIS include order entry system, drug logistics and management information system, patient record system, anesthesia information management system and disease surveillance record among others.

In Malawi, while the national Health Management Information Systems (HMIS) is integrated, at the district level independent sub systems exist. These are the major cause of fragmentation or 'islands of systems' [1]. These 'islands of systems' are

R. Popescu-Zeletin et al. (Eds.) AFRICOMM 2011, LNICST 92, pp. 125–134, 2012.

invariably highly complex, developed over time as a result of disease burdens and administrative, economic, legal or donor pressures [14, 1].

The international donors and Non-Governmental Organizations (NGOs) come into the resource-constrained public health sector with resources to complement governments' efforts in provision of health care services. These resources are directed towards specific areas and therefore they are organized as independent and vertical programmes which are associated with their own information systems [7]. In Malawi, typical examples are District Health Information System (DHIS) and Drug Logistics Management Information System (LMIS) among others. Consequently, HIS is fragmented with multiple and very often overlapping demands of disease-focused and specific services program systems.

DHIS and Drug LMIS are significant information subsystems at the district level which are not linked to each other or other HIS. They operate as separate autonomous subsystems of the HIS. DHIS is targeted at distributed collection of routine health data from primary health facilities to the district office while Drug LMIS stores drug logistics data at each district pharmacy. District health programme managers frequently need access to information from both DHIS and Drug LMIS from a single point of view for better management in improving health service effectiveness and efficiency. DHIS and Drug LMIS lack effective central co-ordination to ensure that the information which they contain is readily available to the district health programme managers when they need it. Studies done by Galimoto [7] and Chikumba [4] reveal that there is a need for a link or integration between DHIS and Drug LMIS for efficiency and effectiveness.

District health managers, as top management at the district level frequently need instant information from all the subsystems for effective and efficient strategic management decisions. For instance, to get information on surveillance diseases the managers have to access DHIS and for information on drugs and medical supplies status they have to access Drug LMIS. Reports from both systems might not be available at the same time when required by the district health officers due to the stipulated reporting requirements in each subsystem. Health managers are therefore inclined to make uninformed decisions based on inadequate information made available to them at the time needed. As a result of this fragmentation in DHIS, the management reports are likely to provide ineffective, irrelevant, unreliable, untimely and therefore inadequate information that is poor in quality.

One way to integrate the two systems is to use GIS as a tool. Therefore, this paper discusses possibilities of using Geographic Information System (GIS) to integrate District Health Information System (DHIS) and Drug Logistics Management Information System (LMIS) at district level in Malawi.

2   Integration of Information Systems

2.1   Integration

The purpose for two or more software systems integration is to facilitate communication among the systems, information sharing or exchange, as well as system inter-operability in order to achieve a common objective. Integration can bring together things such as services, people, data collection tools, data sets, institutions, information systems among others [14, 10]. Systems integration is the arrangement of an organization's information systems in a way that allows them to communicate efficiently and effectively and brings together related parts into a single system [13]. With inter-operability and interconnectivity, data generated by any one party can be properly accessed and interpreted by all other parties with standardisation as an important strategy for its achievement.

The integration provides organizations with information consistency in data and processes for an organization's database. The data can be stored in a central warehouse to be accessed by the entire organization and can be customized with appropriate security and controls using available transactions. Worldwide, business organizations are using collaborative efforts to integrate a variety of information systems for a global view of the organization operational environment from a single source [2].

The integration of different information systems in the health operational environment brings together inputs, organization, management and delivery services functions from a variety of managerial or operational activities to health information system (HIS) with an aim to improve efficiency, reliability, timeliness, effectiveness, adequacy and quality services in medical practice [6,7,10,13,14]. In case of Malawi, there is no integration to the national HIS as each system is developed independent of the other in order to achieve its own goals within its operational setting. There are no stipulated standards in the health sector for system development, which can be used as a basis for any system development at any level of operation. As a result, a number of fragmented, disintegrated and heterogeneous systems exist in HIS. Therefore, instead of being used as supporting tools, these fragmented systems hinder the provision of quality health care services delivery.

Health care organizations need cohesion in inter-operations for an integrated access to health information in a unified view at all levels of management. HIS integration in developing countries is impeded with lack of proper technological communication infrastructures in most of the health sector organizations. Most health sector organizations do not have computers for basic record keeping and therefore data is captured manually from its source of data collection [15, 17]. In most health sector organizations where computers are available, a challenge is the existence of disparate systems which operate in isolation of other systems in different departments. There is no network connectivity among various departments to link systems for communication flow to and from each computer.

2.2   Geographic Information System (GIS)

"Almost everything that happens, happens somewhere. Knowing where something happens can be critically important" [11, p. 4]. Geographic Information System (GIS) can acquire, store, manage, and geographically integrate large amount of information from different sources, programmes and sectors. Each piece of information is related in the system through specific geographical coordinates to a geographical entity, for example health facility, and the information can be displayed in the form of maps, graphs, charts, and tables. GIS is a computer based information system with geographical dimension and it stores, manipulates and analyses spatially linked data and displays summary information on a map [20]. GIS accesses spatial and attribute information, analyses it, and produces output with mapping and visual display [16]. It has very powerful functions such as generating "thematic maps", for example, allowing for overlaying of different pieces of information; creating buffer areas around selected features; calculating distances between two points; and permitting dynamics link between databases and maps so that data updates are automatically reflected on maps.

Many literatures [3,5,8,11,12,18,19] have discussed about challenges, opportunities and strategies of developing and implementing the GIS in developing countries. Government agencies have discovered that how the GIS is implemented influences its successful usage and although implementation involves a considerable degree of technical issues, they are equalled or surpassed by organisational issues [19]. Croswell [3] argues that the technical side of system implementation and operation is considered "minor" as compared to organisational and institutional problems while standards and data integration are considered very important.

Data collection is one of the most time-consuming and expensive tasks of the GIS but very important as emphasised by Saugene [18] that the effectiveness of the GIS depends on the degree of relevant data as input. In many ways data acquisition can potentially be one of the more difficult and costly issues in the implementation of a GIS [12]. Power of the GIS application relies on the scope and quality of data used and the data should be always available and easily accessed when required. To fully realise the capability and benefits of the GIS technology, spatial data needs to be shared and systems must be designed and used by multiple organisations. According to Ginger [8] and Croswell [3], data exchange standards have key role to play for facilitating the integration of datasets from various distributed sources or organisations and lack of these required standards between organisations impedes data sharing.

3   Methodology

The framed experiment was the one used in this research with the focus on the following: (a) non-standard subject pool which consisted of pharmacy technicians, statisticians and pharmacy-in-charge; (b) experiences and information that the subject pool has with emphasis on the GIS and computer operations; (c) the GIS prototype treated as a new commodity to the drug logistics and health staff; and (d) demonstration of the GIS prototype to the subjects in their respective working places and subjects participated and provided feedback and comments.

The interviews were conducted with the aim of understanding working practices of the drug logistics staff and in the hierarchical manner starting from Regional Medical Stores (RMS) in Blantyre, in the southern region of Malawi, down to its district pharmacies and district health offices (DHO) in Blantyre and Mulanje districts, and then two health centres in each of the two districts. Interviews were pharmacy-in-charge, pharmacy technicians, statisticians, and health centre-in-charges respectively. This was supplemented by analysis of health and drug logistics data collection forms and some monthly summary reports from the Drug LMIS software called "Supply Chain Manager" and direct observation on its data entry and reporting at Blantyre district pharmacy aiming on finding out how it handles drug logistics data.

Data was also collected through the evaluation of a GIS prototype whose spatial data was collected from the Department of Survey and Roads Authority. The GIS prototype was demonstrated to pharmacy technicians and statisticians from the Blantyre DHO and the pharmacist-in-charge from RMS in their respective working places. It was performed by applying the DECIDE framework [21] and drug logistics and health data of September 2008 was used. The demonstration focused mainly on (a) reporting and analysis of drug logistics information and (b) integration of spatial, drug logistics and health data. After the demonstration participants were interviewed for their feedback on the proposed GIS.

4   Findings

4.1   The Drug LMIS

The drug LMIS has health facility, district, regional and national levels. The drug logistics data is collected at the health facility level and processed at the district level (district pharmacy) using different tools in order to produce required logistics information for decision making. A responsible level reports in every month to its upper level which is supposed to send feedback to the lower level and concerned stakeholders (*see Fig. 1*).

The drug logistics data is collected at a health facility by health staff using LMIS forms at the end of every month. Then LMIS forms are sent to the district pharmacy for processing and analysis using the computerized system, Supply Chain Manager. This system generates different type of reports that are sent as hard copies to Regional Medical Stores (RMS), district health management team (DHMT), and some stakeholders on monthly basis and on request. The district pharmacy uses these reports to respond to all emergency orders from health facilities and redistribution of some health commodities from overstocked to understocked health facilities. RMS uses the same information to decide on the monthly distribution of health commodities to health facilities.

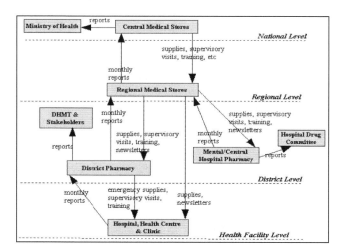

Fig. 1. Information Flow and Feedback between Levels in the Drug LMIS

4.2   Health Management Information System

In the health management information system (HMIS), as shown in the Fig. 2, the information is originated from the health facilities and sent to the district health office (DHO) and then the Ministry of Health. The lower level receives feedback accordingly from the higher level.

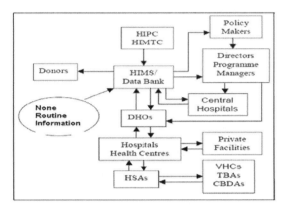

Fig. 2. Information Flow in Health Information System in Malawi
(**Source:** Ministry of Health and Population, 2003b, p. 21)

A catchments health facility collects data from all public and private facilities in its catchments area and performs analysis on monthly basis and takes necessary actions aimed at improvement in management of health programmes. The district health office receives data and reports quarterly from all catchments health facilities in its district. By using a computer system called District Health Information System (DHIS), a statistician compiles reports quarterly which are used for decision making at the district level. The district health offices and central hospitals send the raw health data quarterly to the Ministry of Health for data analysis at the national level.

4.3   Similarities and Differences between Drug LMIS and HMIS

By comparing the HMIS with the drug LMIS, there exist similarities and differences as explained below:

- *Data Collection:* In both systems, data is collected at the health facility level by the same health staff on daily basis while performing their official duties but the drug LMIS uses different forms for data collection from those used in the HMIS. The HMIS uses catchments health facility as a data collection point in a particular catchments area and any other health facilities report to it except the central and mental hospitals. The drug LMIS uses any health facility as a data collection point provided it gets health commodities from a district pharmacy and/or the regional medical stores. At the end of each month the both logistics and health data are aggregated and analysed ready to be forwarded to the upper level.
- *Reporting:* Both logistics and health data from the health facilities in a district are sent to the district health office for data analysis at the district level and then to be

used by the district health management team and stakeholders. The logistics data is sent monthly to the pharmacy technician or assistant while the health data is sent quarterly to the statistician. From the district health office, the health data is sent quarterly to the Ministry of Health while the logistics data is sent monthly to the regional level (regional medical stores) and then to the Central Medical Stores and Ministry of Health.

- *Data Processing at district health office:* It was observed that the most of data processing is done at the district level using computer software systems. The statistician uses the DHIS to compute the health data and the pharmacy technician uses the Supply Chain Manager to process the logistics data. Both systems were developed in Microsoft Access.

5   Integration of DHIS and Drug LMIS

The data integration is a new work process to be introduced due to the introduction of the GIS. This integration can be analysed in two ways: (1) integration of spatial data and attributes; and (2) integration of spatial data, drug logistics data and health data (*see Fig. 3*). It is also important to integrate the spatial data especially the health facilities with the drug logistics and health data. The GIS prototype has demonstrated this integration but there are some options that could be also considered.

The logistics and health data at the district level is not integrated in any way. The drug LMIS and the health information system are separate systems. The district health management team uses both the logistics and health data for decision making and the drug logistics staff also requires health data. Therefore, the proposed GIS can be used as an integration tool to link the logistics and health data together through a common geographical reference system of health facility. At the district level, the Supply Chain Manager and DHIS are used for logistics and health data management respectively and both systems use Microsoft Access database management system which can easily be linked with majority of GIS databases.

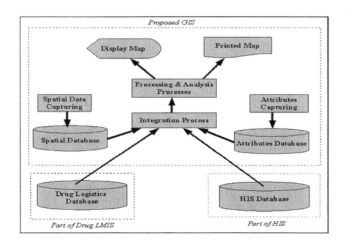

Fig. 3. Integrating Databases of GIS, Drug LMIS and HIS

Two options have been suggested: (1) integrate the spatial data with the drug logistics and health data as shown in Fig. 3 and in this case the proposed GIS requires an interface to access data from all databases; and (2) first integrate the drug logistics data with health data, and then integrate results with the spatial data.

It has been observed that the main new work processes, due to the introduction of the GIS in the drug LMIS, include the spatial data collection, data integration and data management. These processes are the most time-consuming and expensive GIS tasks but very important because effectiveness of the GIS depends on the degree of relevant data as input. For the district health office to successfully implement the GIS in the drug LMIS, it is important to consider carefully data standards and integration between the GIS, drug LMIS and health information system.

As shown in Fig. 3, there are four databases for spatial, attributes, drug logistics data and health data that are integrated at a single point. A common identifier is required in all databases for easy integration and management. It is necessary to determine standards for a common identifier, in this case the health facility and naming of different features such as health facilities, pharmacies and districts. All databases should use common codes and names for health facilities and pharmacies. If this is to be implemented, it means that the district health office will have a lot of work to modify all codes and names of health facilities and pharmacies in the drug LMIS and HIS to match with those in the spatial database.

Hence, the district health office needs to modify some existing policies and standards in the drug LMIS and HIS in order to come with common policies and standards for coding and naming of those health facilities and pharmacies. If there is a certain change in the health facility, it will be necessary to update all databases in order to maintain data consistency and this update will be in hands of two offices which are hard to coordinate, the pharmacy technician (for drug logistics databases) and statistician (for health database). Since both the drug LMIS and HIS will not only be used to feed the GIS, it is important to make sure that the databases have complete data, for example full descriptions of health facilities and pharmacies, for other services. Therefore, when it is needed, for example, to change a name of pharmacy or health facility, all databases should be updated and likely, missing changes in some databases which will result in data inconsistency.

Another challenge is a definition of data collection points in the drug LMIS and HIS as experienced in the GIS experiment. In HIS data is collected from the catchments health facility while in drug LMIS data is collected from any health facility which gets health commodities from either RMS or district pharmacy. It means that to integrate data from the two systems, it is required to define common collection points for both drug logistics and health data. Otherwise data from some health facilities, that are not data collection points in either one of the systems, will not be considered in the GIS because it will be difficult to integrate them.

6   Conclusion

Currently, drug LMIS and DHIS are separate systems at the district level and it is necessary to integrate them in order to be effective to the district health management team and other stakeholders. Both health programme managers and drug logistics staff require both health and drug logistics data in their daily works. It is possible to integrate drug LMIS with DHIS at district level in Malawi using GIS but there are some challenges such as (1) changing of some existing policies and standards in the drug LMIS and HIS in order to come with common policies and standards for coding and naming of those health facilities and pharmacies and also daily work practices; (2) definition of data collection points in the drug LMIS and HIS since each system defines its data collection point differently; and (3) choosing very suitable option for the integration.

References

1. AbouZahr, C., Boerma, T.: Health Information Systems: the foundations of public health. Bulletin of World Health Organisation 83, 578–583 (2005)
2. Chaulagai, C.N., Moyo, C.M., Koot, J., Moyo, H.B.M., Sambakunsi, T.C., Khunga, F.M., Naphini, P.D.: Design and implementation of a health management information system in Malawi: issues, innovations and results. Oxford University Press, London (2005)
3. Croswell, P.: Obstacles to GIS Implementation and Guidelines to Increase the Opportunities for Success. Journal of the Urban and Regional Information Systems Association 3(1), 43–56 (1991)
4. Chikumba, P.A.: Application of the Geographic Information System (GIS) in the Drug Logistics Management Information System (LMIS) at the district level in Malawi: Opportunities and Challenges, Master Thesis, University of Oslo (2009)
5. Forster, M.: Review of the use of Geographical Information Systems in the Marketing and Planning of Logistics Services. Christian Salvesen Logistics Research Paper no. 3 (September 2000)
6. Fumo, T.G.: Health Information Systems Integration: A Data Warehouse Architecture Model for the Ministry of Health in Mozambique. Master Thesis, University of Oslo (2003)
7. Galimoto, M.S.: Integration of Health Information Systems, Case Study from Malawi. Master Thesis, University of Oslo (2007)
8. Ginger, L.J.: Introducing Geographical Information Systems for Health Care in Developing Countries: Challenges and Approaches, A case study from Mozambique. Master Thesis, University of Oslo (2005)
9. Johnson, C.P., Johnson, J.: GIS: A Tool for Monitoring and Management of Epidemics. In: Map India 2001 Conference, New Delhi (2001)
10. Kuhn, K.A., Giuse, D.A.: From Hospital Information System to Health Information System: Problems, Challenges, Perspectives. Method. Inform. Med. (4) (2001)
11. Longley, P., Goodchild, M., Maguire, D., Rhind, D.: Geographic Information Systems and Science, 2nd edn. John Wiley & Sons, Ltd (2005)
12. Mennecke, B.E., Crossland, M.D.: Geographic Information Systems: Applications and Research Opportunities for Information Systems Researchers. In: Proceedings of the 1996 Hawaii International Conference on System Sciences, HICSS-29 (1996)
13. Meyer, M., Levine, W.C., Brzezinski, P., Robbins, J., Lai, F., Spitz, G.: Integration of Hospital Information Systems, Operative and Peri-operative Information Systems, and Operative Equipment into a Single Information display. American Medical Informatics Association (2005)
14. Nyella, E.: Challenges and Opportunities in the Integration of HIS: A case study of Master Thesis, University of Oslo (2007)

15. Odhiambo-Otieno, G.: Evaluation of existing District Health Management Information Systems: a case study of District Health systems in Kenya. International Journal of Medical Informatics 734 (2005)
16. Pick, J.B.: Geographic Information Systems in Business. Idea Group Publishing, Hershey (2005)
17. Sandvand, J.: Organisational Strategies for Improving Health Information at the district level: a field study of management Implemented support structures in Malawi. Master Thesis, University of Oslo (2007)
18. Saugene, Z.B.: Challenges, Opportunities and Strategies for Using Geographic Information Systems for Public Health Management - An Action Research Study from Mozambique. Master Thesis, University of Oslo (2005)
19. Sieber, R.E.: GIS implementation in the grassroots. Journal of the Urban and Regional Information Systems Association 12(1), 15–29 (2000)
20. Wood, D.J., Gatrell, A.C.: Equity of geographical access to inpatient hospice care within North West England: A Geographical Information Systems (GIS) approach. Institute for Health Research, Lancaster University, England (2002)
21. Sharp, H., Preece, J., Rogers, Y.: Interaction Design: Beyond Human Computer Interaction, 2nd edn. John Wiley & Sons (2007)

A Socio-technical Perspective on the Use of Mobile Phones for Remote Data Collection in Home Community Based Care in Developing Countries

Nobubele Angel Shozi, Dalenca Pottas, and Nicky Mostert-Phipps

P.O. Box 77000, Nelson Mandela Metropolitan University, Port Elizabeth, 6031
nobubele.shozi@live.nmmu.ac.za, {dalenca,nmostert}@nmmu.ac.za

Abstract. The adoption of technology into the health care industry has been criticized as being overtly techno-centric. It is assumed that health information technologies will fit into the environment and be easily adopted by the user. This, however, is a fallacy. Research has shown that a socio-technical approach, optimizing the interaction between the relevant social, environmental and technical sub-systems, is preferred. In this paper, a socio-technical perspective is gained on the adoption of health information technologies in the home community based care context, specifically the use of mobile phones for remote data collection. Based on data gathered through interviews with and observations of caregivers administering care in the community, this paper identifies and discusses the social, environmental and technical factors that affect community health care workers while they are using mobile phones to capture patient data in the home community based care environment in developing countries.

Keywords: socio-technical approach, home community based care, remote data collection, mobile phones, community health care worker.

1 Introduction

Health care systems of developing countries have had to carry an extra burden due to the increase of people living with infectious diseases on their already weakened and poor health care systems. Home community based care (HCBC) has been encouraged as an alternative to lessen the burden on the health care systems of developing countries. Information that is collected by the community health care worker (CHCW) in developing countries is in paper-based format and this information cannot be analysed and used efficiently. There are various technological alternatives that can be used to provide for the shift from paper-based to technology-based data collection, but in developing countries it would have to have the ability to overcome problems such as: poor telecommunications infrastructure, lack of resources, lack of electricity and insufficient political commitment and support [1]. The one information and communication technology (ICT) solution that seems to have the ability to overcome the problems listed above is the mobile phone. The use of mobile phones and other mobile technology in the health sector is known as 'mobile health' or 'm-health'.

R. Popescu-Zeletin et al. (Eds.) AFRICOMM 2011, LNICST 92, pp. 135–145, 2012.
© Institute for Computer Sciences, Social Informatics and Telecommunications Engineering 2012

There are six categories of application in m-health namely: education and awareness, remote data collection, remote monitoring, communication and training for health care workers, disease and epidemic outbreak tracking and diagnostic and treatment support [2]. This paper is interested in the use of mobile phones for remote data collection. There has been steady growth of mobile phone subscriptions in developing countries. In 2007, there were 38.5 mobile phone subscriptions per 100 inhabitants and by the year 2010 this had grown to 67.6 mobile phone subscriptions per 100 inhabitants [3]. Botswana has the highest mobile phone subscriptions with 96.12 per 100 inhabitants followed by Tunisia and South Africa with 95.38 and 92.67 respectively [4]. The high number of people who own mobile phones in developing countries gives a clear indication that m-health is a viable technological solution for developing countries and that there is an opportunity to support health care provision through the use of mobile phones. Notably, when introducing a new technology, the user, the technology and the environment where the user will be using the technology must be considered to ensure that all three are in coherence. Socio-technical theory addresses this coherence between the user, environment and the technology.

Socio-technical systems theory was first envisioned by the Tavistock Institute for Human Relations in London in the 1940's [5] and is defined as "a system that involves a complex interaction between humans, machines and the environmental aspects of the work system" [6]. The socio-technical systems theory proposes three interdependent sub-systems namely the social, environmental and technical sub-systems. The social sub-system represents the people that are internal to the organization. In the context of HCBC the people would be the CHCW and other internal people such as supervisors or managers. The environmental sub-system represents the environment that the CHCW and the patients interact in. The technical sub-system defines the technology that is used by the people. This represents the mobile phones that are used by the CHCWs. This paper investigates the use of mobile phones instead of paper-based systems to collect patient data. The paper aims to understand the social, environmental and technical sub-systems in HCBC and identify factors within these sub-systems that affect CHCWs.

2   Research Methodology

The research followed a qualitative approach and was interpretive in nature. This allowed the researcher to understand different aspects in the research: the home community based care environment, the community health care worker as a person, the work that the health care worker does, the factors that affect them while doing this work and how they experience the use of mobile phones to capture data. Emmanuel haven, a non-governmental organization, was investigated as a single case study. A case study was chosen as this type of research strategy allowed the researcher to explore a single phenomenon in its natural setting using to obtain in-depth knowledge about the case study [7]. Semi-structured interviews and observations were used as data collection methods. The structure of the interview questions were divided into three sections that addressed the social, environmental and technical sub-systems. Research ethics were observed during the research process.

3   Case Study Description: Emmanuel Haven

3.1   Background

Motherwell is situated 20km's outside of Port Elizabeth in the Eastern Cape Province of South Africa and is made up of 15 neighbourhood units (NUs); it is home to an estimated 187,680 people [8]. This area is plagued with a high illiteracy level, lack of adequate health service provision such as clinics, high crime rates and poverty. More than 76% of the Motherwell population earn less than R1600 per month with at least 50% of the population being unemployed [9]. Emmanuel haven is a unique community-based project with an integrated marketplace approach that is located in NU 12 of Motherwell Township. The haven currently has approximately 300 volunteer community health care workers who provide a home based care service to patients. The Emmanuel haven has various projects that it runs apart from the home-based care initiative; these include a day care centre, shoe and brick manufacturing, crèche, radio station, computer school, farming and various other initiatives to support its sustainability. The Emmanuel haven was established in 2004 by Dr Mamisa Chabula-Nxiweni with the primary aim of dealing with the growing number of adults and children that are infected or affected by HIV/AIDS [10].

3.2   Data Collection Methods

The interviews were semi-structured to allow for any additional questions to be asked and for the community health care worker (CHCW) to be able to elaborate on their answers. Interviews were conducted with six CHCWs. The interview times ranged from 40 minutes to 105 minutes and were conducted in both isiXhosa and English. The interviews were recorded, translated from isiXhosa to English and transcribed. Three community health care workers were observed in the execution of their daily duties. The observations were recorded on a video recorder and during the observations field notes were made. Each observation lasted approximately 30 minutes. After the observations the video recordings were viewed to validate and supplement the findings from the interviews.

3.3   Interview and Observation Results

Social Sub-system

Gender. The interviewees were all female; this aligns with Simpson's study which shows that most CHCWs are female [11].

Age. The interviewee's ages ranged from 34 to 63. It is important to note that the age is a crucial factor in being a caregiver in developing countries as older people gain the communities respect more easily than younger people.

Language use. The home language of all the interviewees was isiXhosa and they also used the same language to communicate with their patients.

Educational level. None of the interviewees had reached Grade 12 (matric) but one of them was currently in the process of writing examinations to try and complete their Grade 12. The highest grade obtained amongst the community health care workers was Grade 11 and the lowest grade passed being Grade 10.

Community involvement. The CHCWs all lived in Motherwell Township and chose to work in Emmanuel haven as working in the same environment they lived in meant that they would not have to use money for taxi or buses.

Experience in care giving. All the interviewees have had experience in care giving through caring for sick family members from an age as young as 12. This experience of caring for family members has motivated them and built their passion for being caregivers in the community.

Mobile device ownership. All of the interviewees owned a mobile phone. Three of the six interviewees owned basic mobile phones which had limited capabilities. The mobile phone capability usage was evaluated and the most used capabilities were sending SMSes, making calls and using the organizational tools such as calendar and calculator. Taking pictures, videos and listening to music was only used if the phone was capable as was the case with three interviewees. It was noted that the usage of SMS and call capabilities were dependent on airtime and this was sometimes a scarce resource.

Environmental Sub-system

Poverty. The CHCWs stated that because they work in poverty stricken areas, they feel compelled to find means to provide food and clothing to their patients.

Poor road conditions. CHCWs stated that they walk to patients' homes as they do not have enough finances to take taxis or buses. The conditions of the roads in some areas of Motherwell are poor as the roads are not tarred.

Weather conditions. When it rains, the interviewees stated that the road condition deteriorates even further and the roads become slippery, making it even more difficult for them to visit patients.

Remuneration. The CHCWs that were interviewed were all volunteers meaning that they relied on a monthly stipend of R600 to sustain themselves and their families.

Emotional stress. The interviewees reported that working with patients who are sick and living in poverty affects them emotionally. They are unable to provide for the patients as their stipends are barely enough to provide for their own families.

Lack of material. During the interviews, the interviewees reported that sometimes the Emmanuel haven runs out of supplies to refurnish their kits. This includes items such as data collection forms, gloves and aprons which makes it difficult for them to do their work properly.

Discrimination and stigma. The CHCWs stated that some patients face discrimination from their family members and community after they disclose their HIV status. Community health care workers find it hard to work in these environments as seeing the patient being treated badly causes them emotional stress.

Crime. None of the CHCWs reported being directly affected by crime, even though there is a high crime rate and gangsters are known to operate in the area.

Technical Sub-system

The CHCWs were trained to use a mobile phone for remote data collection. The phone that was used during the training was the researcher's Nokia 5130 express music phone. A mobile application was developed using Episurveyor and installed onto this phone. Three CHCWs (labelled A, D and F in the range of CHCWs who were initially interviewed) were followed on one patient visit each and a video recording of the CHCWs using the mobile phone captured. The community health care workers were first required to complete the relevant paper-based forms and were timed, after which they were observed and timed using the mobile device to capture the same data. The recorded times were used as a measure to compare the duration of capturing written data versus capturing data using the mobile device. This cannot be considered as statistically significant though as the sample of CHCWs was very small and except for the training they received, it was the first time they were using the application to capture data. It is to be expected that capturing times using the phone will improve over time.

CHCW A was the oldest of the three CHCWs observed but she had the fastest times overall using the mobile device for data collection. She reported that she struggled to complete the paper-based form more than when using the mobile phone due to the fact that the room that the patients are in is usually dark. She seemed to struggle to enter the letter 'S'. She usually wears glasses and she struggled reading what was on the screen at times due not only to the darkness but also because she did not have her glasses with her. CHCW D found the keypad to be small and ended up using her fingernails instead of fingertips to enter data into the application. Changing to number mode and entering numbers was a problem for this CHCW. She uses a Samsung phone and found that using a Nokia phone was different. She felt that people who are already using a similar phone have an advantage. CHCW F was the youngest and the only CHCW using a Nokia phone therefore she was used to navigating the phone. Even though she was familiar with the phone the entering of numbers was troublesome and time-consuming for her.

This discussion of the social, environmental and technical sub-systems in HCBC leads onto the following discussion of the social, environmental and technical factors that impact the use of mobile devices for remote data collection in the HCBC environment.

4   Socio-technical Factors Affecting the Use of Mobile Phones for Data Collection in the HCBC Environment

The directed content analysis technique was applied to analyse the interview transcripts as there is some pre-existing theory about the phenomenon (although limited). A coding process was used to identify codes. The codes from the interviews along with codes identified from pre-existing literature were used to compile a list of socio-technical factors (Tables 1 – 3) affecting the use of mobile phones for remote data collection in the HCBC environment. The triangulation with literature reported in this section (where available) shows that the findings of this study are valid but also highlights instances where literature differs from the results of the case study.

Table 1. Social factors

Factor	Literature	Case-study
Age	The age of the community health care worker plays a role when determining how effectively they will use mobile phones in the HCBC environment. A study conducted on people (ages 20-35 versus ages 50-64) it was found that older people have a lower navigation performance when compared to younger people [12].	In our case study it was interesting to see that the oldest person was faster when using a mobile phone to capture patient data when compared to her younger counterparts. However, as mentioned, the sample was not statistically significant and although the caregivers had received training, they had only used the application once thereafter.
Language barriers	The use of a common and understood language in a mobile health application is important for the users so they are able to understand it. Language can be a barrier in adoption of technology as user's can sometimes be reluctant to use a technology if it is not in their native language [13].	The paper-based forms used by the community health care workers are in English and therefore using a mobile application that was in English was not a hindrance. During the observations two of the three CHCW's asked what the word "comprehension' meant as it was used in the application. This shows that language remains a factor.
Educational level	A high educational level is required for one to grasp and understand the commonly used language in ICTs i.e. English, as it is the dominant language used in ICTs [14]. The educational level of users must be known so that a mobile application is created with this in mind.	It was gathered from the interview results that most of the CHCWs had achieved a level of education between Grade 10 and 11. Their understanding of the language used in the application can be attributed to the level of education they attained.
Care giving experience	All the CHCWs had vast care giving experience some having started at the tender age of 12. This experience enabled them to better understand the requirements of the mobile health application for data capturing.	
Preference of where to capture data	Four of the six CHCWs use a notebook to write everything that they do at a patient's home. When they get to their homes, they complete the paper forms based on what they wrote in the notebook. The other two CHCWs preferred capturing the patient data during the visit.	
Distance from CHCW to patients	The closer the CHCW lives to the patient, the easier it is for them to travel (regularly) to visit the patient and collect information. Therefore distance between patients and CHCWs has an effect on data collection.	
Mobile device ownership	3.8 out of 5.3 billion mobile phone users in the world belong to developing countries [15]. CHCWs who own mobiles phones find using the phones for data collection to be easier as they already understand it; those who have never used one experience some difficulties [16].	It was gathered from the interviews that all the CHCWs had phones. This made it easier for them to use the mobile application as they were familiar with the use of mobile phones. The CHCW that had a Nokia phone was the most comfortable with the phone.

Table 2. Environmental factors

Factor	Literature	Case-study
Weather conditions and road conditions	Due to poor road conditions patients who live in remote rural areas cannot be reached easily and this becomes worse during rainy seasons as the road condition deteriorates [17]. This literature support shows that the weather conditions and road conditions are interlinked as weather conditions affect the road conditions, which can affect data collection.	The CHCWs considered mobile phones to be able to overcome weather conditions that affect forms. If the forms they use to capture patient data get wet, information is easily lost. The roads that CHCWs use to travel to patients are in a very poor state and during rainy days their condition deteriorates, preventing the CHCW from visiting patients.
Uniformed CHCW	In some countries uniforms make CHCWs approachable as it gives them visibility in the community [18]. However, at times, families deny CHCWs access to their homes, or even insult CHCWs, fearing that their presence would enable the community to identify and stigmatize them [19].	In the Motherwell township there was some stigma attached with a uniformed CHCW being seen entering a patients' home. This can hinder the CHCWs daily work (including data collection) if they are prevented to enter a home due to fear of stigma.
Poverty	The expensive costs and lack of basic commodities make it difficult for CHCWs to replenish their kits; a stable environment is the key for HCBC to be successful [18].	The CHCWs experienced a lack of supplies to replenish their kits. Poverty is a hindrance as CHCWs find it difficult to focus on data collection if a patient is too ill.
Lack of funding	The government, donors, funders and telecommunication operators are all stakeholders that each has a role in ensuring the success of mobile health [20]. Financing structures need to be in place to ensure the use of mobile health.	The CHCWs were affected by a lack of funding as their stipends are occasionally not paid due to a lack of donor funding. The sustainable use of mobile phones for data capturing will depend on the continued availability of funding.
Quality of data collected	During the interviews all the caregivers stated that they write down the detail related to the patient visit at the patient's home. However, during observation of the caregivers, it was noted that none of them captured data at the patients' homes. They indicated that they would do this at their homes. Arguably this could affect the quality of the data that is collected.	
Lack of electricity	Investment into alternative power sources will help to overcome the barrier of not having charged mobile phones [20]. Lack of electricity in developing countries is seen as a constraint [21].	In the Motherwell community, all the houses have access to prepaid electricity but it does sometimes happen that the family cannot afford to buy it.

Table 2. (*continued*)

Factor	Literature	Case-study
Crime	Crime is prevalent in HCBC environments and affects CHCWs in such a way that they have to have paired or escorted patient visitations [22]. When working in crime-ridden areas the CHCWs feel vulnerable to the point that they sometimes end up not carrying the cellphone [16].	In this community none of the CHCWs had been affected by crime directly or in the execution of their duties. However, they did report that some areas that they work in are unsafe.
Transport issues	A lack of transportation does prevent sufficient visitation to a patient as the patient cannot be reached if they live in remote rural areas where transport is scarce [17]. The fewer the visits, the less data collection occurs.	The lack of transport to patients was mentioned by the CHCWs to be a factor in their work as they sometimes have to decrease the number of times they visit a patient due to a lack of transport or a lack of money for transport.

Table 3. Technical factors

Factor	Literature	Case-study
Familiarity	The forms that were created on the mobile phone were based on the paper-based forms that the health care workers used, therefore it was easier for them to understand the application as it was familiar to them.	
Internet connectivity	The lack of telecommunications infrastructure in developing countries can be problematic for the collection of data [21].	Without the existence of an internet connection, data could not be saved onto the server.
Mobile phone support	It was difficult to get a version of Episurveyor that could work on the Nokia 5130 express music phone as not all phones are supported by the Episurveyor application.	
Timing and error rate	The use of mobile phones for data capturing is said to be very efficient and time saving for the CHCW [16].	The time that the CHCWs took to complete the paper forms versus using the mobile phone has been mentioned not to be statistically significant.
Trust in CHCW	It was gathered through the interviews that a certain level of trust in the CHCW is required in order for the patient to be comfortable with the CHCW collecting their private information. If a patient does not trust the CHCW, it will be difficult for the CHCW to collect data.	
Trust in ICT's	Patients find it easier to trust paper-based methods rather than the use of ICTs; even though ICTs can break down certain barriers it does carry some fears along with it [23].	In this case study the CHCW and the patients had not been exposed to the use of ICTs for data collection and therefore this factor was not investigated.

Table 3. (*continued*)

Factor	Literature	Case-study
Portability	CHCWs in developing countries have to work alone in isolated and remote areas with little to no access to information; the use of small portable handheld devices enables CHCWs in remote areas to access up to date information [21].	The CHCWs are required to travel between patients and most CHCWs do not have transportation means. Portability is seen as a technical factor as an ICT solution that is implemented in the HCBC environment must be portable for the CHCW to carry between visits.
Privacy	Although CHCWs assure patients about privacy, they still insist to look at their files to be sure that information such as their HIV status are not recorded; they fear it might be seen by other people[20].	During the interviews the CHCWs stated that a mobile application to capture data would have to be secured through some means. The privacy of the data was well-recognized by the CHCWs.
Mobile phone training	If it is the CHCWs first time using a mobile phone then they will require significant training and education related to this [23].	None of the CHCWs had used a mobile phone for data collection before; therefore training had to be provided.
Airtime dependency	In order for the mobile application to be functional, airtime is a requirement. It was clear that the CHCWs assumed the mobile application would be "for work" and that they assumed airtime would be provided.	
Key size	The size of the keys affected the way that the community health care workers used the mobile phone for data capturing. One CHCW had to use her nails because she felt that the keys were too small.	
Screen size	A small mobile phone screen size can create problems for users as it limits the amount of information that can be put on the screen [24].	One of the CHCWs could only read the screen with her glasses on.
Input mode	The way that information such as numbers was entered during data collection affected the time the CHCWs took to capture patient data.	

5   Conclusion

CHCWs in developing countries still use paper-based systems to collect patient data in the home community based care environment. M-health presents a viable option to introduce a technological solution to replace paper-based data collection. It is being realised that technology is an influencing factor in the health care environment but it cannot stand alone. An approach that is focused purely on technology impacts negatively on its users. The espousal of a socio-technical perspective is more appealing because it encompasses the technology along with understanding the social and environmental factors.

This study has enabled a robust understanding of the social, environmental and technical factors affecting CHCWs when using mobile phones for remote data capturing in HCBC. The factors reflect the sub-systems comprising the context of the study as proposed by socio-technical systems theory. Valid questions still remain on the overlap of the sub-systems; such as are the community health care workershappy to use mobile phones for data collection? Do the emotional stresses of the job vastly outweigh any issues of technology? Is there a bottleneck issue in any of the sub-systems that should be focused on?

It is recommended that the factors identified in this paper be considered when an m-health application for data collection is introduced in an HCBC environment. However, further research is required to enable a comprehensive understanding of the overlap between the social, environmental and technical sub-systems of HCBC. The aim should be adoption and meaningful use of mobile phones to capture data in this environment, which is represented by the intersection of all three the sub-systems.

Acknowledgements. The financial assistance of the South African Government (Department of Science and Technology) and the Government of Finland (Ministry for Foreign Affairs) through SAFIPA (the South Africa - Finland Knowledge Partnership on ICT) is hereby acknowledged. The authors would like to acknowledge the contribution of the SAFIPA Socio-Tech SA project partners, viz. Dr Retha de la Harpe (CPUT), Prof Hugo Lotriet (UP) and Prof Mikko Korpela (UEF).

References

1. Bukachi, F., Pakenham-walsh, N.: Information technology for health in developing countries. Chest 132(5), 1624–1630 (2007)
2. Vital wave consulting. mHealth for Development: The opportunity of mobile technology for healthcare in the developing world. UN Foundation-Vodafone Foundation Partnership, Washington, D.C., Bekshire, UK (2009)
3. International Telecommunications Union (ITU). Key Global Telecom Indicators for the World Telecommunication Service Sector (2010a), http://www.itu.int/ITU-D/ict/statistics/at_glance/KeyTelecom.html (retrieved September 16, 2011)
4. International Telecommunications Union (ITU). Mobile Cellular Subscriptions (2010b), http://www.itu.int/ITU-D/ict/statistics/material/excel/MobileCellularSubscriptions00-09.xls (retrieved September 16, 2011)
5. Scacchi, W.: Socio-Technical Design. In: Bainbridge, W.S. (ed.) Encyclopedia of Human-Computer Interaction, pp. 656–659 (2003)
6. Baxter, G., Sommerville, I.: Socio-technical systems: From design methods to systems engineering. Submitted to The Journal of Human-Computer Studies (2008)
7. Collis, J., Hussey, R.: Business Research: A practical guide for undergraduate and postgraduate students, 3rd edn. Palgrave Macmillan, UK (2009)
8. Department of local and provincial government (n.d). Economic snapshot: Motherwell, Eastern Cape, http://www.thedplg.gov.za/urp/index2.php?option=com_docman&task=doc_view&gid=87&Itemid=54 (retrieved September 16, 2011)
9. Department of local and provincial government (n.d). Motherwell urban renewal programme, http://www.thedplg.gov.za/urp/Reports/Cabinet%20Lekgotla/Motherwellv2.pdf (retrieved September 16, 2011)
10. Emmanuel haven (n.d), http://www.emmanuelhaven.org (retrieved May 30, 2011)

11. Simpson, S.: A technical report exploring whether caregivers of people living with HIV/AIDS receive sufficient psycho-social support: A South African descriptive study at community care project, `http://etd.sun.ac.za/handle/10019/126` (retrieved September 16, 2011)

12. Ziefle, M., Bay, S.: How older adults meet complexity: Aging effects on the usability of different mobile phones. Behaviour and Information Technology 24, 375–389 (2005)

13. Beekhuyzen, J., von Hellens, L., Siedle, M.: Cultural Barriers in the Adoption of Emerging Technologies (2005), `http://www.ucd.smartinternet.com.au/ Documents/Cultural_Barriers.pdf` (retrieved September 16, 2011)

14. Jiyane, V., Mostert, J.: Use of Information and Communication Technologies by Women Hawkers and Vendors in South Africa. African Journal of Library, Archives & Information Science 20(1), 53–61 (2010)

15. International Telecommunications Union (ITU). Mobile cellular subscriptions (2011), `http://www.itu.int/ITU-D/ict/statistics/` (retrieved September 16, 2011)

16. Skinner, D., Rivette, U., Bloomberg, C.: Evaluation of use of cellphones to aid compliance with drug therapy for HIV patients. AIDS Care 19, 605–607 (2007), doi:10.1080/09540120701203378

17. Browning, E.: Bringing HIV/AIDS Care Home: Investigating the Value and Impact of Community Home-Based Care in Botswana. Macalester Abroad: Research and Writing from Study Away 2(1), article 4 (2009)

18. Caring from within: Key findings and policy recommendations on home-based care in Zimbabwe. Southern African HIV and AIDS Information Dissemination Services (2008), `http://www.safaids.net/files/Caring_from_within_Zimbabwe%20H BC%20findings%20and%20policy%20recommendations.pdf` (retrieved January 17, 2011)

19. Akintola, O.: Policy Brief: The gendered burden of home-based caregiving. Health Economics and HIV\AIDS Research Division. Health Economics and HIV/AIDS Research Division (HEARD), University of KwaZulu-Natal, Durban, South Africa (2004)

20. Mechael, P.N., Batavia, H., Kaonga, N., Searle, S., Kwan, A., Fu, L., Ossman, J.: Barriers and Gaps Affecting mHealth in Low and Middle Income Countries: Policy White Paper. Center for Global Health and Economic Development, Earth Institute, Columbia University (2010)

21. Chetley, A. (ed.) Improving health, connecting people: The role of ICT's in the health sector of developing countries. A framework paper. Infodev (2006)

22. Snow, D.A., Kleinman, L.S.: The impact of crime on home care services. American Journal of Public Health 77(2), 209–210 (1987)

23. Tapia, A.H., Maitland, C.: Wireless devices for humanitarian data collection: the socio-technical implications for multi-level organizational change. Information Communication & Society 12(4), 584–604 (2009), doi:10.1080/13691180902857637

24. Acton, T., Golden, W., Gudea, S., Scott, M.: Usability and acceptance in small screen information systems. In: Proceedings of the 9th European Collabarative Electronic Commerce Technology and Research Conference, Guildford, Surrey, UK (2004)

Open Source Software Solution for Healthcare: The Case of Health Information System in Zanzibar

Yahya Hamad Sheikh[1] and Abubakar Diwani Bakar[2]

[1] Department of Informatics
University of Oslo
`hamadys@ifi.uio.no`
[2] Department of Computer Science
The State University of Zanzibar
`abubakar.bakari@suza.ac.tz`

Abstract. Through a case study of health information system in Zanzibar, Tanzania, the article discusses adoption of free and open source software (FOSS) through strategic transition from a free Microsoft based application to a full-fledged java based FOSS application. Throughout the article, the adoption challenges and opportunities are discussed. The article contributes to approaches to FOSS adoption. Three areas are identified: the technical capacity of the software surpassing licensing terms, the role of local champions in initiating changes, and the importance of user capacity building prior to project adoption especially for a transitional project.

Keywords: open source software, health information systems, healthcare, integration, capacity building.

1 Introduction

Computer software has become the backbone of human interaction in their activities [1]. However, costs of ownership and freedom to maintain the software have become a major concern [2]. With proprietary software, which is the traditional way of computing, clients are forced to pay high licence costs under strict copyright laws. The strict laws, accompanied with technical procedures to hide the source code, clients are left with no choice of alternative paths. Free and open source software (FOSS) philosophy is a counter approach to computerisation of information systems [3], [4], [5]. In developing countries, especially in the public sector, this is indeed a necessity. The poor countries characterised by high budget deficits cannot afford the expensive software for the automation of their information systems (IS).

This study focuses on the computerisation of public healthcare sector in developing countries. It is part of global efforts to develop health information systems (HIS) in developing countries, known as Health Information System Programme (HISP). HISP has been involved in developing HIS and the use of software data warehouse for HIS automation. Realising the financial situation of the healthcare sector and the need for creating dependable manpower to sustain the HIS, HISP adopted FOSS approach to

R. Popescu-Zeletin et al. (Eds.) AFRICOMM 2011, LNICST 92, pp. 146–155, 2012.

its software products and strategy [6]. The article presents a case study for the HISP project in Zanzibar, Tanzania. The study outlines the implementation of FOSS through strategic transition from a free Microsoft based application that is distributed as open source to a full-fledged FOSS. The paper contributes to approaches to FOSS implementation.

2   Open Source Software for Health and HISP Agenda

While there is an increased awareness on how computers can help to improve healthcare service provision and management, there is also a huge increase on commercial investment for software products to support the sector. FOSS can therefore be an obvious choice in order to serve the larger number of population whose fate remains in the hand of poorly financed healthcare sector of their respective countries [7]. FOSS adaptation has recently seemed to be best alternative in healthcare sector. Many countries have made a considerable shift from proprietary to open source software [7], [8].

FOSS has two major benefits that have attracted this paradigm shift; first, the ability of client organization to have software with lower total cost of ownership, since the organisation will not buy the software, and that the availability of the source code reduces dependency to the business companies. Second, FOSS are believed to catalyse innovation since staff in the client organisation are encouraged to work to improve the software since the code is available and that various open source developer forums exist. [9], [10], [11]. These forums are the primary source of skill sharing among the developers' communities.

Thus, FOSS provides users with option to self support. These benefits give user freedom from 'vendor trap' [3]. Lungo and Kaasbøl [3] discuss a situation in the Tanzanian Ministry of Health where a hard coded software that was developed by a commercial organisation resulted into HIS failure because serious bugs that led to software malfunctioning could not be rectified. This was due to the fact that the licensing terms did not allow for the release of the code.

The HISP project is based on providing support to less resourced countries in the global south by developing and implementing software solution for the public healthcare sector and strengthening information use to facilitate healthcare planning, monitoring and evaluation. From the beginning HISP adopted FOSS approach where a software data warehouse solution called District Health Information Software (DHIS) was developed and distributed freely with code available and free to change [6]. The first version of DHIS, (released as DHIS 1.3 and later DHIS 1.4) was Microsoft Access based. The software development and distribution followed FOSS philosophy, although underneath it used proprietary software at both the database and operating system level. Thus the software was extended and adapted to reflect requirements of specific countries. In India, for example, the local HISP team employed the local capacity to develop a range of add on functionalities related to reporting, presentation, and visualization of data [6].

Despite its wide use, DHIS version 1 had one major setback; the reliance of Microsoft Office locked the departments of health in HISP implementation countries to rely on one operating system and forced the purchase of Office package for all computers. This was an indirect cost to the free software. In turn DHIS version 2 –a java based application which is platform independent was developed. In addition the new version is web based and enhances integration with geographical information systems (GIS). At the database level, DHIS 2 uses PostgreSQL and MySQL, both are free databases systems. A number of countries have shifted from DHIS 1 to DHIS 2, and newly enrolled countries have directly adopted DHIS 2.

3   Research Settings and Methods

This research was conducted in Zanzibar, Tanzania as part of HISP efforts to develop HIS in developing countries. The management of HIS in Zanzibar is shaped by the healthcare administration hierarchy. Data are usually collected and collated into monthly reporting forms at the health facilities that are later sent to the district for entry into the software data warehouse. Data from the districts are transmitted to the higher levels –zonal offices, HMIS Unit and the health programmes. This reporting structure, in principle, gives authority for data quality check and analysis at all levels. There are ten districts (same as political administrative districts) two zones (Unguja and Pemba).

The paper presents a case study for the project implementation from the period of 2008 to April 2011. Data collection is based on first hand experience by both authors who have intensively involved in day to day activities, which involve software configuration and installation, user training, support and supervision, and project planning and management. Thus, data collection is based on qualitative methods mainly participant observations, discussions, and meetings. During all these activities, notes were kept and later analysed. In order to build a deep understanding of the process of FOSS adoption, we adopted interpretive approach guiding both data collection and analysis. Walsham [12] describes the capacity of interpretive approach in understanding social phenomena where the subject attributes meaning to such phenomena.

4   Analysis of HIS Project Implementation in Zanzibar

Efforts to computerise HIS in Zanzibar dates back to 2005 when HISP was assigned the task to develop and implement integrated information system for collecting and processing routine health management data. For the software solution, DHIS 1.4 was adapted and installed for routine use at the district, zonal and national levels as well as the hospitals [13], [14]. For certain reasons, both administrative and technical, the development led to designing two distinct information systems operating in two separate databases, although the guiding principle was that of integration. The first database comprised primary healthcare data mainly from the small health facilities. The system comprised data from general outpatient, immunisation, maternity, and reproductive and child health. This system was commonly known as district system. The second database comprised hospital data collected from various wards and specialisation clinics of all hospitals, commonly known as hospital system. The two systems share data collected from maternity wards, general outpatient (OPD), Sexually Transmitted Infections (STI), and HIV testing and counselling.

This posed a consistency challenge since data are manually entered into the two systems and when updates are made they are not made in both. The two systems have different database files but share the same application (front-end) making users able to switch different databases from the same computer using the same application. Reports were prepared using built in DHIS custom reports and pivot tables. Pivot tables provided reporting tools with great flexibility where users could adjust the templates to prepare different reports.

4.1   Limitations to DHIS 1.4

DHIS 1.4 faced several constraints that lead to technical and managerial problems. Technically DHIS 1.4 was based on Microsoft Access and runs on Microsoft Windows platform. Although the software customisation is possible, this forced the ministry of health to commit itself to buying license for Microsoft Office. While this was supposed to be the case, the implementation team often ended up using pirates since the computers were already installed with pirate software. With the tendency of using pirates, the implementation team also faced another challenge –the compatibility challenge. DHIS is developed within the HISP network reflecting needs and requirements of several implementation countries. The availability of pirates often resulted into districts and other implementation sites to have higher version of Microsoft Office compared to what a particular DHIS release is optimised for.

For example, when Microsoft released Office 2007, licenses and even pirates were readily available but DHIS releases were developed under Office 2003. This caused several problems leading to DHIS to malfunction. The implementation team had to either roll back to Office 2003, the case of which users were never happy, or keep DHIS malfunction and report to global DHIS developers. For a long period pivot tables that were developed in Excel 2007 could not work in 2003 despite saving in compatibility mode, until DHIS was enhanced for Office 2007. In a nutshell, despite its unprecedented use, DHIS 1.4 lacked version flexibility in relation to Microsoft Office computing –its platform.

Another setback is related to the systems settings. Although working under integration slogan, under DHIS 1.4 two databases were developed and operated as independent information systems sharing only the data entry interface. This was mainly caused by DHIS technical capabilities to integrate the two systems which according to DHIS terms had two different organisational levels. DHIS registered organisation units in levels. Level one as the highest administrative level and the last level as the data collection level where data have to be registered. The hospital system had three levels (ward/clinic, hospital and national) while the district had four levels (health facility, district, zone and national). The software was designed to enter data at one common level only. This could be solved by introducing 'zone' dummy level, but it was opposed by the administration claiming that putting a referral hospital (Mnazi Mmoja) under zonal management is against the set guidelines. In addition, integrating the two systems into one database could result into huge number of data elements, which after data entry for some time; the Microsoft Access database capacity would be surpassed. Thus, developing two systems remained the only choice.

As a consequence, the two systems led to data inconsistencies for those data that are required to be entered into both databases. For example, maternity data for every hospital had to be entered at two places; at the hospital itself (in hospital database) and at district office (for the district database). In the end these data must be similar. However, since updates for missing or incorrect data are usually made, in the end the two data sets representing the same hospital are never the same as updates in one database do not necessarily reflect the other. Different people were involved in data entry for the two systems. During the preparation of annual health information bulletin the two were totally different. The hospital officers had to be called to clarify. This scenario repeated itself every year.

In DHIS 1.4, reporting is done manually, though in electronic form. District officers, after entering the data have to export into txt or xml files that will later be emailed or sent using flash disk to higher levels (zones and HMIS office) which must download and import into their database. Programmes also rely on this procedure where HMIS office will export data and submit to them. This introduced unnecessary delay of the data. While in the past, programmes had direct access to data, the new procedures, while being successful in terms of coverage and capacity to share; were not good in dealing with timeliness. Timeliness was the emerging problem. The unnecessary bureaucracy in reporting caused mistrust from health programmes that contribute them to diverge from mainstream HIS. The HIV/AIDS programme for example, used this as an excuse for diverting from the mainstream HIS.

4.2   Adoption of DHIS 2

DHIS 2 was introduced to overcome the above stated problems and also to exploit the power of web applications as well as prospects of FOSS. The DHIS 2, a java-based software application that has option to use either MySQL or PostgreSQL database systems. In Zanzibar, PostgreSQL was chosen because it is more commonly used in HISP network, hence it has larger user and support base.

The first instance of DHIS 2 in Zanzibar was installed in 2008. The software was introduced by the international HISP consultants to solve the existing problems. The consultants also wanted to use the potentials the Zanzibar context give in order to make real use test of the software which by that time was relatively unstable. These attempts were unsuccessful due to concerns raised by the local HISP and HMIS staff on the capacity to leverage the change of software by the DHIS users. The local team emphasised on building user capacity using the previous software version (DHIS 1.4) focusing on capacity to analyse data and to prepare reports, the task which is very important irrespective of technology in use. Further, the team was not prepared to adopt new technologies by that time, weighing the workload the team already had.

Following evaluation of the project implementation in the beginning of 2010, the local HISP team agreed to upgrade from DHIS 1.4 to DHIS 2. The local team contacted the HISP international team to discuss the trends in DHIS technologies and share experience from countries who has implemented DHIS 2, notably India, which was in advanced stage in both development and use. The developers and implementers workshop that was held in Oslo, Norway in April 2010 was highly productive. A new database was configured and installed in the web server located at the HMIS office. This database deployed the advanced technical capabilities of DHIS 2 that gave opportunity to configure a comprehensive and integrated database that takes data sets from both the district and hospital databases that in the past had to be separately deployed.

The team agreed to pilot the new database for the period of one year. At the beginning, the decision was to select two hospitals and four districts, but later it was agreed to train all data entry staff in order to give time to practice before the official launching, and phasing out the DHIS 1.4. Data entry started in May but it was decided to include the January – April backlog, in order to have a full year coverage. Throughout the whole piloting period, the data entry staff were entering data twice. First, they had to enter data into DHIS 1.4, which was the official data reporting system and later enter the same data into DHIS 2. While this can be seen as a tiring work, the purpose was to expose users to the software in order to give them enough experience, at the same time the technical team (local HISP) used feedback as the way to enhance the software as well as learning user perception to the new technology. The data entry staff were paid for the extra work, this motivated them towards the new software. This was in contrary with the recommendations of international HISP team, which saw the task as redundant and wanted direct data import from DHIS 1.4 to DHIS 2.

4.3   Technological and Organisational Implication of DHIS 2

This section presents impacts of implementing DHIS 2 for the Zanzibar healthcare sector and focus on the advantages the software brought compared to its predecessor as well as challenges encountered.

Advantages. Although it is too early to assess the benefits that DHIS 2 has brought in comparison to its predecessor, initial advantages include:

Seamless integration. Due to technological capacity of DHIS 2, the problems resulting from deploying two systems –the district and hospital systems were solved. The new system comprises of only one database installed at a central server and all data can be easily accessed and shared between programmes and other stakeholders. This has been possible regardless of the differences in the organisational level between the systems because DHIS 2 is designed to allow data entry at different levels. In turn, this will result in improved data consistency since data entry and updates take place in a central server. DHIS 2 also came with new phenomenon of data element category meant to solve the problem of huge number of data elements.

Data element is the atomic unit of data which can routinely be recorded for a particular health facility, e.g. Malaria cases for pregnant women.

DHIS 2 combines several data elements as defined in DHIS 1.4 into only one data element with a matrix of categories. For example, confirmed malaria cases is considered to be one data element with three categories: sex (male or female), age (under 5 or 5 years and above) and attendance status (new or re-attendance). In DHIS 1.4 these were eight data elements, reduced to only one in DHIS 2. This has highly improved the database efficiency due to reduced workload. The data entry form has remained with the same format.

Efficiency in data reporting and feedback. The Web has revolutionised the reporting procedure. The aim here is to reduce the time taken from data entry until the programmes receive data. With the web application data are directly entered into central server and all authenticated users including programmes can directly access the data that they are authorised to access. This will attract those programmes which saw the integrated HIS as barrier to a timely reporting of data. Despite the fact that in 2010 the software was still in piloting stage, the immunisation programme decided to take initiatives to promote the application by deciding to directly shift to DHIS 2. Looking for the champion of change, the local HISP team provides constant support to the programme. The fact that the application is web based and run on one server provides opportunity for feedback to the district staff. Staff at the district can measure performance of their districts in comparison with other districts.

Improved data and information access. The web capacity of DHIS 2 enables data access beyond geographical limitations. The nature of the work of healthcare managers requires them to have frequent travel both within and outside the country. This will, and as the case has been for immunization programme, revolutionise data access and will guarantee data access at all the time regardless of where users are. This is a big success from the DHIS 1.4 which was a standalone system.

Improved information visualisation. One component of epidemiological questions is where diseases or certain health problems occur. Geographical information systems (GIS) add value to answering these types of questions. While DHIS 1.4 had GIS module functioning, the problem was that the underlying technologies were proprietary. In DHIS 2, GIS is embedded and uses a range of software applications ranging from proprietary to free and open source. The use of FOSS application in Zanzibar has made data visualisation easier and cheaper. The immunization programme, for example, has used the GIS to map immunisation coverage, identifying the risk factors, and planning for intervention.

Challenges. Despite the relatively short period of implementation, challenges have been evident. These are discussed below.

Internet speed. Despite a contract with the local Internet Service Provider (ISP) to provide a broadband internet to the ministry of health, the speed of the internet provided has been deteriorating every day posing doubt over the reliability of data. This challenge has been dealt by negotiating with the ISP to provide the reliable service as agreed, while at the same time making backup solutions. One back up solution is to buy internet modem provided by local telecom operator and in case of severe shortfall staff can always use the services at the HMIS Unit headquarters or HMIS office in Pemba, thanks to the short distances from the offices to the district offices and hospitals.

Technical capacity at the HMIS office. Although DHIS 2 requires less technical support to operate compared to its predecessor, the shortage of skilled information technology personnel at the HMIS offices puts the situation into nearly the same risk. While the centralised database system has an advantage of centralised diagnostic system, hence reducing diagnostic efforts, it also poses a critical challenge when the personnel with that skill (currently one assisted by voluntary local HISP staff) fail to support the infrastructure.

5   Adoption of FOSS for Zanzibar HIS

In this paper software migration process to open source software for Zanzibar HIS has been analysed. We now turn into the discussion over the FOSS adoption as experienced in the project. The project implementation process, challenges and opportunities identified shed light into how FOSS have been perceived and adopted.

5.1   Strategies for Adopting FOSS

From the beginning of project implementation DHIS 1.4 was implemented as open source, though did not meet all the criteria, for example, relying on Microsoft Access and Windows platform. The software enjoyed acceptance by its 'free' marketing banner but more importantly, the capacity of the software in handling the local HIS as well as the human resource base that accompany the software located in the global network of developers, implementers and users. Thus, apart from being free, that is, the ministry was not imposed with license fee, the attractor was also on the technical capability of the software to handle the newly designed HIS and its rich support base –the HISP network.

The process to adopt a full fledged FOSS, DHIS 2 seems to follow the same path. The motivations and arguments built were mainly on the software capability to solve the existing problems as well as a promise to more advanced features. In the study of the same project in Zanzibar, Lungo [15] pointed out the effects the licensing terms has for adoption of FOSS in information systems project. He asserts that, developers undermines the licensing terms because they do not have use incentives. This is in contrast to the conventional FOSS literature [16] which emphasise on license terms as an attractor to FOSS adoption. Additionally, this study reveals that the technical and functional capacity of the software surpassed the licensing attractor. In particular, the adopters were attracted by the software capability to provide seamless integration of the previously independent systems that caused data inconsistency and redundancy, improving reporting efficiency, improved data and information access and the embedded and flexible GIS features.

5.2   The Role of Local Champions in Adopting FOSS

Local champions play important role in FOSS adoption [15]. The first instance of DHIS 2, installed in 2008 by the international HISP consultants did not work. Local HISP and HMIS staff abandoned the efforts because they were not in line with local priorities, despite the fact that DHIS 2 could alleviate the existing problems and offer new potentials. When the local HISP and HMIS staff initiated the move, the international collaboration worked. Thus, the collaborative spirit of FOSS as shown in the HISP project works well when the local champions lead the move.

In this respect, we argue that whatever the potentials FOSS may give, it is very important to study the implementation environment beforehand. This implies that, there is a need to create local FOSS readiness before implementing the solutions. FOSS are built to improve freedom and independence from vendor reliance [3], [9], [11]. However, this freedom shall not be seen as only the freedom to not rely on the vendors but also freedom to choose the right FOSS solution at the right time. This will also help to build the sense of ownership from the beginning. The case presented has demonstrated rich ground for FOSS philosophy with regards to participation. This participation from the early stage championed by the locals is very important for project sustainability. The decision by the local team to delay adoption of DHIS 2 meant to build user capacity on data analysis was intended to build strong ground for the project takeoff.

5.3   Leveraging User Capacity through Hands on Practice

FOSS implementation for information systems project is different from the common infrastructure projects, due to separation between developers/implementers and users [15]. The case presented in this study demonstrates similar findings. In this regard, we argue that the prospective user base for any information systems project like DHIS 2 has to be well prepared before directly adopting the software, especially if it is the case of transition. The study shows that the decision by local HISP to delay adoption of DHIS 2 and put emphasis on developing user capacity for data processing and information visualization was meant to prepare users when transitioning to DHIS 2. Subsequently, this reduced the time to learn and hence develop user confidence on the new software. If the team had adopted DHIS 2 earlier, it would result in extra efforts in training and hence adding to a belief that FOSS are difficult to learn. The one year parallel running of the two software versions helped to develop confidence before a formal takeover.

6   Conclusion

In this article, we have discussed HIS implementation with a focus on adoption of FOSS for the automation of HIS. The case presented outlined the adoption process through strategic transition from a free Microsoft based application (DHIS 1.4) to a full-fledged java based FOSS application (DHIS 2). With the FOSS philosophy and implementation strategy being used in marketing and implementation of DHIS 1.4, the marketing of DHIS 2 was primarily based on its technical capacity rather than the

FOSS rhetoric. Lessons learned contribute to approaches to FOSS adoption. Three areas were identified: the technical capacity of the software surpassing licensing terms, the role of local champions in initiating changes, and importance of user capacity building prior to project adoption especially for a transitional project.

References

1. Klang, M.: Free Software and Open Source: The Freedom Debate and its Consequences. First Monday 10, 3–7 (2005)
2. Hnizdur, S.: The IDA Open Source Migration Guidelines. European Communities, 1–148 (2003)
3. Lungo, J.H., Kaasbøl, J.: Experiences of Open Source Software in Institutions: Cases From Tanzania and Norway. In: 9th International Conference on Social Implications of Computers in Developing Countries, São Paulo (2007)
4. Lin, L.: Impact of User Skills and Network Effects on the Competition between Open Source and Proprietary Software. Electronic Commerce Research and Applications 7(1), 68–81 (2008)
5. Bhadauria, V.S., Mahapatra, R., Manzar, R.: Factors Influencing Adoption of Open Source Software - An Exploratory Study. In: AMCIS 2009 (2009)
6. Braa, J., Monteiro, E., Sahay, S.: Networks of Action: Sustainable Health Information Systems Across Developing Countries. MIS Quarterly 28(3), 337–369 (2004)
7. Webster, P.C.: The Rise of Open-Source Electronic Health Records. The Lancet 377(9778), 1641–1642 (2011)
8. Kemp, R.: Current Developments in Open Source Software. Computer Law & Security Review 25(6), 569–582 (2009)
9. Shah, S.K.: Motivation, Governance, and the Viability of Hybrid Forms in Open Source Software Development. Management Science 52(7), 1000–1014 (2006)
10. Pitt, L.F., Watson, R.T., Berthon, P., Wynn, D., Zinkhan, G.: The Penguin's Window: Corporate Brands from an Open-Source Perspective. Journal of the Academy of Marketing Science 34(2), 115–127 (2006)
11. Stanford, J., Mikula, R.: A Model for Online Collaborative Cancer Research: Report of the NCI caBIG Project. International Journal of Healthcare Technology and Management 9(3), 231–246 (2008)
12. Walsham, G.: Doing Interpretive Research. European Journal of Information Systems 15(3), 320–330 (2006)
13. Sheikh, Y.H., Titlestad, O.: Implementing Health Information System in Zanzibar: Using Internet for Communication, Information Sharing and Learning. In: IST Africa 2008, IIMC International Information Management Corporation, Windhoek, Namibia (2008)
14. Lungo, J.H., Igira, F.: Development of Health Information System in Zanzibar: Practical Implications. Journal of Health Informatics in Developing Countries 2(1), 24–32 (2008)
15. Lungo, J.H.: Design-Reality Gaps in Open Source Information Systems Development: An Action Research Study of Education and Healthcare Systems in Tanzania. Faculty of Mathematics and Natural Sciences. University of Oslo, Oslo (2008)
16. Feller, J., Fitzgerald, B.: Understanding Open Source Software Development. Addison-Wesley, London (2002)

A Software Business Incubation Model Using ICTs for Sustainable Economic Development in Uganda

Hugh Cameron, Benjamin Kanagwa, and Michael Niyitegeka

College of Computing and Information Sciences
Makerere University, P.O. Box 7062, Kampala, Uganda
{hcameron,bkanagwa,mniyitgeka}@cit.mak.ac.ug

Abstract. In low-income countries, a recurring challenge in the use of mobile and web-based services to foster development is to ensure the economic sustainability of those new services after their initial launch. The Makerere University Software Business Incubation programme tests a novel approach to this challenge, by applying a venture-capital-like management discipline to ICT innovations created by students, recent graduates and staff of the College of Computing and Information Sciences. The incubation process, which has been refined over the past 3 years, has already resulted in six new business start-ups. Scaling up appears feasible, because of the very low capital funding needs of the programme: the new services are profitable from the start. This paper describes the programme's structure and operational processes and gives several examples of the new services created, along with a discussion of the challenges faced and solved by the programme's management.

Keywords: sustainable innovation, business incubation, venture-capital management, mobile services, web applications.

1   Introduction

A recurring challenge for new mobile and web-based applications to foster development in low-income countries is to ensure the economic sustainability of those new services after their initial launch.

Governments, NGOs and private corporations collectively solicit thousands of proposals for worthy new mobile and web applications in sub-Saharan Africa each year, via competitions for research grants, prize money, Millennium Development Goal programmes, innovation centres, job creation schemes, rural poverty eradication programmes, emergency aid support, health and education surveys, and private-sector software development jobs.

Many millions of dollars are awarded each year and hundreds of new applications are trialled. Most of the trials terminate within a year or two, for lack of funds to scale up, or for lack of sufficiently motivated users.

The net results are a few popular and self-sustaining services such as Mobile Money or Frontline SMS, an enduring cadre of program managers and consultants, and thousands of engineering and ICT graduates with experience in making proposals but very few jobs.

R. Popescu-Zeletin et al. (Eds.) AFRICOMM 2011, LNICST 92, pp. 156–166, 2012.
© Institute for Computer Sciences, Social Informatics and Telecommunications Engineering 2012

This paper reports on a different approach to fostering economic development through ICT services and applications, based on the premise that the venture capital management processes that have worked in North America, and are working now in Europe and Asia, can also work in sub-Saharan Africa.

2   Background

We begin with a short summary of the prevailing economic conditions in sub-Saharan Africa, Uganda in particular. These conditions determine how the venture capital management process needs to be localised.

Like many west and east African countries, Uganda has experienced healthy economic growth in the past decade, averaging around 6% per year [1]. The export potential of natural resources and agriculture is attracting investment from Asia. The political environment is still unpredictable, but its volatility is decreasing.

Use of English as the universal language of education, government and business has reinforced this. Multi-party political systems have taken root and will gain strength in upcoming elections, although the opposition parties in most areas probably do not yet have the organization or discipline to outpoll the incumbents.

Unsurprisingly [2], people have migrated to the cities (especially Kampala) because their opportunities are better in the city and because they know relatives who have become relatively prosperous there, even though the cost of living is higher than in the country. Many people hold two or more jobs in order to meet daily expenses.

The use of mobile telecoms and mobile applications is exploding: the spread of phones, internet and credit cards is being compressed into a decade or two, instead of over half a century as in Europe and North America. Over 95% of people in urban areas have access to phones (either their own, or through family and friends), as do about 75% in rural areas. But local capital for investment is scarce – especially for locally managed investment – and interest rates are high.

Potholes, traffic jams, paper records, queues, power outages and stock-outs are universal. City dwellers of all economic levels lose many hours to the resulting inefficiencies; hence are chronically short of time. Patience becomes not so much a virtue as a coping mechanism.

Local software developers and clerical staff are abundantly available, but usually need on-the-job training or coaching. Experience in business planning, modelling and operations management is scarce. Formal qualifications and credentials are highly respected but do not imply practical experience or initiative, so (deservedly) carry less weight than a first-hand knowledge of local conditions and practices. The strong oral tradition in Africa fosters impromptu discussion and seat-of-the-pants management at the expense of writing and regular meetings.

On the other hand, the concentration of raw talent and learning ability among university students is formidable. The public educational system is highly competitive, so about half of all university students are selected from the top 5% of 20-year-olds. In Uganda, most of these go to Makerere University, which is the oldest, largest and has the best reputation. The great majority of Makerere graduates stay in Kampala and do their social networking face-to-face at government round-tables and workshops, industry associations, boards, Rotary clubs and the like. The physical proximity facilitates contacts and introductions among faculty members, government officials, business owners and executives, consultants and NGO representatives.

Overall, a self-reinforcing combination of widespread inefficiencies, reported obstacles to business [3], lack of traditional inputs for industry research or financial assessments, shortage and high cost (~19%) of local investment capital, has led to an abundance of unexploited commercial opportunities – despite the availability of technical and business university graduates and the government's ardent desire to put them to productive work. Most of these opportunities are unknown to foreign investors because information about them is unpublished and uncirculated outside the local word-of-mouth networks [4].

Figure 1 summarizes these principal dynamics of Uganda's current social and economic development.

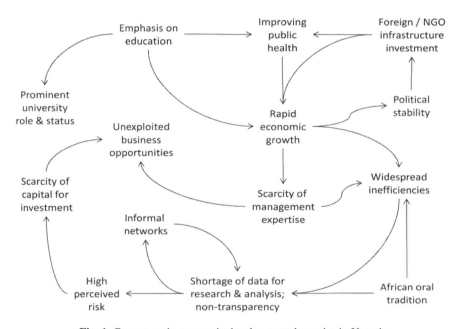

Fig. 1. Current socio-economic development dynamics in Uganda

3   System Description

With the rapid growth of Uganda's economy, the many and obvious inefficiencies represent opportunities to create wealth. The burgeoning of interactive SMS and mobile money services has illustrated this. In the coming decade, as computing and software become pervasive in government, industry and education, there will be many, many more software business opportunities.

A mechanism is needed for bringing together the owners of problems, the creators of solutions, experienced managers and sales people, and financial backers or investors. Out of this confluence, new businesses can be created.

An early-stage venture capital scheme is a proven way to do this.

Rather than proceeding (as in most contests and incubation centres) directly to software development on projects that appear original, the Makerere programme requires its applicants to function as follows.

1	Working from suggestions of students, college partners or faculty members, a) identify a problem in an existing enterprise that prevents it from carrying out its business more effectively, or causes it some undesired expense; or b) identify an opportunity for the enterprise to sell an additional service or product to its existing customers.
2	Engage the enterprise, to understand this problem or opportunity intimately, from the viewpoint of its owner.
3	Conceive a cost-effective solution through discussion with the enterprise. Illustrate with a prototype if needed.
4	Make a business proposal, to seek financial backing.
5	Contract with the enterprise to deliver the solution.
6	Implement the solution and deploy it.

The key difference is – *sell before you build* – so that only what a client is paying for gets built. The college facilities and the available mentors are limited – and any stakeholders want to be sure these resources are marshalled to commercial value. Otherwise the participants lose motivation.

The first 4 steps may take several months to accomplish. But the process avoids the building of solutions to the wrong problem, or to a problem that turns out not to exist for the intended clients.

The project staging from conception to viable business can be summarized as follows:

- First meeting: review and screening of verbal proposals are done on request from any applicant to the programme. Accepted projects will proceed to:
- Stage 0: Project team formation and exploratory research, concluding with a business plan. No funding is offered to the entrepreneurs in the project team during this exploratory stage. As soon as a project team prepares its business proposal, its members can request a review by the Incubation Review Board.
- Stage 1: Business plan approved by the Incubation Review Board. Seed money is advanced to project team to work toward a contract with a lead customer, and an experienced business mentor begins working regularly with the group.
- Stage 2: For B2B projects, contract signed with first customer; for B2C projects, prototype built and agreement signed with any key supplier(s). The new start-up is

incorporated and additional funding advanced to the project team to work toward implementation.

- Stage 3: For B2B projects, the lead customer has implemented the new product or service and begun using it; for B2C projects, the new service has gone live – giving the start-up its first revenue. The business mentor continues with frequent coaching and some additional funding is advanced to the project team.
- Stage 4: For B2B projects, lead customer has formally reviewed the performance of the new product or service, and has declared it to be satisfactory; thus is ready to recommend the new product or service to other clients. For B2C projects, sales have increased steadily for 3 months and a high-confidence date is known for positive operational cash flow. At this point the start-up should have a sales funnel of additional clients and will be able to tap conventional funding sources.

As in the management of venture capital, incremental funding for each stage depends on passing the checkpoint at the end of the preceding stage, according to plan. Figure 2 summarizes the progress of a successful project from proposal to established, growing business.

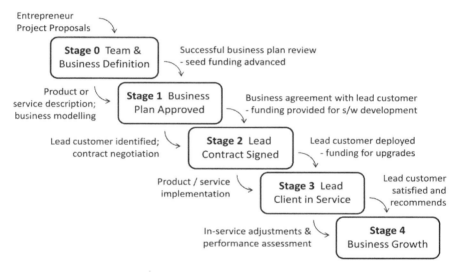

Fig. 2. Progress of a successful B2B incubation project. Below each box is the main work done in that stage; and to the right of each box is the event that enables promotion to the next stage.

The purposes of this process are (i) to provide frequent checkpoints for assessing the viability and progress of each start-up; and (ii) to weed out incipient failures early, so that the available funds can be focussed on those start-ups (and teams) most likely to repay investment. Originality of the entrepreneur's idea is not the key factor: success depends mainly on execution. *The process is more important than any particular business concept it incubates.*

In contrast to existing African venture capital firms and NGOs like Kiva.org and BidNetwork.org that target operational businesses needing cash for expansion [5], our investment focuses on the seeding and early-stage phases of their start-up businesses.

Ownership and management structure of the Software Business Incubation (SBI) programme are similar to that of venture capital firms, as in Figure 3 below. The investment funds are limited partnerships managed by the SBI Ventures firm. They are set up to manage groups of related start-up projects and capitalized with cash contributions from SBI Ventures, college partners, faculty members and other external investors. Their capital can be raised in repeated rounds. When an investment fund reaches its capacity of start-ups to manage, SBI Ventures may open a new fund. The investment funds pay SBI Ventures for facilities for their start-ups. Each fund doles out its capital by stages to its start-ups, like a venture capital fund.

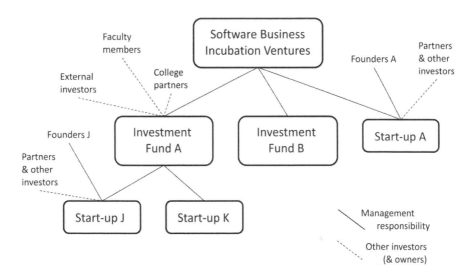

Fig. 3. Legal structure of the Software Business Incubation programme

The SBI Ventures management controls the allocation of resources: technical and business mentors, facilities, computers, software development environment and support, legal services, etc. Money from an SBI Ventures investment fund or directly from the SBI Ventures firm may be advanced to pay for these resources.

Following a successful business proposal review, college partners or other investors may also take a stake in the start-up by advancing funds to it.

When a project succeeds in contracting its first sale, the new start-up can be formally launched and incorporated. Its founders (the project team) receive a majority share of the new company; and SBI Ventures (or its investment fund) also takes a share representing its investment to date in the project plus the additional investment required to support the software development and implementation. The project team is paid a larger stipend from this time forward. Drawing on SBI Ventures' share in the start-ups to pay the founders helps cover their personal expenses and motivates them. Alternatively, other investors in the start-up may raise their stake at this point, or may make a loan to the start-up.

The focus on software business opportunities is not only because the programme originated in an ICT faculty. Software and IT enterprises have long been the most fertile area for venture capitalists. Compared to other businesses, their start-up capital costs are also lower.

As a part of Makerere University, the College of Computing and IS offers several tangible assets of value to software start-ups:

- Office space, computers, network and communications infrastructure, software development environment and support for project teams
- An SMS service platform
- The OpenXdata applications platform (a tool set for structured data collection using mobile phones) and varied application experience with it
- Technical experts and programming coaches and for software development groups
- A constant and renewable supply of the country's top software development graduates (about 1200 per year)
- Ability to host web sites, SMS and database servers
- Some financial capital

To minimize the start-ups' requirement for cash, the college provides these assets as in-kind contributions to the start-ups' equity. Other contributions of expertise – for example in accounting, business modelling, financial planning, coaching in sales and operations management – are credited as in-kind equity contributions wherever this can reduce the need for cash. These other areas of expertise are all locally available.

The college's intangible assets are also valuable in the local Ugandan setting:

- Existing satisfied customers of past software development contracts
- Reputation of success in delivering software and IT services
- Connections with Uganda's political and business elite

The overall aim here, on a smaller scale, is to copy the American experience ("Close relations between universities and industry … with proliferating science parks, technology offices, business incubators and venture funds. About half of the start-ups in the [Silicon] Valley have their roots in the [Stanford] university." [6])

4   Discussion

The Ugandan setting constrains several of the success factors for business incubation, as noted in Table 1. Operationalising the SBI programme has involved mitigating or circumventing some of these challenges, as follows.

First, seed funding from within the university has been quite limited, and is also subject to the accounting rules for public institutions. The SBI programme therefore minimized its cash requirements by negotiating in-kind compensation for business mentors and other contributors; and diversified its funding sources through private placements and continuing applications to NGOs.

Second, the programme's cash flow is irregular and somewhat unpredictable – both for income and expenses. Given these vagaries, a separately managed account became necessary to shield the programme from other demands on college funds.

To fit the natural rhythm of the academic year, the main intake for the programme was moved to October, when final-year ICT students are choosing their major hands-on software projects. For the minority of students who prefer to pursue a project with commercial potential, this timing allows them to apply to the SBI programme with the same project. (As noted earlier, however, any aspiring individual or group of entrepreneurs can apply to the programme at any time.)

Table 1. Business Incubator success factors - comparison

Success factor	Typical university business incubator	High-performance business lab [7]	SBI-Makerere
Business opportunity focus	technology based service or product / licensing	solution for a problem or market failure	solution for a problem or market gap
Intellectual property focus	high	low	low
Business concept differentiation	technology	market segment, pricing, channel	end user cost, delay, pricing
Business model	required	required	required
Relative infrastructure costs	low-medium	low	medium-high
Founders' personal capital	wealthy, variable	wealthy, fairly equal	poor, unequal
Founders' education and business skills	medium-high	high	medium-low
"Soft" resource availability	medium	high	low-medium
Access to finance	medium-good	good	medium-poor
Assumed founder intensity	variable	full time	part time
Concept time to market	12-24 months	3-5 months	3-10 months

In the university setting, many would-be entrepreneurs lack business maturity and often have idealized preconceptions about mass market services, or desire to solve global problems. There is also a tendency (typical in university settings and not limited to Africa) to place excessive value on intellectual property and to focus more on technology than on barriers to uptake. All aspiring entrepreneurs in the programme hence attend a non-credit lecture series on business creation and management.

A related challenge is the lack of financial modelling experience among almost all of the start-up groups. Spreadsheet business models are a crucial tool for exploring product pricing options, determining criteria for profitability and building pro-forma financial statements. To date this has been addressed with individual group tutorials; but a more scalable approach involving visiting business-school interns is under way.

Even with the most sophisticated business models, accurate valuation of start-up businesses is virtually impossible. Hence the use of valuations to compensate start-up supporters like business mentors is unfeasible. To avoid such conundrums, the equity shares of both the College and the business mentors in the start-ups are thus flat-rated.

The operating expenses for the SBI programme cover the following people's time:

- Programme management (2 faculty members part time): about $1,000 per month
- Software development environment, internet access and support for hosting (covered by the College)
- Review Board members (6 local business people, serving as volunteers)
- Business mentors (drawn from the local business community through contacts of Incubation Review Board members): in kind: flat rate 8% equity share in start-ups
- Technical mentors for software development (some volunteers from the College Department of Innovations and Software Development)
- Legal expenses for start-up incorporation, registration, contracts (paid at local market rates, with some pro bono assistance from a Canadian business law firm)
- Day-to-day administration (one college employee part time)

Total operational expenses can amount to as little as $2,000 per month plus about $2,500 per established start-up (from Stage 1 onward).

As such, the funds needed to run the SBI programme have been within the capacity of local investors for the small-scale pilot that was begun in the spring of 2010 and for its expansion in 2011. In absolute terms, they were significantly smaller than the 2009 foundation grant that equipped and launched the College's National Software Incubation Lab.

These numbers reflect the fact that there is some attrition at each stage in the SBI process; i.e. not all approved business plans get executed.

However, we are finding that over successive iterations of the SBI process to deal with operational challenges, the "yield" at each stage can be raised by continuous improvement of the SBI process, so that the portion of start-ups executing successfully and thus promoted to the next stage can rise over time.

In sum, by capitalizing on the existing features and dynamics of Ugandan society, this scheme creates some new positive feedback loops, as diagrammed in Figure 4 – and its investment of money and time can thus have disproportionate leverage.

As examples of this leverage, some of current start-up businesses in operation are:

- Sales/fulfilment and reporting system for booking and playing of radio adverts for radio stations and their clients.
- Web based skills-jobs matching service for job seekers and employers/recruiters
- Travel saving service for patients needing laboratory tests. (The innovation is in technology and channel to market.)
- Interactive SMS service for Makerere and other university results (plus additional information), similar to the secondary school national examination results service
- Targeted local-proximity marketing service for small-medium enterprises (that find traditional media unsuited for advertising their products).
- System for sports fans and other bettors to place bets and collect winnings from their mobile phones.

- Service to allow bus companies and their passengers to query, reserve and pay for intercity travel by mobile phone.

Notably, the role of new intellectual property in these solutions is negligible.

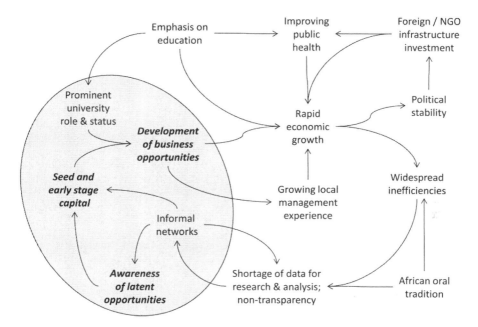

Fig. 4. Effect of new early stage venture funding and management in Uganda

5   Conclusion

This approach to software business incubation is a novelty in Africa. While aiming to emulate the role of universities in North America and Europe, it is adapted for the on-the-ground realities of Uganda's current society and economy, with all its constraints and opportunities. As such, it addresses a gap in current domestic investment and NGO activity in Uganda.

The Makerere University College of Computing and IS has developed this software business incubation programme as a part of its local mission; but in addition, the college would be delighted to collaborate through it with academic and professional partner organizations outside Uganda.

The cost of the SBI programme is small in comparison to foreign-funded education and public health programmes in Uganda, and its potential benefits are disproportionate. At minimum, the programme results in an annual human capacity creation of about 100 people with software venturing experience. At maximum, it will have a multiplier effect throughout the local economy and provide a handsome return for all the cash and in-kind investors involved. As a success, it can certainly be adapted for application in other African countries with similar local conditions.

References

1. Nationmaster, Development statistics for African nations,
   http://www.nationmaster.com
2. Jacobs, J.: Cities and the Wealth of Nations. Random House, New York (1984)
3. World Bank, Doing Business in Africa,
   http://www.doingbusiness.org/economyrankings/
4. Indian Association of Uganda: Doing Business in Uganda,
   http://www.ia-uganda.com/doing_business_in_uganda.html
5. Reuters: Private equity in high-risk markets, May 26 (2010),
   http://af.reuters.com/article/nigeriaNews/
   idAFLDE63I22720100526?sp=true
6. The Economist: Survey of Entrepreneurship, March 12 (2009)
7. Personal communication, Mikael Samuelsson, Stockholm School of Economics

Crowdsourcing ICTD Best Practices

Aaron Ciaghi and Adolfo Villafiorita

Fondazione Bruno Kessler,
via Sommarive 18, 38123 Povo (TN), Italy
{ciaghi,adolfo.villafiorita}@fbk.eu
http://ict4g.fbk.eu

Abstract. A large number of projects in ICT for development include software development to a certain degree. A review of the literature highlights how most of these projects ultimately fail to be sustainable. In this paper, we expose our views on the need for a more structured approach to software development in ICTD and we present our plan to collect best practices from software project managers through a crowdsourcing web portal. This will provide input to a broader study that aims at adapting existing software development processes to the ICTD context.

Keywords: ICT for Development, software engineering, software development process, crowdsourcing.

1 Introduction

Information and Communication Technologies for Development (ICTD) [1] is an emerging discipline that studies how ICTs can stimulate socio-economic development in marginalized communities. This generally means developing projects aimed at improving the quality of life of people living in rural areas in Third World countries. This segment of the world's population is often called the "Bottom Billion" [2].

ICTD is a highly interdisciplinary field that brings together competences from technical (e.g., engineering, computer science) and non-technical (e.g., social sciences) disciplines to address the numerous challenges of bringing ICTs to communities in which resources are scarce by definition and most of the population is illiterate. Some notable areas of research are e-Health, e-Agriculture, e-Learning, communications and infrastructure and e-Governance, addressed by various disciplines such as UI design, user studies, accessibility and localization [3].

As the recent growth in penetration of mobile technologies in developing countries (especially in Sub-Saharan Africa and India) sparked a so-called "mobile revolution" [4], the access to ICTs has become even more crucial in guaranteeing inclusion. As Heeks [5] points out, an already marginalized community lacking ICT access risks being further excluded from the rest of society. As a result, ICTD initiatives based on low-end mobile phones that harness the often unconventional usages of such devices in developing countries have spread [6].

Despite the evidently strong connection with mobile technologies (up to the point that the World Wide Web Consortium has activated an interest group

R. Popescu-Zeletin et al. (Eds.) AFRICOMM 2011, LNICST 92, pp. 167–176, 2012.

in Mobile Web for Development [7]), ICTD project development should not be technology driven but it should include the input of end-users in all phases [5, 8]. However, the trend of considering the technical aspects secondary has led to a lack of documentation, metrics and tools to evaluate solutions. As a result, customizable, reusable and sustainable methodologies to address the problems of the "Bottom Billion" are not available, leading to a continuous re-implementation and repetition of very similar projects that die when their donor funding period is over. Therefore, a high failure rate due to limited or lack of sustainability strategies can be observed [9–11].

Although it is impossible to find a unified recipe, we argue that defining a structured approach to software development for the "Bottom Billion" can reduce the probability of failure of ICTD projects. However, simply copy&pasting techniques from "First World" environments (e.g. customizing the Rational Unified Process [12]) does not work [13]. We thus need to investigate how we can learn from best field practices in ICTD and from First World best practices to formalize an appropriate and customizable development process.

In this paper, we present our observations of the results of several surveys of ICTD projects to motivate the need for a structured approach to software design and development in the ICTD context. We then present our idea to incrementally build a knowledge base of software development best practices in ICTD by developing a web portal to collect and share such information.

In section 2 we present the background of this work and the ICTD experiences we are aware of with a strongly structured computer science approach. In section 3 we discuss our motivations stemming from our considerations on the state-of-the-art of ICTD practice and in section 4 we outline a proposed crowdsourcing web portal to share and collect information about ICTD software projects. In section 5 we present some related works of mapping and surveying such projects. We finally draw our conclusions and outline possible future directions in section 6.

2   Background

The rural areas of developing regions often lack appropriate access to ICTs due to poor infrastructure, illiteracy and – in general – scarcity of resources. As business and social interactions become more an more dependent on digital transactions, providing access to ICTs to the people of such areas is becoming critical to stimulate socio-economic development and prevent their further exclusion from economic, social and political life [5].

Telecenters have represented the archetypal implementation of ICTD in the 90s and in the first decade of the 21st century [3, 5]. Their goal was to overcome the digital divide by providing a common place for a group of people to use and be trained in the use of ICTs. However, several surveys and studies [3, 5, 14] have shown that most telecenters lacked sustainability, scalability and evaluation of benefits.

With the recent skyrocketing of the penetration of mobile technologies in emerging economies, most ICTD initiatives have switched to mobile service delivery [4, 6, 9, 15–17]. The focus of ICTD has thus switched from providing infrastructure to providing services based on actually used technologies [5].

Gakuru et al. [10] produced an extensive report on innovative farmers advisory systems) [18] and identified the top-down approach mentioned above as the main reason for project failures. In fact, most of the systems developed by NGOs do not involve the end-users in the requirements elicitation process. Another analysis of the same inventory [11] points out how the short life-cycle for which projects are designed seriously hinders their possibility of surviving the pilot period. Moreover, no project deals with the whole agricultural cycle and is not interoperable with other solution, thus resulting in a significant overlapping of services and a lack of reuse of effective solutions. For example, new market prices information systems are continuously developed even though very effective systems already exist [19]. Furthermore, only a very small number of these systems are integrated with other services, such as logistics [20], resulting in significant fragmentation and confusion among the end-users.

In a survey of the usage of mobile technologies in East Africa [17], the authors describe the revolution that is happening in countries like Kenya, Tanzania, Uganda and Rwanda, especially with respect to the adoption of mobile banking. However, the authors point out how there is a need for marketing, education and scalability from a technological point of view in order for mobile technologies to truly take off.

More extensive surveys [6] highlight an almost complete lack of communication among different project groups, a lack of documentation and almost no reusability of either the technologies and the methodologies. The current literature on ICTD projects "lacks descriptions of research problems, requirements and definitions" and it is essentially based on assumptions [8]. Moreover, solutions are not always able to adapt to a heterogeneous infrastructure quality, despite being multi-channel and targeting low-end mobile phones. Lack of quality control, standardization and irregular updates of the data sources strongly affect most projects [17, 19].

Only a few examples of clearly defined methodologies [8, 21] and architectures [13, 22] can be found in ICTD practice. Dörflinger [8] advocates the use of user-centric design through all the development phases, drawing from Mobile HCI (Human Computer Interaction) and proposing a tight interaction with real users through participatory design. The methodology includes the use of Living Labs [23, 24] and "local champions" to continuously test functional prototypes at the end of each iteration. The involvement of a "local champion" – or Infopreneur[TM]– should go along with a hub-node-satellite development mode of implementation [25].

Evaluation and monitoring through direct observation, workshops and logging is also envisaged as a critical tool to adjust requirements at runtime. This has been applied at Sekhukhune Rural Living Lab (SRLL) [24] to implement a mobile procurement system for Spaza shops in South Africa [13]. However, these recommendations are in contrast with most of the rest of the literature in ICTD, which is more concerned with the social impact of a given project rather than its requirements, design and evaluation [8].

Another architectural solution worth mentioning is the CAM framework [22], which is based on barcodes captured using a phone's camera. The CAM framework addresses technical limitations commonly found in rural areas, such as intermittent power, intermittent connectivity, and lack of secure storage. Limited education and limited disposable income are among the user limitations that CAM intends to overcome. The CAM architecture includes a mobile phone application used to assist form-based data entry. Data is initially recorded on paper forms from which it is processed by the CAM application with the aid of barcodes placed near each field of the form. CAM has been designed to transmit data asynchronously and to be applicable to multiple use cases, generally connected to data collection.

3   Motivation

We conceptualize an ICT for Development (or rather, "ICT for Good" [26]) solution as a system that directly or indirectly affects a (marginalized) community, improving its quality of life. This can be achieved by a variety of technologies, policies and interventions widely described in literature [3]. In our work, we focus on the subset of these solutions, i.e. those that impact societies by developing and deploying new software systems.

Most projects fail or have low to zero impact on the target communities [27, 28]. Lack of documentation, lack of reuse of common solutions and lack of end-user involvement seem to be among the main shortcomings of most of the current ICTD projects. While this is a recognized fact among scholars, we believe that the field has become too focused on the social aspects of ICTD endeavors rather than on the technical aspects. This is due to the fact that at the beginning of ICTD, projects were mainly technocentric, while now the trend has been reversed with an almost completely sociological approach in which software development is done with a "just do it" philosophy. We do not suggest reversing this trend again, but rather follow the multidisciplinarity idea proposed in [5], in which ICTD is a conceptual merger of computer science, information systems and development studies.

Well documented success stories are hard to find [29] and publicly available documentation on methodologies applied, development processes, sustainability plans, or the solutions themselves is essentially unavailable. By contrast, the social impact of projects is often documented and several frameworks for impact assessment have been applied and proposed to evaluate projects (see, for example, [30]). ICTD projects are in fact unbalanced towards describing the target environment and assessing the impact of the solutions. A clear cut process that goes from a problem of a target community to the delivery of a solution and ultimately impact the community is missing.

The available documentation is limited to surveys conducted by researchers looking for qualitative data about mostly sociological aspects of projects, almost completely ignoring technical (e.g. technologies adopted, software/hardware architectures, etc.), procedural (e.g. design process, time management, team management, project management, etc.) and quantitative aspects (e.g. team size, software metrics, adoption, etc.).

We observe that projects often apply an unstructured approach to software development, likely due to an unbalance of technical and non-technical competences involved. This results in frequent unsustainability issues that could be prevented by adapting software engineering and software project management techniques.

However, "First World techniques" cannot be applied as-is [13]. We claim that ICTD software projects are fundamentally different from any software project by types of stakeholders (typically with a large cultural gap with developers), environmental and technical constraints, and objective (the improvement of the quality of life is not easily measurable, unlike more traditional objectives). Therefore, a custom development process adapted from well established best practices in software engineering must be devised. Such process needs to include both the best practices of software engineering and the best practices of ICTD, with a strong focus on requirements collection, monitoring and sustainability planning.

Requirements collection and sustainability play a key role in the process. The collection of requirements is particularly critical when there is a large cultural gap between the development team and the end users. User-centric design, rapid prototyping and field testing can be of great help in ensuring that the wants of the target community are met. With respect to sustainability, an ICTD software development process has to include support activities not directly concerned with the production of software artifacts or documentation. These activities can create the appropriate environment in which the project is expected to be deployed, for example by building capacity through knowledge transfer.

We have evidence that the Living Lab open innovation model [31] and Agile methodologies such as SCRUM can be successfully applied in ICTD [24]. However, we intend to investigate the best practices that can contribute to the success of a project to include them in a set of custom activities to be performed inside an ICTD software development process. Moreover, the open source development and innovation model can be of further benefit to the ICTD community as it increases the possibility to reuse effective technologies and it is based on collaboration [32].

4   Collecting ICTD Best Practices

While ICTD may have a long history of failures, a number of successful and trendsetting experiencing can be found. See, for example, FrontlineSMS[1], txtEagle[2] and Esoko[3] [20].

---

[1] http://www.frontlinesms.com
[2] http://txteagle.com
[3] http://www.esoko.com

In order to devise an appropriate development process for ICTD software projects, we need to collect lessons learned and best practices from successful examples. This is not an easy task, as collaboration and reuse are rarely seen in the field and most of the sharing of ideas currently happens through informal channels such as Twitter[4]. As a result, success stories are mostly anecdotal and without a technical perspective.

Surveys and questionnaires are frequently used in ICTD practice to understand the target community. Therefore, we plan to use a similar system to reach project managers and teams and collect quantitative and qualitative data about projects. We propose an online crowdsourcing website – called *ict4gHub* – to allow project managers and developers involved in ICTD software projects to share their practices and information about their projects. In this way, we expect to start a continuously growing knowledge base that will benefit not only our study, but the whole community. *ict4gHub* will primarily support data collection. This is what will allow us to obtain information to design our software development process. However, in order to become an added value for the whole community, *ict4gHub* will also work as a showcase of ICTD projects and techniques. This will help increase visibility of initiatives and collaboration among different groups.

The goal of this data collection is to identify the critical success factors and failure factors in ICTD project development to build a set of recommendations that will ultimately constitute a customizable software development process. We are well aware that ICTD cannot be standardized. However, we argue that several commonalities can be found among different projects, therefore paving the way for the design of a customizable development process or a set of development processes.

Table 1 summarizes the data that we want to collect as an ICTD project's factsheet and that we expect to be ultimately able to produce as output. We plan to complement the data collected through *ict4gHub* with direct interviews and questionnaires with the managers of particularly active initiatives.

Figure 1 shows an early mockup of how *ict4gHub* will look like. We intend to show aggregated statistics on the homepage and publicize particularly active projects as "featured projects". All the other projects will be presented in a catalog.

5   Related Work

Several surveys have described ICTD projects in the recent years [6, 10, 11, 19], with particular interest towards mobile technologies and their application in rural contexts (see, for example, [17]). These surveys cover about 200 projects and identify several common aspects of all projects and discuss the reasons behind project failures.

Patra et al. [3] compiled probably the most complete survey of ICTD projects to describe the general direction of ICTD work and its validity. The survey

---

[4] http://twitter.com/#!/search/%23ict4d%20OR%20%23ictd

Table 1. ICTD project factsheet template

Quantitative Data	
Software metrics	Development time
Team size	Adoption (# of users)
Target community demographics	
Qualitative Data	
Project phases	Technologies
Team	Lessons learned
Sustainability plan	Target community
Estimation techniques	Tools (e.g. for planning, designing)

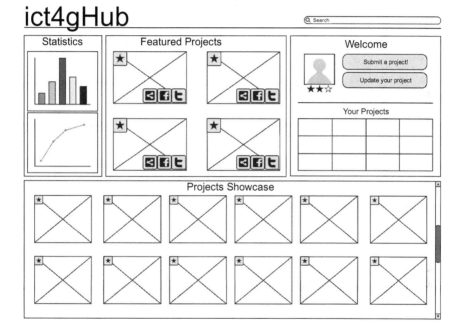

Fig. 1. Mockup of *ict4gHub*

analyzes projects in different areas, providing data about the role of governements in their development, the impact achieved and articles published at conferences.

A more local attempt at mapping ICTD projects has been carried out in the Philippines by Tiglao & Alampay [33] using a well defined taxonomy by Curtain [29]. Curtain describes a checklist of key components for best practices in ICTD. However, while the checklist is fairly extensive and can be applied to project management, it fails to address the specific and concrete issues of ICTD software projects.

Van Reijswoud presented in [34] the concept of "appropriate ICT" and some tools and methodologies to support design and development of ICTD solutions.

Methodologies such as Mobile HCI, user-centric design and Agile methodologies have been applied at Sekhukhune Living Lab [8, 13, 24], which is currently the only environment where software engineering techniques are applied to ICTD and documented.

Our work differs from previous attempts to categorize ICTD projects by taking a software engineering perspective, based on the hypothesis that the analysis can provide us with insights on how to tailor a software development process to the ICTD domain. Furthermore, our work adds value to the survey by making a knowledge base available to ICTD practitioners.

A similar approach has been adopted by eHub for web applications[5] and by MobileActive[6] for mobile tools for social change. More recently, the portal "SMS in action" was set up to map projects based on SMS platforms, using the Ushahidi crowdsourcing platform [35]. The portal we propose aims at taking a more technical perspective, mapping techniques rather than single projects.

6   Conclusion

In this paper, we have presented our views on the shortcomings of software projects in ICTD. We believe that an unstructured approach to software development is among the main causes of failure and we claim that applying software engineering and software project management techniques, without shifting to a completely technocentric approach, can greatly improve the quality of solutions for marginalized communities.

However, the limited documentation available and the lack of concreteness in most ICTD publications require us to devise a method to collect quantitative data on top of the more generally available qualitative data to understand the success factors of solutions in terms of software process.

We have presented the concept for *ict4gHub*, a crowdsourcing web portal to collect data about projects and to facilitate sharing of common solutions and best practices among ICTD researchers and practitioners. Our goals are:

- to classify projects by means of measurable properties.
- to identify a set of best practices and recommendations in ICTD software design and development.
- to provide added value to practitioners and researchers by creating a publicly available knowledge base, therefore encouraging participation to the survey.

We plan to use the results of this survey to design a software development process for the ICTD domain, based on best practices collected through *ict4gHub* and consolidated software engineering techniques.

References

1. Unwin, T.: ICT4D: Information and communication technology for development. Cambridge Univ. Pr. (2009)

---

[5] http://emilychang.com/ehub/
[6] http://www.mobileactive.org

2. Collier, P.: The bottom billion: Why the poorest countries are failing and what can be done about it. Oxford University Press, USA (2007)
3. Patra, R., Pal, J., Nedevschi, S.: ICTD state of the union: where have we reached and where are we headed. In: 2009 International Conference on Information and Communication Technologies and Development (ICTD), pp. 357–366. IEEE (2009)
4. Kalil, T.: Harnessing the Mobile Revolution. Innovations: Technology, Governance, Globalization 4(1), 9–23 (2009)
5. Heeks, R.: The ICT4D 2.0 Manifesto: where next for ICTs and international development. Institute for Development Policy and Management Working Papers, Manchester, UK (2009)
6. Donner, J.: Research Approaches to Mobile Use in the Developing World: A Review of the Literature. The Information Society 24(3) (2008)
7. Boyera, S.: Mobile Web for Social Development Roadmap. Technical report, World Wide Web Consortium (2009)
8. Doerflinger, J., Gross, T.: Technical ICTD - A User Centered Lifecycle. In: Pont, A., Pujolle, G., Raghavan, S.V. (eds.) WCITD 2010. IFIP AICT, vol. 327, pp. 72–83. Springer, Heidelberg (2010)
9. Cranston, P., Painting, K.: Mobile Services in a Wireless World: The CTA 2009 ICT Observatory Meeting. Agricultural Information Worldwide 3(1), 44–50 (2010)
10. Gakuru, M., Winters, K., Stepman, F.: Innovative farmer advisory services using ICT. In: Cunningham, P., Cunningham, M. (eds.) IST-Africa 2009 Conference Proceedings. IIMC International Information Management Corporation, Citeseer (2009)
11. Aker, J.: Dial "A" for Agriculture: Using Information and Communication Technologies for Agricultural Extension in Developing countries. In: Conference on Agriculture for Development - Revisited, University of California at Berkeley (2010)
12. Kruchten, P.: The rational unified process: an introduction. Addison-Wesley Professional (2004)
13. Dörflinger, J., Gross, T.: Bottom Billion Architecture: An Extensible Software Architecture for ICT Access in the Rural Developing World (2010)
14. Heeks, R.: ICTs and the MDGs: On the wrong track? Information for Development, Noida, Inde (2005)
15. Gandhi, S., Mittal, S., Tripathi, G.: The impact of mobiles on agricultural productivity. India: The Impact of Mobile Phones, The Vodafone Policy Paper Series 9, 21–33 (2009)
16. Dick, M.: Weaving the "Mobile Web" in the Context of ICT4D: A Preliminary Exploration of the State of the Art. Proceedings of the American Society for Information Science and Technology 47(1), 1–7 (2010)
17. Hellström, J., Tröften, P.: The innovative use of mobile applications in East Africa. Swedish International Development Cooperation Agency, Sida (2010)
18. Gakuru, M., Winters, K., Stepman, F.: Inventory of innovative farmer advisory services using ICTs. In: Forum for Agricultural Research in Africa (FARA), Accra, GH (2009)
19. Sirajul Islam, M., Grönlund, Å.: Agriculture Market Information Services (AMIS) in the Least Developed Countries (LDCs): Nature, Scopes, and Challenges. In: Wimmer, M.A., Chappelet, J.-L., Janssen, M., Scholl, H.J. (eds.) EGOV 2010. LNCS, vol. 6228, pp. 109–120. Springer, Heidelberg (2010)
20. David-West, O.: Esoko Networks: Facilitating Agriculture Through Technology. GIM Case Study No. B061. Technical report, New York: United Nations Development Programme (2011)

21. Parikh, T.S.: Engineering rural development. Commun. ACM 52, 54–63 (2009)
22. Parikh, T., Lazowska, E.: Designing an architecture for delivering mobile information services to the rural developing world. In: Proceedings of the 15th International Conference on World Wide Web, pp. 791–800. ACM (2006)
23. Guzman, J., Schaffers, H., Bilicki, V., Merz, C., Valenzuela, M.: Living Labs. fostering open innovation and rural development: Methodology and results. In: The 14th International Conference on Concurrent Enterprising (ICE 2008), Lisboa, Portugal, pp. 23–25 (2008)
24. Van Greunen, D., De Louw, R., Dörflinger, J., Friedland, C., Christian, M.: Sekhukhune living lab: Lessons learnt from end user community building and interaction. In: IST-Africa 2009 Conference Proceedings (2009)
25. van Rensburg, J., Veldsman, A., Jenkins, M.: From technologists to social enterprise developers: Our journey as "ICT for development" practitioners in Southern Africa. Information Technology for Development 14(1), 76–89 (2008)
26. Eshete, B., Mattioli, A., Villafiorita, A., Weldemariam, K.: ICT for Good: Opportunities, Challenges and the Way Forward. In: Proceedings of the Fourth International Conference on Digital Society, ICDS (2010)
27. Heeks, R.: Information systems and developing countries: Failure, success, and local improvisations. The Information Society 18(2), 101–112 (2002)
28. Avgerou, C.: Information systems in developing countries: a critical research review. Journal of Information Technology 23(3), 133–146 (2008)
29. Curtain, R.: Information and communications technologies and development: Help or hindrance. AusAID Virtual Colombo Plan (2004)
30. Heeks, R., Molla, A.: Compendium on impact assessment of ict-for-development projects. Development Informatics Working Paper Series. Institute for Development Policy and Management, Manchester (2009)
31. Eriksson, M., Niitamo, V., Kulkki, S.: State-of-the-art in utilizing living labs approach to user-centric ict innovation–a european approach. Working Paper (2005)
32. van Reijswoud, V., de Jager, A.: Free and open source software for development. CoRR abs/0808.3717 (2008)
33. Tiglao, N., Alampay, E.: Mapping ICT4D Projects in the Philippines. Philippine Journal of Public Administration 129, 26-4 (2009)
34. van Reijswoud, V.: Appropriate ICT as a tool to increase effectiveness in ICT4D: theoretical considerations and illustrating cases. The Electronic Journal of Information Systems in Developing Countries 38(9), 1–18 (2009)
35. Okolloh, O.: Ushahidi, or'testimony': Web 2.0 tools for crowdsourcing crisis information. Participatory Learning and Action 59(1), 65–70 (2009)

Information and Communication Technologies and Firms Productivity in Cameroon[*]

Pierre Valére Nketcha Nana[1] and Christophe Péguy Choub Faha[1,2,**]

[1] Department of Economics, Université Laval, Canada
{vnketcha,fpeguy}@yahoo.fr
[2] 2276, Place Versailles, G1V1S1, QC, Canada

Abstract. Using panel data from manufacturing firms in Cameroon, this study investigates the impact of Information and Communication Technologies (ICTs) on firms' productivity in Cameroon. The empirical model is derived from the flexible Translog production function. The strategic complementarities between ICT-capital and organizational changes are accounted for. We estimate our model using the System-Generalized Method of Moments (GMMS) estimator as it is adequate to deal with endogeneity issues. Our results reveal that the effects of ICT on productivity are catalyzed by the implementation of organizational changes. Moreover, we identified the specific organizational changes that deliver the highest benefits.

Keywords: ICT, Productivity, System-GMM Estimators, Organisational Changes.

1 Introduction

In 1995, Cameroon has launched a nationwide program to promote the adoption of Information and Communication Technologies (ICTs) by local firms. A recent survey, carried out by the National Institute of Statistics in 2006, reveals that 56% of companies have invested in at least a basic form of ICTs. However, it is unclear whether and to what extent these technologies have contributed to the growth of productivity. This issue is ever more important since about 40% of local firms are still reluctant to use ICTs [1].

The role of ICT in improving business productivity is however at the forefront of development strategies. Theoretically, ICTs can significantly contribute to firms' productivity through the improvement of production processes; especially by facilitating transactions and by stimulating labour productivity and multifactor productivity.

Yet, recent empirical evidence from developing countries suggests that increased investment in ICTs does not necessarily lead to higher productivity,

---

[*] We acknowledge the grant support from ICBE through the joint project of TrustAfrica and IDRC.

[**] Corresponding author.

R. Popescu-Zeletin et al. (Eds.) AFRICOMM 2011, LNICST 92, pp. 177–186, 2012.

[2,3]. This might reduce firms' incentives to use ICTs, especially when they are facing tight budgetary constraints. In addition, many firms are still using traditional methods and these firms can switch to use ICTs only if the benefits derived are higher than the investment and maintenance costs.

In the light of developed countries' experience, it appeared that the mere accumulation of ICT capital is not enough. How those technologies are used within the firm is determinant. For example, if firms introduce complementary organizational changes along with investments in ICT, the productivity gains will be more important, [5,6]. Note that these complementary investments require technical expertise and financial resources that might be limited in small and medium enterprises.

At the macroeconomic level, a set of conditions should also be ensured to allow productivity use of ICT at the firm level, namely, the availability of skilled labor, regular electricity supply, adequate telecommunication infrastructure, etc. Thus, in the absence of an enabling environment, it might not be very productive to invest in ICT; may be one reason why firms' investments in ICT are still very low in Cameroon.

In fact, between 2000 and 2006, investments in ICT represent an average of 7% of total firm's investments in our sample. As shown in Fig. 1, ICT-investments decreased by 12% during this period[1], while total investment felt by 3.6% only. This suggests a kind of distrust of the firms with regard to ICT.

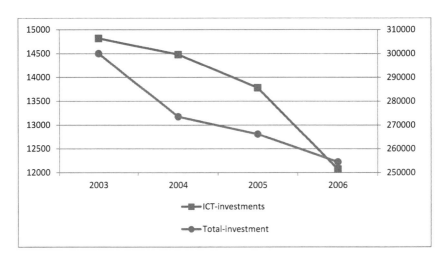

Fig. 1. Evolution of Investments (in Millions of Francs)

This study proposes to examine closely the impact of ICTs on firm productivity in Cameroon, paying particular attention to the role of organizational change. Specifically, our aims are to:

---

[1] Conjuncture Survey, Ministry of Economy and Finance.

- estimate the elasticity of output with respect to ICT capital;
- determine if the implementation of organizational changes improve the productivity gains from the ICT-capital;
- identify the different types of organizational changes that are more likely to maximize the benefits of ICT investment in Cameroon.

The paper is organized as follows: The next section reviews the literature on the impacts of ICTs on firms' productivity. Section 3 presents the methodological framework. Section 4 describes the data. Section 5 presents and discusses the preliminary results, and Section 6 concludes.

2   Literature Review

In the early 1980s, most studies on the relationship between ICTs and productivity led to the statement of the paradox of productivity [7]. This "lack of ICTs in the productivity statistics" ultimately turns to be a problem of measurement of ICTs and the value they create, particularly in the sector of services where output is particularly difficult to identify.

Subsequent studies on manufacturing firms have in fact led to positive results [4,8], particularly because of improvements in the measurement of output so as to account for qualitative aspect of ICTs'[2] impact.

In developing countries on the contrary, the efficiency of ICTs as a factor in firm performance is still hampered by the lack of a solid empirical foundation. [9] and [6] on the contrary report a negative impact of ICTs on labour productivity in Small and Medium Scale Enterprises (SMEs) in Kenya and Tanzania. Such a result would indicate that on average the use of ICTs is not beneficial for firms in developing countries.

More generally, ICTs have higher impacts primarily where skills in ICT were improved, and where organizational changes were implemented. Therefore, the productivity paradox that have been highlighted by [9] and [2] for the case of Eastern African firms may be due to the fact that organizational changes or qualification of employees in using ICT were not accounted for in the underlying empirical models.

In a nutshell, if we have convincing evidence for developed countries that ICTs contribute to higher productivity in firms, the issue is still unresolved as far as developing countries are concerned. This may be due to the paucity of robust empirical analyses. In a study on Brazil and India, [10] have taken into consideration the impact of organizational changes while estimating the impact of ICTs on firms' productivity. Yet, their results may be biased because they do not deal with the potential issue of simultaneity in the input and output choices at the firm level. Clearly, for the purpose of effective policy making, we need robust evidence about the real economic impacts of ICTs on firms' productivity, as well as the necessary conditions to ensure the highest positive impacts.

---

[2] This is in particularly the improvement of the quality of output and labor input, the variety of products, quality customer service, reducing delays.

3   Methodology

The theoretical framework commonly used is the production function theory
[8]. The underlying assumption is that the firm has a method for transforming
various inputs into output, and the process can be represented by a production
function. This requires a particular specification of the relationship between the
inputs and the outputs.

The Cobb-Douglas specification is commonly used in previous studies, particularly because of its simplicity. It is however a very restrictive specification,
compared to the Translog specification that offers the advantage of being more
flexible [11,12]. Hence, we will use a Translog-based specification in this study.
The resulting empirical model is specified as follows:

$$LnY_{it} = \mu_{it} + \beta_1 LnN_{it} + \beta_{11}(LnN_{it})^2 + \beta_2 LnTIC_{it} \qquad (1)$$
$$+\beta_{22}(LnTIC_{it})^2 + \beta_3 LnK_{it} + \beta_{33}(LnK_{it})^2 + \beta_{12} LnN_{it}LnTIC_{it}$$
$$+\beta_{13}LnN_{it}LnK_{it} + \beta_{23}LnTIC_{it}LnK_{it} + \beta_4 TIC_{it}ORG_i$$

$$\mu_{it} = \eta_i + \gamma_t + \epsilon_{it} \qquad (2)$$

The index i refers to the individual units of firms, and index t the temporal
observations. The variables η_i are time-invariant firm-specific effects. The variables γ_t are time-specific effects, strictly identical across individuals. ϵ_{it} is the
component of the residual term which is orthogonal to η_i and γ_t . A key assumption we maintain throughout is that ϵ_{it} is a disturbance term independently and
identically distributed, which satisfy the following assumptions:

$$E(\epsilon_{it}) = 0 \qquad (3)$$

$$E(\epsilon_{it}, \epsilon_{js}) = 0, \quad \forall j \neq i, \quad \forall (t, s) \qquad (4)$$

$$E(\epsilon_{it}, \epsilon_{is}) = \begin{cases} \sigma_\epsilon^2 & si\ t=s \\ 0 & \forall t \neq s \end{cases}, \quad which\ implies\ that\ E(\epsilon_i, \epsilon_i) = \sigma_\epsilon^2 I_T \qquad (5)$$

Y is the output: This variable is defined by the value added calculated before
tax. This definition takes into account improvements in the quality of output in
relation to the use of ICTs.

N is employment: It is measured by the number of employees including staff
employed full time, part time or seasonally.

K and TIC are respectively the stock of ICT-capital and ordinary capital :
Capital stocks are calculated using a proportional downgrading model that will
easily express the amount of capital of a period depending on the capital of the
previous period and the volume of investment in the previous period.

$TIC_{it}ORG_i$ is a multiplicative dummy variable. It captures the indirect impact of ICTs on productivity resulting from the strategic complementarities between organizational changes[3] (measured by ORG_i) and ICT see [11] and [10].

---

[3] Detailed definition is presented below.

In general, taking into account the organizational changes in empirical studies is controversial and this is due to the absence of a universally accepted definition of the concept [13]. Indeed, the concept of organizational change refers to a complex set of changes affecting not only the internal organization of the firm but also its relationships with its customers or business partners. Concretely, it is when a firm redefines or restructures a number of factors such as the hierarchical structure, the political incentive to work, or the management of customer services.

In this study, it is still possible to evaluate the appropriateness of some practices identified in the literature as "best practices". In fact, these practices have effectiveness in obtaining high yields of investments in ICTs in the context of developed countries [14,15]. The focus here will be to question the relevance of these practices for Cameroonian firms that have invested in ICTs. Similar approach by [10] has rightly questioned the relevance of some of these practices in the case of Indian firms. What about the case of Cameroon?

To assess the impact of organizational practices on the marginal return of ICTs capital, the corresponding dummy variables are taken into account in estimating the following model (1). Following methodologies [10], [13] and [15], organizational variables will be taken into account individually.

The marginal contribution of an input to total output depends on the level of utilization of all factors of production. They are expressed as follows, respectively for employment, ICT capital and ordinary capital:

$$\overline{\alpha}_N = \frac{\partial Y_{it}}{\partial N_{it}} = \beta_1 + 2\beta_{11}\overline{LnN_{it}} + \beta_{12}\overline{LnTIC_{it}} + \beta_{13}\overline{LnK_{it}} \tag{6}$$

$$\overline{\alpha}_{TIC} = \frac{\partial Y_{it}}{\partial TIC_{it}} = \beta_2 + 2\beta_{22}\overline{LnTIC_{it}} + \beta_{12}\overline{LnN_{it}} + \beta_{23}\overline{LnK_{it}} \tag{7}$$

$$\overline{\alpha}_K = \frac{\partial Y_{it}}{\partial K_{it}} = \beta_3 + 2\beta_{33}\overline{LnK_{it}} + \beta_{13}\overline{LnTIC_{it}} + \beta_{23}\overline{LnK_{it}} \tag{8}$$

To estimate the parameters of the production function, several studies [9,2] have used the approach of Ordinary Least Squares (OLS). However, in the presence of simultaneity and/or unobserved heterogeneity, the standard OLS estimators generally turns to be unsatisfactory and the resulting estimates are less efficient in terms of statistical properties [16].

The unobserved heterogeneity bias is possible because the strategies of highly productive firms are usually different from the strategies of firms that are not in such a way that if highly productive firms, invest more in ICTs, the results will be overestimated. The simultaneity bias arises because the choice of inputs is often a function of the level of output that the company wants to achieve and therefore the capital stock and productivity are correlated.

The estimation of a production function on individual data by taking into account the simultaneity bias and/or heterogeneity does not always produce satisfactory results [16]. In this context, the estimator of the Generalized Method of Moments in first Differences (GMMD) is generally used. However, [17] show that the properties of the estimator are weak when the variables are highly persistent, as it is usually the case with series of sales, added value, capital and employment. In this case, delayed variables in levels are weakly correlated with the equations in first differences (weak instruments).

[17] also show that the implementation of the Generalised Method of Moments in System (GMMS), by combining information from first-difference equations (standard instruments) and level (instruments in first differences) and by imposing initial conditions can significantly improve the quality of results.

[18] applied the GMMS method to assess the impact of ICTs on firms' productivity in Europe and discovered that GMMS estimators are more efficient than OLS estimators and GMMD. In the context of this work, we will use the GMMS method. From what we know, this estimation approach has not yet been used in previous studies assessing the impact of ICT on productivity in the context of developing countries. GMMS estimations of parameters of production function will be obtained using the GAUSS DPD98 program developed by [19].

Finally, the quality of the estimated coefficients of the model (1) depends on the validity of instruments that should not be correlated with the disturbance in order to correct the regression. This hypothesis will be tested using a Sargan test. In addition, since the equation of reference is passed in first difference, the residues thus obtained are supposed to be correlated to the order 1, but not to order 2. The tests AR (1) and AR (2) [20] can be used to verify this.

4   Data

To implement our empirical methodology, we used data obtained from a field survey in addition to the data already available from the Fiscal and Statistics Statements (FSS) at the National Institute of Statistics. From the FSS, we collect all the necessary quantitative information. After all the statistical treatments[4] , we came out with an unbalanced panel of 344 firms with annual observations from 2003 to 2007.

From the survey, we collect the necessary qualitative variables to complete our database. The treatment of qualitative variables consists in attributing the value one to the variable measuring organizational change when a change is made in the company organization and zero otherwise. At the time of the survey, 320 of the 344 firms of our first database have been identified, and 261 were able to provide qualitative information necessary to measure the organizational changes. Finally, we merged the two databases and obtain an unbalanced panel of 261 firms over 5 years[5] . The main descriptive statistics of the panel are presented as follows:

---

[4] Firstly, from the raw dataset, firms with inconsistent information in the FSS have been removed. Secondly, to account for the entry-exit in the population of firms, only firms that produced their FSS for at least two consecutive years between 2003 and 2007 have been considered.

[5] Data for the more recent years are not included because the recent FSS are not officially released by the National Institute of Statistics yet.

Table 1. Descriptive Statistics of Key Variables (Log)

Variables	Obs.	Firms	Mean	Med.	S.d.	Min	Max
value added	1238	261	2.313	1.497	6.693	0.003	5.560
Employment	1238	261	6.001	5.540	6.693	2.303	9.327
ICT-Capital	1238	261	1.908	3.009	4.067	0.001	6.778
Non ICT-Capital	1238	261	6.777	5.743	4.250	3.196	13.749

Source: Authors' Calculations

5   Estimation Results

Table 2 presents in a concise manner the estimation results of our empirical Translog model by GMMS on the entire sample.

Table 2. Estimation Results for the Translog by GMMS

Dependent variable: lnY			
	ORG= Decentralization	ORG= Workplace organization	ORG= Human resources practices
LnN	$1,258^{***}$	$1,385^{***}$	$1,238^{***}$
	(0,157)	(0,156)	(0,153)
$LnICT$	-0,042	-0,019	-0,027
	(0,061)	(0,063)	(0.059)
LnK	$0,153^{***}$	$0,198^{***}$	$0,111^{***}$
	(0,083)	(0,088)	(0,08)
$(LnN)^2$	$-0,033^{***}$	$0,011^{***}$	$0,028^{***}$
	(0,017)	(0,016)	(0,014)
$(LnICT)^2$	$0,002^{**}$	$0,001^{***}$	$0,005^{**}$
	(0,007)	(0,004)	(0,006)
$(LnK)^2$	0,011	0,014	0,018
	(0,006)	(0,007)	(0,003)
$LnN*LnICT$	$0,034^{***}$	$0,042^{**}$	$0,024^{***}$
	(0,017)	(0,015)	(0,021)
$LnN*LnK$	-0,009	-0,005	$-0,008^*$
	(0,006)	(0,001)	(0,007)
$LnICT*LnK$	-0,007	-0,003	-0,004
	(0,005)	(0,008)	(0,007)
$ICT*ORG$	0,017	$0,019^{**}$	0,018
	(0,012)	(0,02)	(0,014)
R^2	0,831	0,798	0,856
Dif. Sargan (p-values)	0,56	0,572	0,479
AR(1)	0,008	0,006	0,009
AR(2)	0,033	0,037	0,041

Source: Authors' estimation from the DPD98 program running in GAUSS.
$***$, $**$ and $*$ denote significance at 1, 5 and 10% level, respectively.
Values in parentheses represent standard deviations. The results are those of the two-step GMMS estimator.

As discussed in the "methodology" section, the GMMS estimator is robust to potential endogeneity issues, which allows us to interpret the results in terms of causality; the results presented in Table 2 show that the direct impact of ICT-capital depends on the level of investment in ICT. In fact, the coefficient of the quadratic term for the ICT-capital is positive and significant; while the coefficient of the simple ICT-capital is negative. Thus, the higher the amount firms invest in ICT, the more the input "ICT-capital" is productive.

Based on a Cobb-Douglas model, [4] had revealed that the direct impact of ICT-capital is negative in the case of firms in the East Africa. Our analysis enables to understand that their result depends crucially on the level of investment in ICT. We see the advantage of using flexible Translog based empirical model that the more restrictive Cobb-Douglas-based models as in previous studies.

As we indicated earlier, another approach to better understand the impact of ICTs on firm's productivity is to consider the role of organizational changes. Three specific measures of organizational changes are considered, namely the "decentralization of competences", which is a measure of whether the number of hierarchical or reporting levels has decreased, and if employees have autonomy of decision in the company; the "workplace reorganization", which is a measure of whether firms have introduced performance compensation scheme, or a flexibility in programming and management of working hours; and the "human resources practices", which is a measure of whether firms have put more emphasis on the monitoring of individual workers or teams of workers.

The results presented in Table 2 show that the coefficient on the interaction term between ICT capital and organizational changes is positive for all measures of organizational changes that we used. This confirms the view that the productivity of ICT is improved when complementary organizational changes are implemented within the firm. However, only the effect of the "workplace organization" is significant. This suggests that if the organizational changes are important for improving the productivity of ICT, the impacts are not the same for all types of changes. "Workplace organization" seems to be the best type of complementary organizational changes.

6   Conclusion

At the end of this analysis, a number of important results have been established. First, the direct impact of ICT on productivity depends on how much firms spent in these technologies. This can be easily understood when we know that to take advantage of the basic ICT equipment such as computers, it is necessary to invest in the purchase of software, network hardware and other technical means necessary to process and share information. All those other components of the ICT-capital are relatively more expensive than basic computers, but they are important otherwise, investments in computers will not be productive.

Second, our results showed that in addition to contributing directly to firms' productivity, ICT also contributes indirectly through the improvement of labor productivity. In fact, our results have revealed that the elasticity of output with respect to employment increases with the level of investment in ICT.

Finally, our results showed that the implementation of organizational changes can improve the impact of ICT. Furthermore, it appeared that among all types of organizational changes we considered, the introduction of performance compensation is the best.

References

1. Research ICT Africa: Towards an African E-Index: SME E-Access and Usage in 14 African Countries, Johannesburg: The Link Centre,
   `http://www.researchictafrica.net/images/upload/SMEbook-Web.pdf`
2. Chowdhury, S.K.: Investments in ICT-Capital and Economic Performance of Mmall and Medium Scale Enterprises in East Africa. Journal of International Development 18, 533–552 (2006)
3. Dewan, S., Kraemer, K.L.: The Grid: Information Technology and Productivity: Preliminary Evidence from Country-Level Data. Management Science 46(4), 548–562 (2000)
4. Lichtenberg, F.: The output contributions of computer equipment and personal: A firm-level analysis. Economics of Innovation and New Technology 3, 201–217 (1995)
5. Bryjolfsson, E., Hitt, L.: Beyond computation: information technology, organisational transformation and business performance. Journal of Economic Perspectives 14, 23–48 (2000)
6. Brynjolfsson, E., Hitt, L., Yang, S.: Intangible assets: computers and organizational capital. Brooking Papers on Economic Activity 1, 137–199 (2002)
7. Bryjolfsson, E., Yang, S.: Information technology and productivity: A review of the literature. Advances in Computers 43, 179–214 (1996)
8. Bryjolfsson, E., Hitt, L.: Paradox lost? Firm-level evidence on the returns to information systems spending. Management Science 42(4), 541–558 (1996)
9. Matambalya, F., Wolf, S.: The role of ICT for the performance of SMEs in East Africa. Discussion Paper on Development Policy No. 42, ZEF (2001)
10. Basant, R., Commander, S., Harrisson, R., Menezes-Filho, N.: ICT adoption and productivity in developing countries: New firm level evidence from Brazil and India. Discussion Paper No. 2294, IZA (2006)
11. Hempell, T.: Does experience matter? Innovation and the productivity of ICT in German services. Economics of Innovation and New Technology 14(4), 277–303 (2005)
12. Sumit, S., Jung, C.: A study of the impact of information technology on firm performance: a flexible production function approach. Information System Journal 19(3), 313–339 (2007)
13. Black, S.E., Lynch, L.M.: Measuring organizational capital in the new economy. Discussion Paper No. 1524, IZA (2005)
14. Gera, S., Gu, W.: The effect of organizational innovation and information and communications technology on firm performance. International Productivity Monitor 4, 37–51 (2004)
15. Arvanitis, S.: Computerization, workplace organization, skilled Labour and firm productivity: evidence for the Swiss business sector. Economics of Innovation and New Technology 14(4), 225–249 (2005)
16. Griliches, Z., Mairesse, J.: Production functions: the search for identification. In: Strom, S. (ed.) Essays in Honour of Ragnar Frisch. Econometric Society Monograph Series. Cambridge University Press, Cambridge (1997)

17. Blundell, R., Bond, S.: GMM estimation with persistent panel data: an application to production functions. Econometric Reviews 19(3), 321–340 (2000)
18. Hempell, T.: What's spurious, what's real? Measuring the productivity impacts of ICT at the firm-level. Centre for European Economic Research, Discussion Paper, No. 02–42, Zew (2002)
19. Arellano, M., Bond, S.: Dynamic panel data estimation using DPD98 for GAUSS: a guide for users (1998), `http://www.american.edu/academic.depts/` `cas/econ/gaussres/regress/dpd/dpd98.pdf`
20. Arellano, M., Bond, S.: Some tests of specification for Panel Data: Monte Carlo evidence and an application to employment equations. Review of Economic Studies 58(2), 277–297 (1991)

e-Health for Rural Areas in Developing Countries: Lessons from the Sebokeng Experience

Massimiliano Masi[1,2], Rosario Pugliese[1], and Francesco Tiezzi[3]

[1] Università degli Studi di Firenze, Viale Morgagni 65, 50134, Firenze, Italy
[2] Tiani "Spirit" GmbH, Guglgasse 6, Gasometer A, 1110, Vienna, Austria
[3] IMT Advanced Studies Lucca, Piazza S. Ponziano 6, 55100, Lucca, Italy
massimiliano.masi@tiani-spirit.com, rosario.pugliese@unifi.it
francesco.tiezzi@imtlucca.it

Abstract. We report the experience gained in an e-Health project in the Gauteng province, in South Africa. A Proof-of-Concept of the project has been already installed in 3 clinics in the Sebokeng township. The project is now going to be applied to 300 clinics in the whole province. This extension of the Proof-of-Concept can however give rise to security flaws because of the inclusion of rural areas with unreliable Internet connection. We address this problem and propose a safe solution.

Keywords: e-Health systems in developing countries, information security, healthcare technology standards, e-Health experiences.

1 Introduction

In recent years the importance of healthcare systems based on Electronic Health Records (EHRs) has been addressed by governments and institutions. An EHR is a set of sensitive data written in a machine readable format (e.g., the Hl7's CDA [1]) containing the healthcare history of a patient, such as vital signs, prescribed medicines, billing, and the patient summary.

Many projects have been started worldwide with the aim of developing systems for electronic healthcare (e-Health) based on EHRs sharing and capable of providing optimum patient care (see, e.g., [2,3]). To ensure fallbacks and interoperability, such systems need to be built using international, well-known, and open standards, due to the impact on financing and governance that they might have. Large investments are conducted by governments, therefore a good confidence in the project success is needed. For this reason the initiative Integrating the Healthcare Enterprises (IHE, [4]) was founded with the goal of tailoring already existing standards (such as [1,5,6]) in the context of Service-Oriented Architectures for setting up e-Health projects. IHE thus provides a standard methodology for building applications in which EHRs exchange plays a significant role.

By adopting standard technologies, governments and hospitals obtain significant benefits from both a financial and a practical point of view. E-HR.GP [7] is

R. Popescu-Zeletin et al. (Eds.) AFRICOMM 2011, LNICST 92, pp. 187–196, 2012.
© Institute for Computer Sciences, Social Informatics and Telecommunications Engineering 2012

an example of an ongoing project based on IHE standard technologies aiming at managing EHRs of patients from the Gauteng province, South Africa. A Proof-of-Concept (PoC) of such project has been successfully installed in the Sebokeng township [8]. The next step of the E-HR.GP project is the extension of the PoC implementation to cover the clinics of the overall Gauteng province.

The process of creating e-Health systems, however, is not just a merely adoption of healthcare standards. Indeed, these standards are often designed with the assumption of a high-speed network infrastructure in place, which is not always the case when considering rural areas of developing countries. This can result in a set of security flaws in the authentication process of healthcare professionals due to missing requirements on technology (e.g., implicit assumptions on communication channels, such as availability and reliability). Therefore, since a considerable area of the Gauteng province suffers from the above mentioned connectivity problems, we believe that such security flaws would occur in the extension of the PoC, unless suitable measures are taken. In this paper, we tackle the problem of amending the system developed in the E-HR.GP's PoC by proposing the use of a formally-proved correct IHE-based protocol [9], so to include also clinics in rural areas with low or absent Internet connectivity and reachable only by hundred of kilometers of sand tracks.

To sum up, the main contributions of this work are: 1) the presentation of the outcome of the current status of the E-HR.GP's PoC; 2) the identification of potential authentication problems that can arise in the extension of the PoC; 3) the proposal of adopting of a formally-proved secure protocol for connecting clinics in rural environments.

The rest of the paper is structured as follows. In Section 2, we provide an overview of the E-HR.GP project. In Section 3, we discuss major problems to tackle when extending the application of the project to include more clinics and how to solve them by means of an IHE-based protocol. In Section 4, we touch upon more closely related work. Finally, in Section 5, we conclude the paper.

2   The E-HR.GP Project

Before the starting of the E-HR.GP project, some clinics of the Gauteng region were already equipped with Clinical Information Systems [7]. These systems, however, were not interoperable and were not based on international standards, resulting in an high cost of ownership. In fact, in each clinic, long patient queues and slow response times were experienced, which often led to preventable deaths.

To provide a better patient care, in 2007 the Gauteng Department of Health (GDoH) issued a request for proposal (RFP) for enabling e-Health in the region. Fourteen companies answered to the RFP, and six of them were shortlisted. At the end, one preferred supplier and one reserve were chosen. The preferred supplier (the Baoki Consortium[1]) realized the PoC within the time frame defined (from august 2007 to august 2008). The project is divided in three phases: the

---

[1] Baoki is a consortium created by two South African resellers, Equiton Investment (Pty) Ltd and AMEtHST (Pty) Ltd.

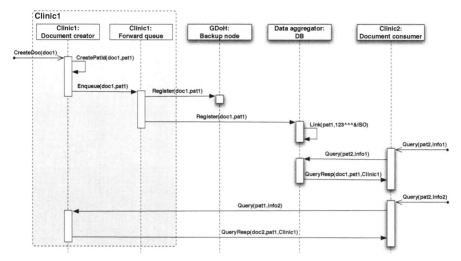

Fig. 1. Messages exchange in the E-HR.GP Proof-of-Concept

first phase consists of the definition of the PoC, the second is the full implementation of the PoC, and the third the application to the whole region. In the
first two phases, three clinics (Johan Deo, Levai Mbatha, and Dr. Helga Kuhn
Clinic) and the 700-beds Sebokeng hospital were involved.

2.1   Proof-of-Concept Software Architecture

The three clinics and the hospital run the same software components (actually,
the hospital is considered as a 'big' clinic). The common messages exchange in
such an architecture is depicted in Figure 1, where a clinic creates a document
belonging to an EHR, which is spread over the clinic's network, and then another
clinic tries to fetch it.

Specifically, a document doc1, e.g., a patient summary, is created (and locally
stored) in a generic clinic, Clinic1. The document belongs to a patient, whose
identifier pat1 is chosen by Clinic1. The document, its metadata and the newly
created patient identifier are enveloped in a message queued in a software actor,
named Forward queue. When the Forward queue processes the message, this is
duplicated: one copy is sent through the IHE-based transaction Register to a node
located into the GDoH offices, while using the same transaction a second copy is
sent to the Data aggregator. The Backup node installed at the GDoH offices has
the task to provide a working backup image for each clinic. This reliable node
should contain the data of all clinics. The Data aggregator is another reliable
node that instead acts as a forwarder: whenever a request for a given patient
is received, it returns its copy of the document and the link to the clinic where
the data were originally stored; every subsequent query about the patient will
be delivered directly to the clinic, without passing through the Data aggregator.

Notably, the Data aggregator contains all the patients' local identifiers and
their data as registered in the clinics. These local identifiers are linked together

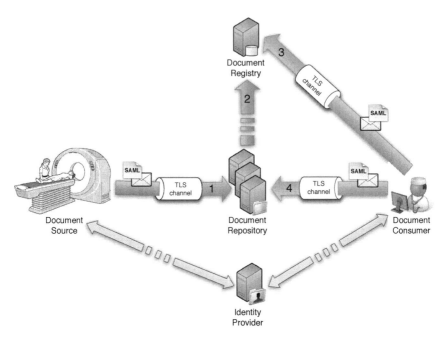

Fig. 2. The XDS model grouped with ATNA and XUA profiles

(through a Link transaction) by means of an identifier that is unique for the whole Gauteng province. In our example pat1 is linked to 123^^^&ISO (the patient identifier is written using a notation *à la* Hl7 [1]).

Now, suppose that a doctor sitting in Clinic2 wants to retrieve a document containing information info1 for a patient identified by pat2. Clinic2 does not know where information about the patient pat2 can be retrieved, therefore the Data aggregator is contacted, using the IHE-based transaction named Query. The Data aggregator knows the patient identifier, which is actually linked to 123^^^&ISO too (i.e. pat1 and pat2 identify the same patient, resolved by means of *demographics queries* [4]). This patient has documents into Clinic1 and, hence, the Data aggregator returns this information to Clinic2, together with the patient identifier pat1. For a given amount of time, this information is cached in Clinic2 and all the subsequent queries for pat2 will be sent to Clinic1 directly. Indeed, in the last pair of Query/QueryResp transactions in Figure 1, a document consumer asks for information info2 for patient pat2; Clinic2 now is informed that the patient is known as pat1 at Clinic1 and, hence, directly sends the query to Clinic1 for patient pat1.

2.2 The IHE Model

Each clinic involved in the PoC uses an e-Health system based on the IHE Cross Enterprise Document Sharing (XDS) model [4], depicted in Figure 2. The XDS model uses a central document registry that acts as a catalogue for the data. The document source (e.g., a medical device) produces healthcare data for patients and store data into one or more document repositories (e.g., databases). The repositories extract metadata and update the registry. Then, possibly quite long time later, the document consumer (e.g., a doctor's workstation) queries the registry and obtains a link to the repositories from where data can be downloaded and displayed to the doctor.

In IHE standards, building blocks of e-Health systems are defined in *profiles* that expose a set of requirements. Two or more profiles are *grouped* together by merging their respective requirements. The resulting system can be grouped again with other profiles for building a complete e-Health solution.

When dealing with such sensible data as EHRs, security and privacy play a crucial role. Aspects like confidentiality, authentication, integrity and authorization are crucial for the success of any e-Health project. The IHE security model is based on the Audit Trail and Node Authentication (ATNA) profile [4]: each system is classified as either *secure application* or *secure node*. A secure application is a system that permits to establish Transport Layer Security (TLS) channels for exchanging medical records using IHE-defined transactions. A secure node is a secure application where no other way to access patient's data exists (i.e. there is no physical access to the machine). With these requirements, each actor (e.g. a document consumer) is authenticated by exchanging X509 certificates and corresponding private keys. Instead, healthcare professional authentication is defined in the Cross Enterprise Document Assertion (XUA) profile [4]. If a system is grouped with this profile, each message must contain a Security Assertion Markup Language (SAML) assertion [6], i.e., a security token encoded using the XML language, providing the digital identity of the professional and issued by a trusted third party named *identity provider*.

Creating a system grouping standard IHE profiles permits to drastically reduce errors due to missing healthcare information in paper-based clinics. EHRs are always available to every patient and authorized healthcare professional across the clinics. The probability to perform, e.g., duplicate medical tests and examinations is then reduced significantly. The hardware running in each clinic is reduced in costs: with an investment of a few thousands of U.S. dollars for off-the-shelf components, a clinic can start to be operational in a few days.

3   Applying the Protocol for Disconnected Clinics

The roadmap of the programme after the PoC phases is to increase the number of hospitals and clinics involved in the E-HR.GP project. Although the Gauteng province is the geographically smallest province in South Africa, nowadays it is the most densely populated[2]. Thus, up to 38 hospitals, 30 community health clinics and around 300 clinics will participate in the exchange of medical records.

The PoC setting described in Section 2 fits perfectly within regions with a high-speed Internet connection. Indeed, healthcare documents usually have important dimensions (e.g., the size of DICOM [5] images can be larger than one

---

[2] Around 9 millions, of which 90% are urbanized.

gigabyte) and, thus, their real-time exchange is expensive. For this reason, nightly transfers to the central repository (i.e. the backup node) of the GDoH are scheduled. Each transaction passes through a forward queue (see Section 2.1) that duplicates the messages: a copy is sent to the local XDS affinity domain, while the duplicated message is queued waiting to be transferred when the connection link is operating. Unfortunately, in Gauteng, due to the limitations of the Internet connectivity in some spots of the region (where network connection is mainly based on GPRS and 56k modems), nightly transfers among clinics and the repositories may not reach the termination, due to the large size of files.

The IHE initiative solves the above problem by introducing the Cross Enterprise Document Sharing using Portable Media (XDM) profile [4]. This specification enables the usage of different types of electronic support, like CDs, DVDs, and USB drivers, for the transmission of EHRs. By using the IHE grouping mechanism mentioned in Section 2.2, XDM replaces in the XDS model the TLS channels established from the forward queue to the endpoint of Data aggregator and Backup node with out-of-band channels, based on a car transportation system. However, simply adopting the newly created system is not sufficient. In fact a new security flaw would be introduced: by dropping the TLS channel, the system would miss the authentication of the remote peer (the clinic). The receiving system would not be able to trust the message carried by the portable media because no key material is present that enforces authenticity. This flaw would introduce serious drawbacks: a malicious intermediary could change the message on the channel (resulting in a compromission of the safety of the patient) or could replay messages to get more medicines prescribed (e.g., for the illegal market). In this way, the system security would be totally demanded to the security of the out-of-band channel. Usually this channel is represented by a van travelling among clinics for collecting portable media to be stored in the central repository. The van is then a critical actor in the project security model.

A possible solution of such an authentication flaw, which does not put any requirement on the security of the van itself, is presented in [9]. This work introduces an ad-hoc protocol for exchanging medical records that exploits the XDM standard. The protocol does not affect software already in production stage and its adoption has a reduced impact on costs. Security of the protocol is proved by using the formal methods described in [10], in particular the process calculus COWS for formally modeling the protocol, the temporal logic SocL for expressing the protocol's security properties, and the model checker CMC for verifying the properties over the model.

The protocol is depicted in Figure 3. Each clinic has its own information system where the communication channel between the actors Creator and Receiver and the corresponding *Audit Record Repositories (ARRs)*[3] is assumed to be secure. Indeed, a clinic in a rural area is usually built in an environment composed of a single machine or a few machines running in the same private local network disconnected from the Internet, where network intrusions cannot be performed.

---

[3] The role of ARR A and ARR B, as well as the role of the Security Officer, will be explained later on.

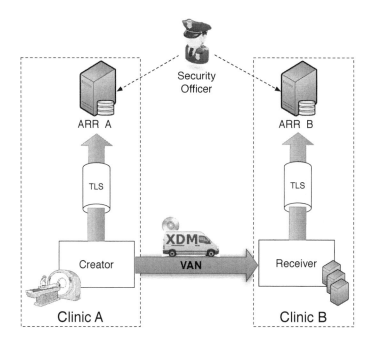

Fig. 3. The protocol for sharing medical records in disconnected clinics

On the other hand, if a clinic is connected to the Internet (e.g., an hospital), software like Intrusion Detection Systems (IDS) [11] can assure the authenticity of the above mentioned channel. The scenario in Figure 3 is common for clinics in rural areas, in which the information systems are running on ATNA secure nodes. XDM, ATNA and XUA are grouped together, therefore the security token that authenticates each message is a SAML assertion as per the XUA profile.

The protocol is based on an end-to-end scenario, where clinics cooperate together to exchange messages. In the communication scenario, the clinic that produces a document is named **Creator** and the clinic that receives the document is named **Receiver**. Each clinic contains a security token service that is able to authenticate the healthcare professional, and an ARR, as part of ATNA. The ARR is a tamperproof hardware that stores the logging entries (i.e., the audit trails) for all the transactions performed. The software components establish a TLS channel with the ARR, as per ATNA specifications [4]. Whenever a document is created, or a document needs to be retrieved, the corresponding XDS message is enqueued into the forward queue. When the forward queue needs to be transferred, the XDM component writes the messages to the portable media. This media is transferred to the receiver along the 'communication channel' represented by the van. The protocol, indeed, abstracts this car-transportation system as a communication channel that permits to send a single chunck of data. In fact, this channel does not satisfy any mutual authentication properties [12]. Each message contains a cryptographic secret created by the identity provider of the creator clinic and encrypted for the clinic acting as a receiver. The secret is also stored in the ARR of both clinics and it is the key used for tracing the transaction and the message exchange in the channel represented by the van. No information about the van or its driver needs to be stored in the messages or in the associated audit trails. The message structure is maintained as per the XDS/XDM specifications.

In order to perform analysis on the security of the protocol, a threat model is proposed in [9]. In such a model, an attacker à la Dolev-Yao [13] is used. Based on the past experience of other e-Health projects (see, e.g., the NHIN threat model [14]), our threat model identifies four different attacks with a particular attention to the scenario in rural areas. Most of the attacks are performed (sometimes physically) to the car-transportation system. In the first attack, the intruder suppresses a message (e.g., a submission for a new rare form of allergy). In the second attack, the intruder is trying to impersonate an healthcare professional by reusing a token found in a stolen portable media. In the third attack, the payload of the message is manipulated so to reuse the authentication token for obtaining different resources (e.g., different prescribed medicines). In the fourth attack the intruder tries to replicate the message for obtaining the same resource multiple times.

All the attacks are discovered by the design of the protocol, except the first. In fact, in the scenario under study, where assuming clinics' clocks be synchronized is a too strong requirement, a new actor, called *security officer*, is introduced to discover the threat. This officer, that can be enacted by an human being polling the clinics in a round-robin fashion, reads the audit record repository to keep track of the logging entries. By performing this action, he/she recognizes time differences between the message sent and the message received by the clinic nodes and is thus able to discover attacks based on message suppression. Notably, the security officer is assumed to be a trustworthy actor. This assumption is reasonable in the considered scenario. In fact, the security officer can only manage signed and encrypted data and, moreover, a suppression of logging entries is detected by the protocol.

It is worth noticing that the protocol can scale with a large number of clinics. Indeed, we can apply the XDM-based protocol between disconnected clinics and the classic XDS model in the other cases, and then exploit the hierarchical organization of clinics enabled by XDS. The protocol is also designed to scale with a great number of patients, by relying on the fact that a van can carry many portable media and that, nowadays, electronic supports like DVDs and USB drivers can store significant amounts of data.

4   Related Work

Providing EHRs for rural areas and disconnected clinics is a challenging research field. An approach using Mesh networks is proposed in [15]. This approach has a great benefit: a Mesh network infrastructure, which can be exploited for e-Health purposes, is implementable with low-cost hardware. Our approach instead acts at the software infrastructure level rather than at the hardware one, and has basically no additional costs, except those for adapting the software infrastructure to be able to fulfill the requirements of [9] (to register secrets into ARRs and to copy authentication tokens into portable media). If detection of lost messages is needed, a security officer must be employed and trained.

Our protocol, firstly proposed in [9], has the advantage to be formally proved against errors in a specific threat model. Formal analysis on security protocols has given very good results in the last years (see, e.g., [16,17,18,19]). A more complete survey can be found in [20,21]. The work closest to ours is [22] where a generic communication infrastructure is proposed within a governmental project in Mozambique. In that work, a "fat" client approach is taken, in which the application and persistency layer reside on the local machine. Differently from our approach, data exchanged are partially anonymized, since they are used for statistical purposes, while we adopt a protocol that ensures authentication and confidentiality of sensitive data.

5   Conclusions

In this paper we reported the experience on the first phases of the project E-HR.GP running in Sebokeng, Gauteng, a province of South Africa. This project aims at giving optimum patient care in the province by enabling an e-Health solution based on international standards. The major drawback of this and other similar projects in developing countries with rural areas is the low or absent network connectivity. To cope with problems due to the lack of connectivity, we propose to exchange messages by exploiting the international IHE standard XDM, which permits the usage of portable media to share EHRs. However, adopting this standard drops the requirement of having authenticated channels. To recover authentication, we propose the use of a formally-proved secure protocol that amends the standard in order to provide a secure EHRs exchange with disconnected clinics using a car-transportation system to bear portable media.

As we show in this work, just adopting international standards for the establishment of e-Health projects is not sufficient, because new security flaws can be introduced. Our aim is to continue to use formal methods to analyse e-Health projects for developing countries in order to tailor secure solutions with an important level of technology and reduced costs.

References

1. Health Level Seven organization: Hl7 standards (2009), http://www.hl7.org
2. The epSOS project: An European eHealth Project (2010), http://www.epsos.eu
3. The Nationwide Health Information Network (NHIN): An American eHealth Project (2009), http://healthit.hhs.gov/portal/server.pt
   (last visited on July 4, 2011)
4. The IHE Initiative: IT Infrastructure Technical Framework (2009), http://www.ihe.net
5. ACR-NEMA: Digital Imaging and Communications in Medicine (DICOM) (1995)

6. OASIS Security Services TC: Assertions and protocols for the OASIS security assertion markup language (SAML) v2.02 (2005),
   http://docs.oasis-open.org/security/saml/v2.0/saml-core-2.0-os.pdf.
7. Mosupi, M.: Gauteng Department of Health (GDoH): E-HR.GP, System Implementation (2008),
   http://www.ihe-austria.at/fileadmin/user_upload/CAT2009/
   documents/MmakgosiMosupiIHE_Conference_Presentation_220409.pdf
   (last visited on July 4, 2011)
8. Wikipedia, the free encyclopedia: Sebokeng, Gauteng. Wikipedia entry,
   http://en.wikipedia.org/wiki/Sebokeng,_Gauteng
   (last visited on July 4, 2011)
9. Masi, M., Pugliese, R., Tiezzi, F.: Security analysis of standard- driven communication protocols for healthcare scenarios. In: Healthcom, pp. 308–315. IEEE (2011)
10. Fantechi, A., Gnesi, S., Lapadula, A., Mazzanti, F., Pugliese, R., Tiezzi, F.: A Logical Verification Methodology for Service-Oriented Computing. ACM Transactions on Software Engineering and Methodology (2011) (to appear)
11. Wikipedia, the free encyclopedia: Intrusion Detection Systems. Wikipedia entry,
   http://en.wikipedia.org/wiki/Intrusion_detection_system
   (last visited on July 4, 2011)
12. Lowe, G.: A Hierarchy of Authentication Specifications. In: CSFW, pp. 31–44. IEEE (1997)
13. Dolev, D., Yao, A.: On the security of public key protocols. IEEE Transactions on Information Theory 29(2), 198–207 (1983)
14. The Nationwide Health Information Network (NHIN): Threat models (2009),
   http://wiki.directproject.org/Threat+Models (last visited on July 4, 2011)
15. Yarali, A., Ahsant, B., Rahman, S.: Wireless mesh networking: A key solution for emergency & rural applications. In: MESH, pp. 143–149. IEEE (2009)
16. Armando, A., Carbone, R., Compagna, L., Cuellar, J., Abad, L.: Formal Analysis of SAML 2.0 Web Browser Single Sign-On: Breaking the SAML-based Single Sign-On for Google Apps. In: FMSE, pp. 1–10. ACM (2008)
17. Johnson, J., Langworthy, D., Lamport, L., Vogt, F.: Formal specification of a web services protocol. In: WSFM. ENTCS, vol. 105, pp. 147–158. Elsevier (2004)
18. Blanchet, B.: CryptoVerif: Computationally Sound Mechanized Prover for Cryptographic Protocols. Dagstuhl seminar "Formal Protocol Verification Applied" (2007)
19. Bhargavan, K., Corin, R., Fournet, C., Gordon, A.: Secure sessions for web services. In: SWS, pp. 56–66. ACM (2004)
20. Ma, L., Tsai, J.: Formal verification techniques for computer communication security protocols. Handbook of Software Engineering and Knowledge Engineering 1, 23–46 (2001)
21. Fidge, C.: A Survey of Verification Techniques for Security Protocols. Technical Report 01-22, Software Verification Research Centre, Univ. of Queensland (2001)
22. Armellin, G., Bogoni, L.P., Chiasera, A., Toai, T.J., Zanella, G.: Enabling Business Intelligence Functions over a Loosely Coupled Environment. In: Popescu-Zeletin, R., Rai, I.A., Jonas, K., Villafiorita, A. (eds.) AFRICOMM 2010. LNICST, vol. 64, pp. 122–131. Springer, Heidelberg (2011)

On Development of a Collaborative ICT Infrastructure for Online HIV/AIDS Advisory Service Provision

Simon Samwel Msanjila

ICT Department, Faculty of Science and Technology, Mzumbe University,
Block C, Room 111, P.O. Box 87, Mzumbe-Morogoro, Tanzania
simon.msanjila@gmail.com

Abstract. The initiatives to combat the spread of HIV/AIDS across African society have been following different approaches ranging from workshops and seminars to posters across streets. One of the main challenges has been on the dissemination of relevant information related to HIV/AIDS advices to the appropriate in demand users. However, the advances in ICT have not been benefited in this area and particularly in developing economy countries. This paper first provides an understanding of needs and challenges for developing an online infrastructure (Collaborative Infrastructure for HIV/AIDS Advisory Services – CIHAAS system) that can facilitate the provision of HIV/AIDS advisory services to youths. It also addresses requirement identification, specification of services and functionalities of the proposed ICT infrastructure, and finally, it presents architectural design of the proposed system.

Keywords: ICT, HIV/AIDS advisory services, CIHAAS infrastructure.

1   Introduction

In spite of the promising trends in the establishment and provision of e-services in various higher level education institutions in Tanzania there is still no a harmonized and standardized collaborative ICT platform for this purpose and particularly for knowledge related to HIV/AIDS advisory service provision. The trends on the provision of these e-services to young generation in Tanzania is moving from being limited at an individual university (even at the level of a single unit or department) to a kind of an alliance constituting a number of universities, medical centers and individual medical professionals which intend to use an ICT platform to support the provision of HIV/AIDS advisory services. However in Tanzania, universities have different culture for which regulations are established (public or religious) which shall influence the formulation of guidelines related to content, type and format of knowledge on HIV/AIDS advices that can be uploaded to their repositories or shared and provided outside the respective university through the supporting systems. The systems should have *affective capability* to enable tune itself to match the specific requirements and regulations of each specific university [Afsarmanesh, et al 2011].

Development of ICT platform suitable for supporting the provision of ICT enabled online environment that is capable of facilitating the collaborative delivery of live and

R. Popescu-Zeletin et al. (Eds.) AFRICOMM 2011, LNICST 92, pp. 197–207, 2012.

offline HIV/AIDS advisory services to young generation will reduce the severity of the challenge related to the lack of knowledge in HIV/AIDS prevention. Although it is promising to have such solution in place and perfectly working, however, there is still unclear understanding on the customized technical requirements, and there are no proper architectural designs that could support making decision related to which suitable systems and platforms (ICT- infrastructures) to develop. This paper addresses the requirement analysis and modeling of ICT infrastructure capable of providing or facilitating the provision of HIV/AIDS advisory services. The paper also proposes an architectural ICT platform design based on standards of service oriented architecture.

2   Collaborative Networks

Collaborative network is addressed as a new scientific discipline that covers the study of alliances consisting of a variety of entities (e.g. organizations and individuals) that are largely autonomous, geographically distributed, and heterogeneous in terms of their operating environment, culture, social capital and goals, but that collaborate to better achieve common or compatible goals (e.g. problem solving, production, or innovation), and whose *interactions are supported by computer network* [Camarinha-Matos & Afsarmanesh, 2005]. *A collaborative network (CN) is a network consisting of a variety of entities (e.g. organizations, people, machines) that are largely autonomous, geographically distributed, and heterogeneous in terms of their operating environment, culture, social capital and goals, but that collaborate to better achieve common or compatible goals, thus jointly generating value, and whose interactions are supported by computer network.* [Camarinha-Matos, Afsarmanesh, 2005].Collaborative network paradigm has been increasingly penetrating in market and society due to continuous advances in ICTs and particularly, the internet technology. This paradigm has been evolving with contributions from multiple disciplines including computer science, engineering, management, economy, organizational ecology, sociology, etc. For instance, in terms of ICT application in industry, this new discipline is a natural consequence of a long term evolution ICT-enabled enterprise related developments.

As the health sector in developing countries is continuously being pushed to operate with business mind, the need for establishing joint efforts is surely witnessed to health specialized organizations and professionals. Considering the current trend, these actors can hardly equip themselves to meet current demands in terms of resources, capital, professional experts, required knowledge, etc. for the provision of HIV/AIDS advisory services Thus collaboration is also seen to be amenable.

3   Collaboration Environments for Medical Experts and Youths

This work applies two specific forms of collaborative networks, namely one short-term type and one long-term type constituting medical organizations and medical professionals as entity members, namely: *Temporary Teams of Medical Experts* (TTME) and *Medical Advices Collaborative Environment* (MACE) defined as:

A TTME is an association of (legally) independent individual medical experts that come together and share knowledge and skills to achieve a common goal, such as providing HIV/AIDS advisory services to on demand university students.

In practice, TTME are configured constituting individual medical professionals who are members of the MACE environment and, therefore, the potential TTME partners are selected among the best-fit MACE expert members.

A MACE is defined as a "strategic" alliance of medical organizations, medical professionals, and youths and related supporting institutions adhering to a base long-term cooperation agreement and adopting common operating principles and infrastructures, with the main goal of increasing both their readiness and preparedness such as related to acquiring relevant knowledge and skills enough for collaboration in responding to complex queries of customer students on demanded HIV/AIDS advisory services.

4   Motivation for e-Services for HIV/AIDS Advices

The provision of e-services on advices related HIV/AIDS issues in developing countries is still limited traditional approaches such as face to face contacts. Tanzanian universities for example still do not effectively collaborate through computer network facilitation to share knowledge on these issues. Different universities have different repositories of knowledge such as digital repositories of publications of their academic staffs. However, there are still no inter-accesses of this rich and on demand knowledge among universities and thus stored advisory services on HIV/AIDS could be an example. Consequently, even the much needed web supported services such as for HIV/AIDS advisory e-services are difficult to initiate due to the lack of suitable collaborative ICT infrastructure. Collaborative provision of automated services shall benefit from the advances of collaborative network paradigm and penetration of internet technology within the societies. Fast developments in information technology and computer communications have acted as a boosting factor to the emergence of new forms of collaboration, and for this case collaborative networks applied in the area of HIV/AIDS advisory service provision can be mentioned. However, there exist a number of other common and important aspects that cannot be neglected if the application of this concept in this domain has to be realized. Poor communicational interchanges among partners also lead to mistrust, suspicion and ultimately discouragement and lack of commitments in a MACE environment or TTME consortium. Other related issues include the fairness / transparency / equality / reciprocity, etc., within the MACE. The aspects are also related to value systems, social protocols, etc. and cause negative emotional states.

5   Analysis and Specification of the CIHAAS System

The need for collaborative provision of e-services across Tanzanian universities is amenable, particularly considering the shortage of relevant professional staffs (e.g. those in the field of medicine,). In the same line and so for HIV/AIDS advisory service provision; there are a number of factors hindering students from accessing necessary information and advices physically to their location including following:

- **Feeling shame:** It is still perceived in the society that people with HIV/AIDS got the infection due to their irresponsible behavior related to sexual relations such as having a number of casual sex partners. Such type of life is not culturally supported although it is not legally prohibited. People do feel shame to face to face ask for advices to medical doctors on the ground that they will be seen as they have been misbehaving.
- **Studies' pressure:** Students do feel lacking enough time to handle their studies. Although the HIV/AIDS issue is sensitive, students might take it as less important for the purpose of spending more time in studies.
- **Distance from service centers:** Sometimes universities are located relatively far from centers where good and quality services and qualified medical professionals can be found. Thus students might fail to access such services due to distance reasons.
- **Unavailability of information:** University students have the ability to learn through reading various documents. However as it is still practiced in Tanzania, HIV/AIDS information is still provided through paper based means. Considering the cost of printing, the increasing of number of university students in the country, and the country financial position, printed copies are usually not enough to meet the actual requirements.

5.1   Elicitation of User Requirements for CIHAAS System

Identification of users of the CIHAAS system is based on the analysis of potential stakeholders for three defined general *service objectives* related to the provision of HIV/AIDS advisory services, namely:

Provision of demanded services: This service objective addresses the facilitation and provision of required advisory services including verification of the content of the provided information, verification of the quality of the services, etc. The potential stakeholders for this service objective are: MACE manager, CIHAAS system administrator, TTME planner, medical professional members, medical organizations, and MACE membership applicants.

Accessing of provided services: This service objective addresses the facilitation for access of the services based on user rights. This includes classification of services per user rights, provision of validation techniques to ensure right users, provision of right user interface for different modes of service delivery such as live or offline, etc. The potential stakeholders for this service objective are: MACE manager, system administrator, TTME planner, medical professional members, medical organizations, and university students.

Administration of the collaborative environment: This service objective addresses the services supporting the management and administration of the CIHAAS system. The service objective also addresses the required functionalities for management and administration of the MACE environments. The potential stakeholders for this service objective are: MACE manager, CIHAAS system administrator, TTME planner, medical professional members, and medical organizations.

Seven user groups are classified on the basis of these three general service objectives. These seven User Groups (UG1 to UG7) and their respective user requirements are presented in Table 1.

Table 1. Identification and classification of users of the proposed system

User group	User roles & rights	User requirements (UR)
UG1: CIHAAS administrator	• Highest administrative rights • Can view and execute all services • Can create and change user's rights	1. Viewing and change the rights and indicators for registering a new user of the system 2. View, modify and create advisory provision and accessing services in the system 3. Create, modify and execute services for the management of stored knowledge
UG2: MACE manager	• 2nd highest administrative rights • Can view, execute, modify all services	4. View and execute services for the management of MACE members and memberships 5. Defining, authorizing and assigning rights to users of the system based on their membership level in the MACE environment. 6. Supporting CIHAAS system users, such as the medical professionals or students, in providing or accessing the right content of the HIV/AIDS advices. 7. Managing the advices related data in the CIHAAS system.
UG3: TTME planer	• Third highest administrative rights • Can manipulate advisory provision services	8. Execute services for analyzing and assessing the competencies of medical professionals for establishing an expert temporary team 9. Execute services to change its own MACE membership profile 10. Execute services to provide and view advisory services in the system
UG4: medical professionals	• Basic user rights • Can view advices available • Can upload the requested advices • Can comment of uploaded services	11. Execute services to change its own MACE membership profile 12. Execute services to provide and view advisory services in the system 13. Execute services support accessing knowledge repository in the CHIAAS system
UG5: medical organizations	• Basic user rights • Can view advices available • Can upload the requested advices • Can comment of uploaded services	14. Execute services to change its own MACE membership profile 15. Execute services to provide and view advisory services in the system 16. Execute services support accessing knowledge repository in the CHIAAS system
UG6: students	• Basic user rights • Can view advices available	17. Execute services to view advisory services in the system 18. Execute services to send specific service request to medical professionals
UG7: MACE guests	• Guest user rights • Can view public information only	19. Execute services TO view public information related to HIV/AIDS advisory services in the system

6 Specification of System Requirements for the CIHAAS System

Functional Requirements: Statements of services that the system should provide, how the system should react to particular inputs and how the system should behave in particular situation. Design of the CIHAAS system is based on the service oriented architecture (SOA) and in particular the web service technology. The provision of services related to HIV/AIDS is based on the concepts of e-services and thus acting as a platform supporting collaborative online service provision. Accordingly, the specified functionalities are referred to here as **services**. The system shall provide five integrated learning services namely service S1 to service S5.

Service S1 - Static information provision: The system shall provide or support publishing information that students can access through the web-based CIHAAS system irrespective of time and physical location. Considering the continuously increase of availability of internet accesses in universities in Tanzania such information can easily and efficiently be disseminated to students. Thus the system shall provide a website interface for publishing well categorized and classified information based on the nature of knowledge, user rights, and hosting university.

Service S2 - Offline advisory service provision: It is expected that interested medical professionals will be registered in the system as members on the MACE environment. Their respective physical locations and employers will not be necessary since medical professionals shall join MACE environment on their own will. However, the public profiles and region/district location of each medical professional shall be made known to registered students in the system. This will enhance trust between medical professionals and students who might need services from anonymous providers. Provision of this kind of services adopts following approaches:

> **Service S2.1 - Email exchange:** With this service component, students in need of HIV/AIDS advisory services can select one or more medical professionals and send a private email. Although the emails of medical professionals will be hidden in the system but there will be an interface in the system providing this possibility.
>
> **Service S2.2 - Uploading private request for advisory service:** With this service component, a student may upload a request for advices which can be responded by any registered medical professional. However, a student can also select specific medical professionals to respond to his/her queries. Collaboration among medical professionals is possible while responding to this type of queries through which each can provide additional information to those already provided online by other medical experts. The request is private, so other students cannot see the response.
>
> **Service S2.3 - Uploading public request for advisory service:** With this approach, a student has an option to upload a request for advices to the system and allow both his/her request as well as the responses to be seen by other students. Responding procedure by professionals is the same as stated in service S2.2.
>
> **Service S2.4 - Ongoing discussion forums:** This forum will allow medical professionals to discuss online the ongoing or emerging issues addressing relevant topics related to HIV/AIDS such an emergence of a new disease associated with HIV/AIDS. When sounding results are achieved in these discussions then with the decision and support of the forum convener the relevant content of the results can be made public to all registered students to enhance their knowledge.

Service S3 - Live advisory service provision: This service provides mechanisms and tools for real time discussion among medical professionals themselves or between medical professionals and students. The following methods shall be adopted:

> **Service S3.1 - Live text chat:** The system shall provide mechanisms for students and medical professionals to chat online using text messages. This method is very suitable to students who want to keep their anonymity medical professionals while being advised.
>
> **Service S3.2 - Live voice chat:** With little trust students might be open to chat to a medical professional who they have never met before using voice means. This method might enhance both the speed of chatting and the accuracy of the service delivery to the respective student.

Service S3.3 - Live video chat: A good level of trust between the student and the medical professional is needed for this type of service to be accepted by both parties. This may be achieved after several occasions of voice and text chats. This is most efficient way of providing advisory services but could lead to a problem if a misunderstanding emerges between the two parties considering the fact that already they know each other by face.

Service S4 - Advisory service retrieval: This service supports users of CIHAAS system to access various information and knowledge available in the system. The main beneficiaries of this service are the university students who will use this service to receive advisory information. The information can be accessed as private feedback on questions rose by specific students and responded by specific medical experts. The information can also be accessed as public data for members in the MACE.

Service S5 - MACE environment management: This service supports the MACE manager and CIHAAS administrator to handle issues related information management in the collaborative environment and membership management in the MACE environment. In relation information management this service support the MACE administrator to collect and store data related to medical expert profiles, university regulation profiles, medical organization profiles, students' details, MACE operating principles and regulations, MACE service domain, etc. The service also supports the classification and structuring of members and their membership rights in the system.

Non-functional Requirements: Statements on what need to be obeyed for the system to be capable to provide the required services to the user at the defined quality. Examples of non-functional requirements that shall be met by the intended ICT infrastructure include Privacy, Security, Reliability, and Interoperability.

Domain Requirements: Derived from the application domain of the system rather than from the specific needs of system users. Such requirements usually include specialized domain technology or reference to the domain concepts. They may be new functional requirements, constraints on the existing functional requirements or set out how particular competitions must be carried out. For the CIHAAS system domain requirements are classified into the following categories:

Regulatory requirements: Every university where students are attached has internal regulation on the type, content and format of information which can be shared or exchanged. In Tanzania, a university can be public, private or religious. HIV/AIDS related information might have some terms that might not be acceptable to certain institution such as religious. A particular domain requirement for this case could be content affective capability. In sense that the system must be aware to which university is being accessed and what terms or contents must be filtered to meet the regulation of the specific university.

Health sector requirements: These are international and local regulations that must supported or met with any system dealing with information in this domain. For example; such requirements may include details of students which can be public, type of discussion between medical experts and students that can be handled virtually, how long information of a patient can be stored, etc.

National established regulation on health: Tanzania government has specific regulations on how to handle patient data. HIV/AIDS patients also in one way or another are affected by these regulations. To get permission on advices on HIV/AIDS regulations must be obeyed.

7   Towards Architectural Design of the CIHAAS System

Based on the services presented in Section 6, this section introduces the design of the CIHAAS system, addressing briefly its three architectures, namely: *the process architecture, interoperability architecture*, and *four-layer componential architecture*.

CIHAAS system processes architecture: A process as perceived in the proposed system is defined as an interaction between participants (medical professionals and youths) and the execution of activities according to a defined set of rules in order to achieve a common goal. Figure 1 shows interactions pattern of process. A number of processes shall be supported by the infrastructural system during the provision of advisory services on HIV/AIDS issues to young generation. At conceptual level the processes are categorized as (1) among medical professionals and young generation, (2) among medical professionals, (3) among medical professionals and stakeholders.

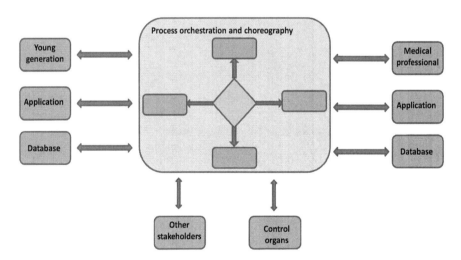

Fig. 1. Processes for the ICT infrastructure on HIV/AIDS advices provision

Interoperability architecture for the CIHAAS infrastructure: CIHAAS shall interact with local systems at the user site. As shown in Figure 2, interaction will occur for four main purposes: *(a) acquiring the local needed data, (b) exporting information from executed service to local repositories, (c) accessing basic services provided by the ICT-Infrastructure, and (d) supporting human user access.*

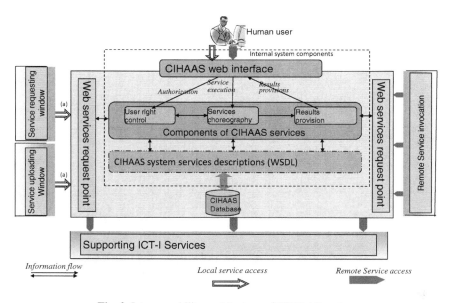

Fig. 2. Interoperability architecture of CIHAAS system

External interactions are supported by a number of internal components of CIHAAS system that are grouped into three categories, namely the component for: *(1) User right control, (2) Services choreography, and (3) Results provision.* The components for *user right control* provide functionalities for authorizing users (both human and system users) that wish to access the CIHAAS infrastructure. For the authorized users, these components also provide functionalities for classifying the services on the basis of the user rights as well as providing access to those services that each user is allowed to view or execute (such as public, restricted or administrative services).

The components for *services choreography* provide internal mechanisms and/or functionalities to organize the order and time for the execution of a number of services in response to each received user's request. The components for *results provision* organize and provide proper responses to requests received by the system, such as returning specific results for the successful requests, or returning negative response for the rejected requests.

The four-layer componential architecture of the CIHAAS system: The four-layer componential architecture of the CIHAAS system adopts the standard definitions for web service technology. Thus it addresses the classification of internal components (system modules) into four layers. The components of CIHAAS system, as shown in Figure 3, are classified into these four main layers, namely: the *presentation layer, the process layer, the description layer,* and *the message layer,* as described below.

Layer 1- Presentation layer: This layer deals with the delivery of HIV/AIDS advisory information from the process layer to the web interface in a format that is readable by humans. The layer also handles the transformation of data submitted by

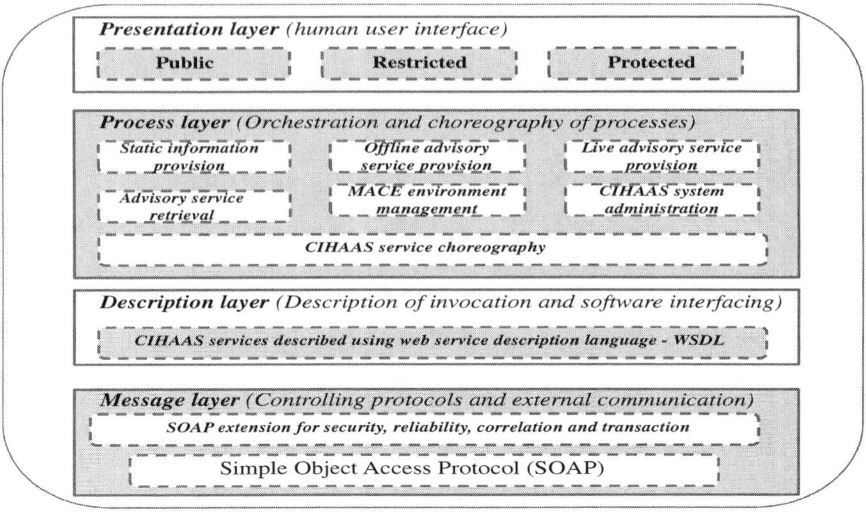

Fig. 3. Four-layer componential architecture of the CIHAAS system

human users, such as medical experts and university students, to the format that is acceptable by various modules at the process layer [Field & Hoffner, 2003]. The CIHAAS system manages and deals with some sensitive and ethically protected information that in most cases the owners may consider as proprietary, such as results of discussion on *personal sickness history*. The access of the system is classified into the *public interface, the restricted interface* and *the protected interface.*

Layer 2 - Process layer: The process layer is responsible for defining the logic of the invocation of various processes that need to be executed in order to provide the requested integrated service. The process scheduling constitutes *orchestration and choreography processes.* [Papazoglou & Georgakopoulus, 2003; Peltz, 2003].

Layer 3 - Description layer: Description layer deals with the provision of the grammatical specifications of the services provided by the CIHAAS system, to support the external invocations by remote systems.

Layer 4 - Message layer: The message layer defines the protocols for communication among systems and exchanging information across the network so that a receiving server/client may be able to interpret it [Peltz, 2003]. The standard applied communication protocol for web services is SOAP (Simple Object Access Protocol). Besides the standard SOAP protocol, additional mechanisms can be added to improve the security, reliability, adaptability, and so forth, of the system.

8   Conclusion

This paper has addressed the challenge on specification and design of a collaborative ICT infrastructure aimed at supporting the online provision of HIV/AIDS advisory services. The paper also presented the needs for e-services in this domain as well as the configuration of collaborative network for supporting joint initiatives of members.

References

1. Afsarmanesh, H., Msanjila, S.S.: ePAL Vision 2020 for Active Ageing of Senior Professionals. In: Camarinha-Matos, L.M., Boucher, X., Afsarmanesh, H. (eds.) PRO-VE 2010. IFIP AICT, vol. 336, pp. 60–72. Springer, Heidelberg (2010)
2. Afsarmanesh, H., Camarinha-Matos, L.M.: A framework for management of virtual organization breeding environments. In: The Proceedings of the Collaborative Networks and their Breeding Environments, PRO–VE 2005, Spain, pp. 35–49 (2005)
3. Camarinha-Matos, L.M., Afsarmanesh, H.: Collaborative Networks: Value creation in a knowledge society. In: Knowledge Enterprise: Intelligent Strategies in Product Design, Manufacturing and Management, pp. 26–40. Springer, Heidelberg (2006)
4. Camarinha-Matos, L.M., Afsarmanesh, H.: Collaborative networks: a new scientific discipline. The Journal Intelligent Manufacturing 16, 439–452 (2005)
5. Field, S., Hoffner, Y.: Web services and matchmaking. The International Journal of Networking and Virtual Organizations, Inderscience 2(1), 16–32 (2003)
6. Msanjila, S.S., Afsarmanesh, H.: On Architectural Design of TrustMan System Applying HICI Analysis Results. The case of technological perspective in VBEs. The International Journal of Software, 17–30 (April 2008) ISSN 1796-217X
7. Papazoglou, M.P., Georgakopoulus, D.: Service-Oriented Computing. The Communications of the ACM 46(10) (2003)
8. Peltz, C.: Web services orchestration and choreography. The IEEE Computers 36 (2003)

Socio-technical Arrangements for mHealth: Extending the Mobile Device Use and Adoption Framework

Tiwonge Davis Manda[1,2] and Yamiko Msosa[3]

[1] Department of Informatics, University of Oslo, Norway
[2] Department of Mathematical Sciences, Chancellor College, University of Malawi
tiomanda@gmail.com
[3] Baobab Health Trust, P.O. Box 31797, Lilongwe 3, Malawi
yamiko.msosa@baobabhealth.org

Abstract. This paper extends the mobile device adoption model by Sarker & Wells [1]. We extend this model from being focused on individuals, to discuss intra and extra organisational socio-technical arrangements that interplay with mHealth solution implementation and adoption, in low resource contexts. Among others, highlighted factors include user characteristics, influence of supported work, modality of user mobility, technological characteristics, change management, and other contextual factors such as economic, social, and political factors. This is done by reviewing an mHealth initiative from Malawi and related mHealth literature. We argue that the above mentioned factors form the installed base on which solutions are built, and continuously interplay with the use of mHealth solutions, thereby influencing adoption outcomes.

Keywords: mHealth, heterogeneous, information infrastructure, socio-technical.

1 Introduction

The penetration of mobile phones and other mobile technologies in developing countries has spurred increased diffusion of mHealth applications [2, 3]. Some areas of application include the use of mobile phones to enhance communication between medical personnel and community health workers [4], digitization of records and data reporting [3, 5], education and awareness, remote monitoring, communication and training for healthcare workers, disease and epidemic outbreak tracking, as well as diagnostic and treatment support [3].

Despite the promise shown by mHealth as regards enhancing care delivery in low resource contexts, the implementation of such solutions is not always easy and smooth sailing. The adoption and use of mobile devices interacts with and is influenced by a multiplicity of factors [1, 6, 7]. Similarly, mHealth involves the convergence of heterogeneous socio-technical arrangements. These, among others, include mobile and desktop health information systems, as well as people and healthcare processes, facilitated by both wired and wireless connectivity [8]. Thus, mHealth implementations can be considered information infrastructures. Information

R. Popescu-Zeletin et al. (Eds.) AFRICOMM 2011, LNICST 92, pp. 208–217, 2012.
© Institute for Computer Sciences, Social Informatics and Telecommunications Engineering 2012

infrastructures are *"shared, evolving, heterogeneous installed bases of IT capabilities among a set of user communities based on open and/or standardized interfaces"* [9:pp 208]. This necessitates the need to understand and continuously investigate multiple system development and implementation issues, to enhance the continued adoption and use of mHealth solutions. According to Yu et al. [8] such issues include healthcare workers' information needs, workflow and usability requirements, available technology options, and how best technology can be adapted to suit these needs and requirements. The ensemble of such heterogeneous socio-technical factors, can be referred to as an *installed base* [9], through which solutions are constructed. Thus, the complexities of the installed base are critical to successful implementation of mHealth solutions.

This paper extends the mobile device adoption model, proposed by Sarker and Wells [1], which is individual user-centric, to discuss mHealth use and adoption, which interacts with multiple intra and extra organisational arrangements. Sarker and Wells [1], argue that mobile device use and adoption is influenced by factors such as user characteristics, modality of user mobility, type of supported work, technological characteristics, as well as economic, social, and political factors. In extending their model, we have added extensions to some of these factors but also added the dimensions *change management and research*, to the model. Our arguments have been developed by applying the model by Sarker and Wells [1] to an mHealth implementation from Malawi, as well as reviewing extant literature on mHealth. The rest of this paper is organised as follows: firstly, we present the methodology employed by this research. This is followed by a review of relevant literature. Following the literature review, we present the mHealth solution from Malawi. This is then followed by a discussion of our findings. Lastly we present our conclusions.

2   Research Methodology

This paper is based on a review of literature and a mobile phone-based Anti-Retroviral Therapy (ART) protocol developed by Baobab Health Trust. The solution was developed to automate a paper-based protocol used by HIV/AIDS counsellors, under the Malawi AIDS Counselling and Resource Organization, during consultations with patients and when deciding on referrals for the patients. This case review is partly based on first hand experience of the second author, who is the solution's lead developer. The author's experiences were supplemented by in-depth discussions, on the solution, between the two authors. In addition, we have reviewed literature on mHealth adoption and associated challenges, with a focus on developing countries. Sense making of findings used in this paper is guided by the interpretive paradigm. The paradigm builds on the fundamental assumption that knowledge is socially constructed [10]. Interpretive research is therefore focused on investigating and understanding phenomena by considering meanings subjects under study attribute to such phenomena [11]. This, allows a researcher to describe, interpret, analyze, and understand the social context of elements under study [12]. Adopting this paradigm was therefore critical to this study's analysis of socio-technical factors of interest that together shape the implementation, management and use of mHealth information infrastructures.

3   Literature Review

mHealth comprises multiple socio-technical arrangements, which, among others, include workers' information needs, workflow and usability requirements, available technology options, and how best technology can be adapted to suit these needs and requirements [8]. Sarker and Wells [1] argue that user interaction with mobile devices is influenced by user characteristics, modality of mobility, communication and task characteristics, technology characteristics, network externalities, as well as context-centric social and economic factors [1]. Efforts to implement mHealth solutions therefore, need to consider particularities and sensitivities of the socio-technical ensemble of factors that interact with such solutions [5]. The interaction of these factors to influence mobile device use is modelled in **Fig. 1.**

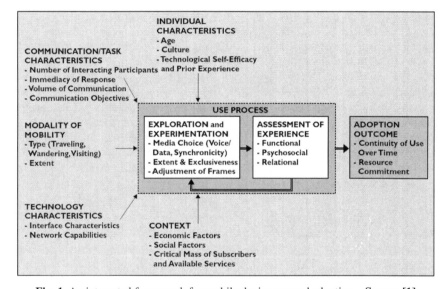

Fig. 1. An integrated framework for mobile device use and adoption – **Source [1]**

Under the model, the use process comprises *exploration and experimentation*, and *assessment of experience*. Under *exploration and experimentation,* users choose a medium of communication and desired synchronicity, as well as extent and exclusiveness of use. They also improvise and develop new ways of using mobiles as new motivations, modes, and consequences of applying technology emerge [1].

Assessment of experience is done along at least three dimensions: *functional, psychosocial, and relational* [1]. The *functional* dimension evaluates the effectiveness and efficiency with which people can perform their work and manage interpersonal relationships, using implemented mobile technologies. The *psychosocial* outcomes relate to less tangible impacts of mobile technology use, such as sense of security, as well as professional and social self-worth. The *relational* dimension assesses how mobile technology use impacts the establishment and maintenance of functional ties, as well as frequency, volume, and coordination of communication [1]. The totality of the use process, then, informs long-term user adoption of mobile devices. We now review the factors influencing the use process, and link them to mHealth.

3.1   User Competencies/Individual Characteristics

User characteristics such as demographics, technology-related skills, and culture substantially influence the implementation and acceptance of mobile devices [1]. Literacy also affects how well people can use certain solutions. SMS-based solutions, for example require a good level of writing skills [4]. Furthermore, for medical practitioners to effectively use mHealth applications, they need to posses a sufficient level of technological competencies [13]. The standardisation of required technology-related competencies is however not a straightforward matter. Thus, the advancement of mHealth is to an extent hindered by inadequate availability of expertise to bridge the gulf between health and technology [8].

3.2   Technology Characteristics

Usability aspects of applications and the extent of mobile network coverage have considerable impact on the use and adoption of mobile devices [4, 8]. The level of integration between solutions also impacts users, considering that there is a multiplicity of mHealth solutions [8]. It is therefore imperative that health care providers and health authorities are able to integrate new technological capabilities to existing settings in order to leverage their capacities and quality of services [13].

Although mobile technologies have made inroads within low resource contexts, certain areas that would benefit the most from mHealth solutions remain underserved in terms telecommunication capabilities [13] and access to electricity [4].

3.3   Desired Communication and Supported Work

Mobile device-led communication is sensitive to the number of interacting participants, immediacy of response desired, volume of communication desired, and communication objectives [1]. It is therefore imperative that mHealth solutions be designed with users' information needs, workflows, and usability requirements in mind [8]. This is of particular interest because mobile devices have become an integral part of people's work and social lives [14]. More than this, the success of mHealth applications significantly depends on how well they are integrated with users' workflows [8].

3.4   Economic Factors

Availability of adequate funding to finance routine operating expenses, maintenance costs and systems upgrades, all intrinsic features of ICT systems, is a vital element towards the sustainability of ICT driven initiatives [15]. For example, solution implementers need to know that users' willingness to use a technology does not imply long term commitment to meeting any adoption or sustainability costs [2]. mHealth projects must therefore implement financial sustainability models for usage beyond pilot level, before project initiation, to understand who will eventually support, maintain and manage the initiatives [2]. To the contrary, most ICT led initiatives for health in low income countries remain heavily reliant on external support [15, 16].

3.5   Additional Factors Not Covered in the Model by Sarker and Wells

We argue that to inform the use and adoption of mHealth solutions beyond individual users, it is necessary to consider the role change management and research play. Next we present an overview of these factors, but elaborate on their relevance when discussing the mHealth solution from Malawi, later in the paper.

3.5.1   Change Management

Change management is vital to the diffusion of information systems, as various socio and political forces impact technology diffusion [5, 8]. For example there has to be sufficient acceptance for a solution from both users and high-level managers. When people have adopted solutions, there is also need for mechanisms to manage knowledge related to adopted solutions, make data from varied sources accessible at the point of care, and ensure that people have access to appropriate devices for the work [13]. Scaling of mHealth initiatives is also not a straight forward thing, as solution pilots do not always portray a complete picture of costs and technical implications associated with scaling [15].

3.5.2   mHealth Research

Common barriers to mHealth scaling and sustainability are a result of limited knowledge of what works, how it works, and how much it costs [17]. Several authors agree that there is a dearth of research on mHealth [5, 17-19].The future of mHealth, therefore, depends on the establishment of a critical knowledge and evidence base that enables key decision makers to make informed decisions on how to invest limited health resources in technology [20]. To achieve this, there is need for the implementation and researching of large scale mHealth solutions to demonstrate where, how, and why mHealth works best [20].

4   The Case: Mobile Phone-Based ART Protocol

Baobab Health Trust has developed a mobile phone-based Anti-Retroviral Therapy (ART) protocol to guide HIV/AIDS counsellors, under the Malawi AIDS Counselling and Resource Organization (MACRO), with decision making and data capture, when consulting with clients. The solution which is currently being piloted in Malawi, seeks to replace paper-based protocols used by the counsellors. Currently the mobile phone-based solution is being used in parallel with the paper-based protocols.

4.1   MACRO and the Work of HIV/AIDS Counsellors

MACRO is a non-governmental organisation providing voluntary counselling and HIV testing (VCT) services in Malawi. MACRO has several testing sites, including mobile sites. Its HIV/AIDS counsellors also go around different busy trading centres to conduct HIV tests and counsel people. They also have door-to-door initiatives as part of their work. When going about their work, the counsellors use a paper-based protocol to collect data and consider patient referrals based on captured data and guidelines on the protocol.

Before the introduction of the automated mobile phone-based protocol, all counsellors only used paper forms for data capture. The data was then recorded in registers and forwarded to the district level. At the district level, data was then manually aggregated to provide a picture of service delivery in the district.

Over time, it has been noted that manual data aggregation is time consuming and there are inconsistencies in referral recommendations by counsellors when using the paper-based protocol. Enforcement of recommendations by paper-based protocols is largely dependent on the user. It has also been noted that, at times, counsellors lose paper forms before reporting collected data.

4.2   The Mobile Phone-Based Protocol

The mobile phone-based protocol was implemented to enhance consistency in referrals as the application makes recommendations based on input data. The mobile phone-based protocol also fast-tracks data reporting and aggregation, as counsellors can immediately send their captured data to a central server. Currently, the solution is implemented in two districts, and plans are underway to extend to two other districts.

Despite its promise, the solution is not without some challenges. Two important challenges include lack of a well developed mHealth solution developer community in Malawi and concerns by data clerks at MACRO for their jobs, fearing that the application would render them redundant. To have the clerks' buy-in, they were trained on how to use the new solution. However, not having a sufficiently developed mHealth developer community limits innovation in that there are very few people on the ground to collaborate with developers at Baobab Health Trust. There are also just a handful of mHealth research publications from Malawi. In addition to these challenges, there is also the challenge of recharging mobile phones in remote sites. In Malawi, only 2.5 % of the rural population has electricity at home [21], despite around 85 % of the country's population residing in rural areas. Furthermore, since the mobile solution has not yet scaled, cost and technical implications associated with such an undertaking remain unknown.

5   Discussion

We now discuss how mHealth solution implementations should be approached by applying the model by Sarker and Wells, and other reviewed literature, to our case.

5.1   Baobab Health Trusts' mHealth Solution

The mobile phone-based ART protocol solution demonstrates an interaction of multiple heterogeneous elements, which form the installed base upon which the solution has been developed and operates. These interactions are what shape this mHealth solution. Firstly, the case demonstrates the importance of technological characteristics and integration with users' workflows. For example, the mobile phone-based protocol builds on an existing paper-based protocol. The use of mobile phones also affords users sufficient mobility and integrates into their mobile work patterns, thereby permitting use of the technology during service delivery. This fits with the proposition by Yu et al. [8] that to enhance adoption, mHealth applications should be designed with users' information needs, workflows, and usability requirements in mind [8]. On the other hand, short battery lives for mobile phones and challenges with recharging them, especially in remote areas, reflect the role of technological characteristics and infrastructural sensitivities in shaping their use. Beyond this, use of the mobile phone-based protocol requires that users possess a sufficient level of literacy and technological skills. This indicates that user characteristics are an important factor in shaping mobile device use, as argued Sarker and Wells [1].

The approach taken by solution implementers to dispel fears by data clerks concerning their job security, by empowering them with new skills to use the mHealth solution, demonstrates the importance of change management and negotiating with users when implementing solutions. Furthermore, by easing the process of data reporting and aggregation, solution implementers have introduced added value for solution, beyond the ART service delivery protocol. mHealth solutions cannot survive without sufficient buy-in from both users and high-level managers [8]. Keeping with change management, it is not easy to tell how well the solution will scale, since it is still in pilot phase. Solution pilots hide cost and technical implications that have the potential of overturning initial success registered by solutions [15]. Furthermore, that the solution will need a sound financial basis to scale and be sustainable over time needs no further argument. Routine operating expenses, maintenance costs and systems upgrades are intrinsic features of ICT systems. Having sufficient funding to cover such costs is a vital element towards the sustainability of ICT driven initiatives [15].

On the other hand, the infancy of Malawi's mHealth community negatively impacts the mHealth solution in question as regards sharing of technical and research expertise. Limited availability of mHealth literature from Malawi also makes it hard for the solution implementers to learn from other initiatives, within their context of operation. Knowledge management is an essential part of mHealth solution implementations [13, 17], as mHealth scaling and sustainability is dependent on solution implementers having the knowledge of what works, how it works, and how much it costs [17].

5.2   Approaching mHealth Implementations

Considering the multiplicity and heterogeneity of socio-technical composite elements and the dynamics involved in managing divergent and competing interests among stakeholders, we argue that mHealth implementations should be considered information infrastructures. Hanseth and Lyttinen [9] define an information infrastructure as *"a shared, evolving, heterogeneous installed base of IT capabilities among a set of user communities based on open and/or standardized interfaces"*

[9:pp 208]. Viewing mHealth solution implementations as such helps highlight associated complexities.

The case and literature review demonstrate that mHealth solutions build on existing installed bases and are impacted by their dynamics. Among others, these include user competencies, workflows, individual and organisational interests, as well as existing technological arrangements. Implemented solutions also grow in importance by supporting integration. The level of integration between solutions impacts users' workflows and adoption of mHealth solutions, considering that there is a multiplicity of mHealth solutions [8]. This does require standardisation of interfaces. We have modified the framework by Sarker and Wells [7], as shown in Fig. 2, to reflect these interactions and their resultant influence on mHealth solution implementations. This is supplemented by insights from our case review.

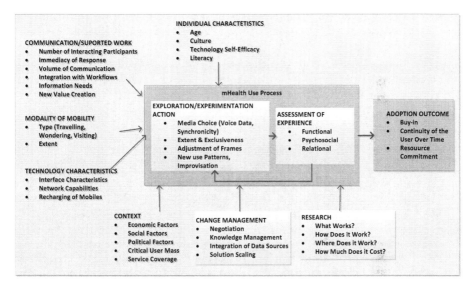

Fig. 2. An integrated framework for mHealth use and adoption – **Adapted from Sarker and Wells [1]**

In line with the propositions by Sarker and Wells, we argue that change management supported work, users' modality of mobility, technology characteristics, research and various other contextual factors, together influence users' interaction with mHealth solutions. In the end, the resultant user experience, as shaped by these factors, determines the adoption of mHealth solutions.

Change management is concerned with negotiation, knowledge management, and integration of data sources. The component on *communication/supported work* is concerned with number of interacting participants, required immediacy of response, volume of communication, integrations of technology with workflows, users' information needs, and value creation for users. *Modality of mobility* assesses extent and types of user mobility. The *technology characteristics* dimension is concerned with interface characteristics -usability and logic, network capabilities, and recharging of mobile devices. The *research* component looks at the questions: what works? How does it work? Where does it work? How much does it cost? Additional *contextual* factors of interest include economic, social, and political factors, adoption by a critical user mass, and service coverage.

6   Conclusions

In this paper, we have extended the *mobile device use and adoption framework* by Sarker and Wells [1] to fit the case of mHealth. We have mostly adjusted the model to give it an organisational and extra-organisation perspective on mHealth solution use, rather the individual user-centric framework proposed by Sarker and Wells [1]. In going about this, we have discussed how socio-technical arrangements such as user characteristics, influence of supported work, modality of user mobility, technological characteristics, change management, and other contextual factors such as economic factors shape mHealth implementation and adoption.

We argue that the above mentioned factors form the *installed base* on which solutions are built. These factors also continuously interplay with the use of mHealth solutions by users, thereby influencing adoption outcomes.

References

1. Sarker, S., Wells, J.D.: Understanding mobile handheld device use and adoption. Commun. ACM 46(12), 35–40 (2003)
2. Hwabamungu, B., Williams, Q.: m-Health adoption and sustainability prognosis from a care givers' and patients' perspective. In: Proceedings of the 2010 Annual Research Conference of the South African Institute of Computer Scientists and Information Technologists, pp. 123–131. ACM, Bela Bela (2010)
3. Vital Wave Consulting, mHealth for Development: The Opportunity of Mobile Technology for Healthcare in the Developing World, UN Foundation-Vodafone Foundation Partnership: Washington, D.C. and Berkshire, UK (2009)
4. Manda, T.D., Herstad, J.: Implementing Mobile Phone Solutions for Health in Resource Constrained Areas: Understanding the Opportunities and Challenges. In: Villafiorita, A., Saint-Paul, R., Zorer, A. (eds.) AFRICOMM 2009. LNICST, vol. 38, pp. 95–104. Springer, Heidelberg (2010)
5. Braa, K., Sanner, T.A.: Making mHealth Happen for Health Information Systems in Low Resource Contexts. In: 11th International Conference on Social Implications of Computers in Developing Countries, IFIP Working Group 9.4: Kathmandu, Nepal (2011)
6. Arnold, M.: On the phenomenology of technology: the "Janus-faces" of mobile phones. Information and Organization 13(4), 231–256 (2003)
7. Jarvenpaa, S.L., Lang, K.R.: Managing the paradoxes of mobile technology. Information Systems Management 22(4), 7–23 (2005)
8. Yu, P., et al.: The Challenges for the Adoption of M-Health. In: IEEE International Conference on Service Operations and Logistics, and Informatics, SOLI 2006 (2006)
9. Hanseth, O., Lyytinen, K.: Theorizing about the Design of Information Infrastructures: Design Kernel Theories and Principles. Sprouts: Working Papers on Information Systems 4, 207–241 (2004)

10. Walsham, G.: Doing Interpretive Research. European Journal of Information Systems 15, 320–330 (2006)
11. Myers, M.D., Avison, D.: An Introduction to Qualitative Research in Information Systems. In: Myers, M.D., Avison, D. (eds.) Qualitative Research in Information Systems: A Reader. SAGE Publications, London (2002)
12. Hanseth, O., Nielsen, P.: Infrastructural Innovation. Flexibility, Generativity and the Mobile Internet, 1–29 (2007)
13. Mishra, S., Singh, I.P.: mHealth: a developing country perspective. In: Making the eHealth Connection, Bellagio, Italy (2008)
14. Hagen, P., et al. Emerging Research Methods for Understanding Mobile Technology Use. In: Annual Conference of the Australian Computer-Human Interaction Special Interest Group (OZCHI 2005), Canbera, Australia (2005)
15. Lucas, H.: Information and communications technology for future health systems in developing countries. Social Science & Medicine 66(10), 2122–2132 (2008)
16. Vital Wave Consulting, Health Information Systems in Developing Countries: A Landscape Analysis. Vital Wave Consulting, California, USA (2009)
17. Mechael, P., et al.: Barriers and Gaps Affecting mHealth in Low and Middle Income Countries: Policy White Paper, Center for Global Health and Economic Development Earth Institute, Columbia University (2010)
18. Donner, J.: Research Approaches to Mobile Use in the Developing World: A Review of the Literature. The Information Society: An International Journal 24(3), 140–159 (2008)
19. Rashid, A.T., Elder, L.: Mobile Phones and Development: An Analysis of IDRC-Supported Projects. The Electronic Journal of Information Systems in Developing Countries 36(2), 1–16 (2009)
20. Mechael, P.N.: The Case for mHealth in Developing Countries. Innovations: Technology, Governance, Globalization 4(1), 103–118 (2009)
21. AICD, Malawi's Infrastructure: A Continental Perspective. The World Bank, Washington, DC (2010)

Power Dynamics in E-commerce Adoption in Least Developing Countries: The Case of Dar-es-Salaam SMEs, Tanzania

Salah Kabanda

Department of Information Systems,
University of Cape Town, South Africa
{salah.kabanda}@uct.ac.za

Abstract. This paper examines power structures that make E-Commerce adoption amongst Small and Medium Enterprises in least developing countries a daunting task. The study adopts structuration theory as a lens, focusing specifically on structures of domination. The results indicate that at organizational level, lack of management support was the reason. However this was caused by government's reluctance to adopt E-Commerce. By not adopting E-Commerce, government creates structures of domination by drawing on both of its allocative and authoritative resources. Further results show education institutions possessing authoritative power - they design the curriculum by determining what to teach and how to teach it; and whilst doing it, fail to take into account the industries and specifically SMEs needs. However with the rapid adoption of mobile technologies, E-Commerce is becoming a reality through the development of mobile enabled trade websites, which gives SMEs numerous ways to diffuse and rejuvenate themselves in the global economy.

Keywords: E-Commerce, Structuration theory, least developing countries, Small and Medium Enterprises, Tanzania.

1 Introduction

Over the past few decades, E-Commerce has been widely believed to be an avenue for integrating communities and countries into the global market economy. E-Commerce in this study is seen as a technological innovation - a tool used by the adopting society to perform tasks more efficiently or to perform new tasks [1]. As a technological innovation, E-Commerce promises to reduce the costs of interbusiness transactions by automating many individual steps in the procurement process; alleviating transaction inefficiencies in the supply chain [2]; and most importantly bridge the existing development gaps between the haves and the have not through integration of information systems [3,4,5,6,7]. However these economic benefits can only be accrued to those who succeed in adopting the technological innovation [1]. Succeeding is usually a daunting task for developing countries, and more so for Least Developing Countries (LDC), who still find it difficult to compete in the global digital exchange as they lack a conducive operating environment in terms of technical, social, economic and political elements [8,9,10]. LDCs constitute a special category

R. Popescu-Zeletin et al. (Eds.) AFRICOMM 2011, LNICST 92, pp. 218–227, 2012.

of the "poorest and weakest segment" of the international community that are characterized by extreme poverty, weak economies, inadequate institutional and human resources and often vulnerable to natural disasters [47]. As such, very few LDCs have adopted E-Commerce and even those that have adopted E-Commerce, most, remain at the initial adoption phase – a level of adoption ranging from being connected (e.g. basic email), having a static website (e.g., simple website) to interactive E-Commerce. A limited number have transcended to the second measure of adoption, institutionalization - the extent of E-Commerce utilization which range from having an interactive, transactive, or integrated E-Commerce status [11].

Tanzania is an example of an LDC that has shown little substantive progress with regard to E-Commerce – specifically at the institutionalization phase. Since E-Commerce adoption is highly affected by contextual factors of the adopting society [44,48], this study focuses on understanding power structures that make E-Commerce adoption amongst SMEs an uphill struggle. To do so, the study adopts structuration theory as a lens, to enrich "the picture of meaning construction—or construction of interpretive schemes—by interrelating the analyses of meaning, power and norms" [12]. The theory is inherently dynamic and grounded in ongoing human action, and therefore indeed has the potential to explain emergence and change in technologies and use [13]. Through this lens, E-Commerce is conceptualized as a structuration process that takes shape through the social construction of E-Commerce rules and resources.

The rest of this paper is structured as follows: the next section provides background study of ICTs and E-Commerce in Tanzania. Section 3 presents theoretical work on structuration theory. Section 4 presents the methodological approach and Section 5 the data analysis. The results are discussed in Section 6. Section 7 concludes the paper.

2   ICTs and the State of E-commerce in Tanzania

Tanzania is located in the eastern coast of Africa with a population of just over 41 million people. Although the country is fairly stable politically with a fully functioning multi-party democracy, economically, the country is among the least developed countries. As in many other developing countries, Tanzania has many Small and Medium Enterprises (SMEs) which play a critical role in the economy especially with respect to employment. As a result, there have been numerous studies investigating internet related technologies and the digital divide as well as the role of ICT for the performance of SMEs. Matambalya and Wolf [14] investigated a sample of 300 SMEs in East Africa. Their result shows that the use of ICT by SMEs in Kenya as well as in Tanzania is increasing over time, with the usage of fixed phone lines nearly reaching the saturation point (although still lower in Tanzania than in Kenya). In Tanzania, Nielinger [4] and Pigato [15] found that computer usage, and the internet in particular still remains very low even in firms that own computers. As for those who have computers and ICTs, under-utilization is a common feature with "a widespread gap between availability and effective use". Nielinger [4] found that 36% of the enterprises had access to a fax-machine and one-third had access to email. However, both means account for only 10% or 9% of total business correspondence, leaving the outstanding 81% of business correspondence to traditional, non-electronic means". Although currently the countries' number of Internet users is increasing steadily, the country still lacks cheap and high-capacity connections to the global Internet despite the large and increasing demand for Internet access [16]. The digital divide is also highly evident. For example, there are 16 times more people per Internet café in the rural regions of Iringa, Mbeya and Songea compared to urban Dar es Salaam, and in the semi-urban region, Morogoro, were there are 7 times more people per café [17].

Of recent, the country is experiencing a rapid rate of mobile phones adoption. Matambalya and Wolf [14] indicate that the percentage of firms that uses mobile phones is increasing fast. Molony [18] explored how mobile phones are being used by informal construction workers in Dar es Salaam, Tanzania. His study reveals that ownership of mobile phones is stratified along employment lines and if properly integrated, a form of mobile E-Commerce could take charge. The increase in mobile telephony has ensured a steady increase in the country's teledensity which went from one per cent in 2000 to 25 per cent in 2008 and has already overtaken that of main line access. Yet the increase in mobile telephony, with high priced tariffs, has not translated into an increase in the use of the Internet, making "telecommunications services only available to the elite rather than everyone" and consequently excluding the poor majority from taking part in the nation's drive to become an ICT-enabled, and a 'knowledge-based society' [19,20].

3   Structuration Theory

Structuration theory developed by Giddens [22] is used to study social phenomena with the purpose of understanding how institutions or behavioral practices are produced and re-produced over time. These practices when routinized over time tend to determine how social realities come about and how social system works [23]. To produce or reproduce these behavioral practices, individuals draw on an array of interconnected rules and resources that may stretch across potentially great spans of time and space [24]. Rules and resources mediate human action, while at the same time are reaffirmed by individuals whose actions simultaneously condition and are conditioned by them [25, 26,27].

To conceptualize the theory, Giddens identifies three dimensions of interaction as: (i) signification (rules of meaning, understandable communication, the ideas and values people hold), (ii) domination (the exercising of power via resources as channeled for example via the financial system and the interrelation of supply and demand), and (iii) legitimation (the sanctioning of each other). Specifically, structures of signification describe the shared understanding of a given phenomenon by a group of people and are communicated via interpretive schemes or stocks of knowledge that serve as cognitive guides for individual action and behavior [28, 29,30,31,32,33]. Structures of domination are provided by structures that enforce established institutional rules to regulate actions and behaviours of individuals using available resources at their disposable which become the basis for acquiring individual power [25,28,29,33]. They are created when actors use power in interaction by drawing on either or both allocative resources (control of material products or aspects of the natural world) and authoritative resources (give the actor power over the actions of others) [22,34]. Structures of legitimization, communicated through norms, are established by organizational conventions that validate whether certain behaviors are desirable and congruent with the goals and values of the organization or not [28,35,36].

4   Research Approach and Method

The study is qualitative in nature. Qualitative methods are useful in generating "multiple interpretations and deep understanding of the often conflicting rationalities of the people involved in IS innovation" [37]; thereby allowing the researcher to gain better understanding of the problem and identify the phenomena, attitudes and influences [38, 39]. Research methods informed by qualitative stance tend to give explicit recognition to the world of consciousness and humanly created meanings within the specific cultural and contextual settings from the perspective of participants. This approach is more suitable for this study as it complements our goal of trying to understand underlying power structures from the participant's (SMEs) viewpoints.

The empirical work was conceived as a combination of a pilot study, followed by interviews that spanned for two months. Targeted participants included SME owners, managers and IT executives as they are most familiar with E-Commerce in their firms and environment. Subsequent interviews lasted between an hour or two. Audio recording and note taking during interviews served as data collecting tools through which we examined the situated production of social action and addressed the visual, material as well as spoken features of the interviewees. The study is limited to SMEs in Dar-es-Salaam, Tanzania, especially to those with a significant ICT presence. Initially, the database of the Bureau of Statistics in Dar-es-Salaam was used as an initial sampling frame to obtain the names of all SMEs in the region. SMEs not registered were contacted through a snowballing technique.

36 different SMEs were interviewed in total from the following industries: Communication Electronics & Computer, Loans & Finance, Service providers (ISP), Safety & Protection, Tourism & Entertainment, Arts, Craft & Curios, Agriculture & Forestry, Fishing & Manufacturing, Transportation, and Insurance respectively. We therefore ensure we sampled per industry and per level of E-Commerce adoption (initial to institutionalization). Many of the SMEs fell under the Communication Electronics & Computer industry (15 SMEs); followed by the tourism sector (5 SMEs). 37% of the SMEs were only targeting the local customer. 25 SMEs had a website and email communication. 53% of SMEs targeted both international and local, and the remaining 47% specifically targeted the East African market (Kenya, Uganda, Rwanda, and Burundi). 56% of the SMEs had their websites hosted abroad. Although many were reluctant to indicate which country their website was hosted in, the common responses were India, Germany and Dubai. SMEs that had no website but had some form of ICT presence such as email communication indicated that despite having email, their most used mode of communication was the mobile. Email was used for personal communication such as checking on friends and occasionally for conducting international business. The industry that solely relied on the mobile was Insurance, followed by transportation services.

5   Data Analysis and Results

At organizational level, SME employees felt there was a lack of top management support for desktop ICTs, specifically the usage of the computer. They indicated that if the support was present, it was purely not for transactive or fully integrated web-based E-Commerce. There was a consensus viewpoint across all industries that management's support with regard to desktops was relatively low and almost insignificant compared with mobile technology. As one SME employee from the Insurance industry indicated, *"our managers are more interested in mobile phones because it is the quickest method to communicate here and most of our clients have phones but few have computers. So phones work for us.* Management showed their support for mobile technology in their businesses by providing employees with *Blackberries loaded with Internet airtime* or airtime credits for their personal phones to enable marketing of the businesses.

At environmental level, SMEs perceived the government to possess the power to initiate E-Commerce and ensure it thrives because they are the biggest single buyer and employer in the country of ICT services; and ideally should be more engaged in the procurement, and delivering services. Despite having these resources, SMEs indicated that the government was reluctant to partake in online related transactions, accept credit payment, and were simply *lazy in checking their emails.* There was consensus that the government was more resistant to technological changes than individual consumers or private companies. As such, SMEs feel that E-Commerce adoption and institutionalization would not result in many returns if the biggest single buyer and employer in the country of ICT services was not adopting E-Commerce.

SMEs also queried the policies set out with regard to ICTs. It was established that they lacked clarity and were incomprehensive to cater for E-Commerce concerns, specifically on security issues. For example, an SME in the Communication Electronics & Computer industry indicated that *there needs to be a clear definition of what the terms computers and peripherals meant to the public and specifically to those in government who will tax you if you come with the CPU - they think that a computer is the monitor! Even if you complain, it depends on whom you find that day because the person responsible to take matters forward will not. So the winner will always be on the other side and you end up having to pay something.* These sentiments were echoed by other SMEs in the same industry and hinted of the existence of power structures which unfortunately lends itself to corruption.

Apart from the government, there was a unanimity complaint amongst SMEs, of a lack of competency and expertise in the ICT sector. They noted that software specific skills were difficult to acquire and even if acquired, difficult to retain and as such, most SMEs did not have software skills experts in their organizations but relied on external support or foreign partners, to develop and host their website, to train employees and for system maintenance. An SME in the tourism and entertainment industry lamented indicating that *the problem is we can't trust the market to provide us with the right person to do the job and who has the right technological skills. We need a great website for our tourism site. So what we do is outsource from outside the country.* It was evident that all SMEs felt powerless with the current available skills and specifically the graduates they receive because according to them, there was a definite mismatch between the industries needs and what the educational institutes were offering. SMEs lamented on the lack of *grooming, experience and exposure to software development* and the potential of having a career in this field. The mismatch between educational curriculum and industrial needs according to SMEs specifically those specializing in software development, resulted in *graduates being very inexperienced, unskilled with practical issues and needing a lot of help. We normally fund them to attend certification courses.* However, few SMEs could provide graduates with the necessary help because ICT training was perceived to be more expensive compared to other professional courses. This is partly because some ICT courses require the usage of the internet which is unfortunately expensive. According to one of the service providers, Internet access is still expensive because of SEACOM monopoly – a privately owned and operated pan-African ICT enabler that is driving the development of the African internet. He indicated that although there are other cables that have arrived, they are still not effective in terms of operation and as such Internet price changes are not yet felt.

6   Discussion

The data analysis reveals that SMEs felt incapable of adopting and ultimately institutionalizing E-Commerce without government's involvement – specifically government's use of E-Commerce. Government's involvement in E-Commerce was seen as necessity because it is projected that if governments begin using E-Commerce for example e-procurement, they can provide an important incentive for SMEs to begin using E-Commerce as well [40]. The government therefore is seen to possess allocative power, in that it has infrastructural resources necessary to implement E-Commerce and has authoritative power in that it has the influence to adopt E-Commerce if it chose to, and the influence to prioritize E-Commerce by ensuring that there is physical infrastructure (road, electricity and traceable physical address), readily available expertise, provision of ICT policies that are clear and comprehensive, and other E-Commerce prerequisites. By not adopting E-Commerce, and any form of electronic transactions, the government creates structures of domination by drawing on both of its allocative and authoritative resources causing SMEs to feel inadequate as they are unable to influence the government in adopting E-Commerce. The inability to influence does not give SMEs the power to make a difference on how to propagate E-Commerce but clearly demonstrates how the state is an instrument of domination as it has the power to implement desirable changes [41] – such as adopt E-Commerce. Further results show education institutions, possessing authoritative power – they determine what to teach and how to teach it; they design the curriculum and whilst doing it fail to take into account the industry's needs. SMEs feel powerless because they are at the receiving end and have no say in what students should be competent in prior to graduating. As a result, SMEs receive graduates who are short of various important and sometimes basic ICT skills. This is a concern because, factors such as presence of an IT labor force and general IT literacy are enabling conditions for E-Commerce, although these are influenced by demographic factors [43].

These results echo those of Hambrick [42] who indicates that institutions that have access and control over scarce resources tend to be more dominant in the business industry than those that do not, even though the forms of domination may differ. This study however indicates that such institutions do not necessary have to use their power to exploit the means of production (resources) at their disposal, but can choose to remain silent, and reluctant in exploiting those means of production, such as the government in this instance. In so doing, the government consciously or unconsciously retains its power by not changing the status quo, of which if changed, could jeopardize their authority.

Despite these power structures, SMEs have not remained stagnant in the usage of ICTs but have moved on to mobile technology – a technology they find capable of meeting most of their business needs quite efficiently and effectively by allowing them to top-up mobile phone credits for themselves and their employees, airtime transfers between mobile phones, corporate bill payments and access to new markets, specifically rural poor people who have no traditional bank accounts. In order to tap further into these benefits, mobile phone companies are now facilitating E-Commerce by allowing SMEs to interact and conclude business transactions online, sending money to each other through mobile financial services already available in the local market. Mobile financial services have gained enormous popularity and SME owners see no other means of transacting economically. They have now articulated and reinforced their firm belief in the technology by ensuring that employees abide by the businesses' unwritten regulation of utilizing their personal mobiles for business venture. SME managers find mobile financial services a safe technology for business transactions despite there being no proper law to guide and regulate the mobile banking industry since its introduction in Tanzania in 2008 [44]. This is a clear indication that businesses would rather take the risk of mobile banking than wait for the government to amend the physical and telecommunication infrastructure and other traditional E-Commerce prerequisite. Through mobile technology, SMEs have gained the power to transform existing structures using resources (mobile phone) that have recently become available to them. They have shown that despite their political, culture and business contextual constraints, they can still craft their own destiny. To them, mobile telephony has been the most significant contributor to regional market expansion [21] and the path towards E-Commerce. As agents, SMEs have shown the ability to "make causal contribution to their own motivation and action within a system of triadic reciprocal causation" [22,45]. They have the capacity of forethought or consciousness which allows them to "monitor their own actions and their consequences, the actions of others [46], set goals for themselves, and plan courses of action likely to produce desired outcomes [45].

7   Conclusion

E-Commerce in least developing countries is still at a developing stage. This study specifically investigated structures that make propagations of E-Commerce an impossible task. The empirical analysis indicates that LDCs governments still have the largest ICT infrastructure and the prerequisite resources necessary for E-Commerce adoption as compared to SMEs. However, SMEs are faced by an ongoing resistance from government in the adoption of E-Commerce – even at the basic level of email communication. This study shows that institutions in power do not necessary have to use their power to exploit the means of production (resources) at their disposal, but can choose to remain silent, and reluctant in exploiting those means of production, such as the government in this instance. By doing so, they strengthen their position and reaffirm their authority. In addition, SMEs are faced by further challenges from the educational institutions which tend to reaffirm their authoritative power by designing their ICT curriculum without taking into account the industries and specifically the SMEs needs. By not being included in the curriculum design, SMEs feel powerless because they are at the receiving end and have no say in what students should be competent in prior to graduating. That is, students finish their studies with degrees that are not context specific.

SME however have found an alternative solution that befits their business context – the mobile phone. Mobile technology has attempted to mitigate the adverse effects of government's political domination on SMEs. With the rapid adoption of mobile technologies in Tanzania and other LDCs by both consumers and businesses, E-Commerce can now become a reality through the development of mobile enabled trade websites, thereby giving SMEs numerous ways to diffuse and rejuvenate themselves in the global economy.

References

1. Mugodi, T.Z., Fleming, D.R.: A study of ICT diffusion into South Africa's platinum mining sector. Application of Computers and Operations Research in the Minerals Industries, South African Institute of Mining and Metallurgy (2003)
2. Barkley, D.L., Markley, D.M., Lamie, R.D.: E-Commerce as a Business Strategy: Lessons Learned From Case Studies Of Rural And Small Town Businesses, http://www.energizingentrepreneurs.org/site/images/research/cp/cs/cs7.pdf
3. Ojukwu, D., Georgiadou, E.: Towards Improving Inter-Organisational Trust (IOT) amongst SMEs: A Case Study from Developing Countries. In: The International Federation for Information Processing (IFIP) 9th International Conference on "Social Implications of Computers in Developing Countries", Sao Paulo, Brazil, May 28-30 (2007)
4. Nielinger, O.: Fact Sheet: ICT-utilisation of Small and Medium Enterprises (SME) in Tanzania, http://www.ourtanzania.com/smes%20ICT%20utilisation.pdf
5. Pare, J.D.: B2B E-Commerce Services and Developing Countries: Disentangling Myth from Reality, http://www.ids.ac.uk/UserFiles/File/globalisation_team/DraftAoIR3.pdf
6. Wolf, S.: Determinants and Impact of ICT use for African SMEs: Implications for Rural South Africa. Center for Development Research (ZEF Bonn). Paper prepared for TIPS Forum (2001)
7. Esselaar, P., Miller, J.: Towards Electronic Commerce in Africa: A Perspective from three country studies. Southern African Journal of Information and Communication 2, 1 (2001)

8. Jennex, M.E., Amoroso, D., Adelakun, O.: E-Commerce Infrastructure Success Factors for Small Companies in Developing Economies. Electronic Commerce Research 4, 263–286 (2004)
9. Hawk, S.: A comparison of B2C E-Commerce in developing countries. Electronic Commerce Research 4, 181–199 (2004)
10. Efendioglu, M.A., Yip, F.V., Murray, W.L.: E-Commerce in Developing Countries: Issues and Influences, http://userwww.sfsu.edu/~ibec/papers/25.pdf
11. Molla, A., Licker, P.S.: eCommerce adoption in developing countries: a model and instrument. Information and Management 42, 877–899 (2005)
12. Karsten, H.: "It's like everyone working around the same desk": Organisational Readings of Lotus Notes. Scandinavian Journal of Information Systems 7(1), Article 3 (1995)
13. Orlikowski, W.J.: Using Technology and Constituting Structures: A Practice Lens for Studying Technology in Organizations. Organization Science 11(4), 404 (2000)
14. Matambalya, F., Wolf, S.: The Role Of ICT For The Performance Of SMEs In East Africa. Empirical Evidence from Kenya and Tanzania, http://purl.umn.edu/18717
15. Pigato, M.: Information and Communication Technology, Poverty and Development in Sub-Saharan Africa and South Asia. World Bank, Washington, DC (2001)
16. Tanzania Ministry of Communications and Transport, http://www.uwaba.or.tz/nationaltransportpolicy.pdf
17. Furuholt, B., Kristiansen, S.: A rural-urban Digital Divide? Regional aspects of Internet use in Tanzania. The Electronic Journal of Information Systems in Developing Countries 31 (2007)
18. Molony, T.: Running out of credit: the limitations of mobile telephony in a Tanzanian agricultural marketing system. J. of Modern African Studies 46(4), 1–22 (2008)
19. Mercer, C.: Telecentres And Transformations: Modernizing Tanzania through the Internet. J. African Affairs 105(419), 243–264 (2005)
20. Chitamu, P.J., Van Olst, R., Vannucci, D.E.: How Can The Cost Of Telecommunications Access In Africa Be Driven Downwards?, http://Www.Satnac.Org.Za/Proceedings/2003/Other/648%20-%20chitamu.Pdf
21. Carmody, P.: A New Socio-Economy in Africa? The integration and the Mobile Phone Revolution. Institute for International Integration Studies (279) (February 2009)
22. Giddens, A.: The Constitution of Society, Polity, Cambridge (1984)
23. Brooks, L.: Structuration theory and new technology: analysing organizationally situated computer-aided design (CAD). Information Systems Journal 7, 133–151 (1997)
24. Ogden, D., Rose, R.A.: Using Giddens's Structuration Theory to Examine the Waning Participation of African Americans in Baseball. J. of Black Studies 35(4), 225–245 (2005)
25. Crowston, K., Sawyer, S., Wigand, R.: Investigating the interplay between structure and information and communications technology in the real estate industry. J. Information Technology & People 14(2), 163–183 (2001)
26. Giddens, A.: Profiles and Critiques in Social Theory. Macmillan, London (1982)
27. Devadoss, P.R., Pan, S.L., Huang, J.C.: Structurational analysis of e-government initiatives: a case study of SCO. Decision Support Systems 34, 253–269 (2002)
28. Rai, A., Brown, P., Tang, X.: Organizational Assimilation of Electronic Procurement Innovations. J. Management Information Systems 26(1), 257–296 (2009)
29. Chu, C., Smithson, S.: Organisational structure and e-business: a structurational analysis. In: Proceedings of the 5th International Conference on Electronic Commerce, pp. 205–212 (2003)

30. Wu, S., Kersten, G.E.: A Structuration View of E-Negotiation System Use. InterNeg Research Papers INR02/08, http://interneg.concordia.ca/views/bodyfiles/paper/2008/02.pdf
31. Sydow, J., Windeler, A.: Organizing and Evaluating Interfirm Networks: A Structurationist Perspective on Network Processes and Effectiveness. J. Organization Science 9(3), 265–284 (1998); Special Issue: Managing Partnerships and Strategic Alliances
32. Scheepers, R., Damsgaard, J.: Using Internet technology within the organization: a structurational analysis of intranets. In: International Conference on Supporting Group Work - GROUP, Phoenix Arizona USA, pp. 9–18 (1997)
33. Willmott, H.: The Structuring of Organizational Structure: A Note. Administrative Science Quarterly 26(3), 470–474 (1981), http://www.jstor.org/stable/pdfplus/2392518.pdf
34. Montealegre, R.: The interplay of information technology and the social milieu. Information Technology & People 10(2), 106–131 (1997)
35. Jones, M.R., Karsten, H.: Giddens's structuration theory and information systems research. MIS Quarterly 32(1), 127–157 (2008)
36. Pozzebon, M., Pinsonneault, A.: Structuration Theory In the IS Field: An Assessment Of Research Strategies. Global Co-Operation in the New Millennium. In: Proceedings of the 9th European Conference on Information Systems Bled, Slovenia, June 27-29 (2001)
37. McGrath, K.: Doing critical research in information systems: a case of theory and practice not informing each other. J. Info. Systems 15, 85–101 (2005)
38. Rotchanakitumnuai, S., Speece, M.: Barriers to Internet banking adoption: a qualitative study among corporate customers in Thailand. International J. Bank Marketing 21(6/7), 312–323 (2003)
39. Flick, U.: An introduction to qualitative research. SAGE, Thousand Oaks (2009)
40. UNCTD: United Nations Conference on Trade and Development. Selected examples of e-enterprises in LDCs. Based on survey prepared for the Third United Nations Conference on Least Developed Countries, Brussels (2001)
41. Sarasona, Y., Dean, T., Dillard, J.F.: Entrepreneurship as the nexus of individual and opportunity: A structuration view. J. Business Venturing 21, 286–305 (2006)
42. Hambrick, D.C.: Environment, Strategy, and Power within Top Management Teams. Administrative Science Quarterly 26(2), 253–275 (1981)
43. Gibbs, J., Kraemer, K.L., Dedrick, J.: Environment and Policy Factors Shaping E-Commerce Diffusion: A Cross-Country Comparison. Uc Irvine: Center for Research on Information Technology and Organizations (2002), http://www.escholarship.org/uc/item/2x73003z
44. Mutarubukwa, A.: Govt to table bill on mobile banking regulations. The Citizen (2011), http://thecitizen.co.tz/magazines/-/8517-govt-to-table-bill-on-mobile-banking-regulations
45. Bandura, A.: Human Agency in Social Cognitive Theory. American Psychologist 44(9), 1175–1184 (1989)
46. Lyytinen, K., Ngwenyama, O.: What does computer support for cooperative work mean? a structurational analysis of computer supported cooperative work. Accounting, Management and Information Technologies 2(1), 19–37 (1992)
47. The United Nations.: Least Developed Countries, http://portal.unesco.org/
48. Avgerou, C.: The significance of context in information systems and organizational change. Info. Systems J. 11, 43–63 (2001)

The Expansion of the Siyakhula Living Lab: A Holistic Perspective

Lorenzo Dalvit[1,2], Ingrid Siebörger[3], and Hannah Thinyane[3]

[1] ICT Education, Education Department, Rhodes University
[2] MTN Chair of Media and Mobile Communication, School of Journalism and Media Studies,
Rhodes University
[3] Telkom Centre of Excellence, Computer Science Department, Rhodes University
6140 Grahamstown, South Africa
{l.dalvit,i.sieborger,h.thinyane}@ru.ac.za

Abstract. In this paper we discuss the recent expansion of network connectivity within the Siyakhula Living Lab. This is part of an ICT-for-development project located in a rural area on the Wild Coast of South Africa. Thus far, five schools in the area have been the primary points of access to the network for the surrounding communities. Thanks to external funding, eleven more schools will be connected. Consistent with the Living Lab approach, the expansion needs to take into account technical as well as social aspects. Technical challenges relate mainly to the constraints of working in a rugged, mountainous terrain with poor road and electricity infrastructure and harsh environmental conditions such as dust and temperature variances. Social challenges relate to obtaining the buy-in of the local community and to reaching consensus on the criteria for the expansion. In this paper we account for the preliminary work which led to the implementation plan. We hope our experience will inform similar interventions in other parts of Africa.

Keywords: Living Labs, ICT-for-development, wireless networks, WiMAX, social aspects, community involvement.

1 Introduction

Internet penetration in Africa is low compared to other parts of the World. Despite its strong economy and first-World infrastructure in metropolitan areas, South Africa only averages an Internet penetration of 10% [1]. This is largely due to poor ICT infrastructure in rural areas where a vast portion of the population (approximately 42.5% according to the 2001 census [2]) lives. The fixed-line teledensity in rural areas is less than 5% [3] and the high cost of deploying and maintaining copper and fibre plants make it risky for telecommunication operators to roll out traditional wired technology into these rural areas [4]. For these reasons wireless technologies appear to be a more viable solution [5].

Access to the Internet has recently been recognised by the UN as a human right [6]. Information and knowledge are key strategic resources for social and economic

R. Popescu-Zeletin et al. (Eds.) AFRICOMM 2011, LNICST 92, pp. 228–238, 2012.

development. Rural communities could be empowered by participating in the knowledge society through the use of ICTs. In order for ICT interventions to be effective and sustainable, the local community of prospective users needs to be involved in shaping and supporting the intervention [7].

In this paper we discuss the current (Aug – Nov 2011) expansion of an existing ICT-for-development (ICT4D) project with a strong telecommunication focus. The expansion is funded by a company who specialise as a telecommunications solution provider [8] as an exploration of possible technical and social challenges in network provision in rural communities. We couple the use of wireless technologies like WiMAX, WiFi with a focus on social integration within the framework of the Siyakhula Living Lab (SLL) based in Dwesa/Cwebe, a rural area of South Africa.

The work covered in this paper is part of an overarching project, the SLL. For more information on the project as a whole, or for specifics on the wireless technologies that are used, refer to [7] and [4] (respectively). This paper differs from past publications as it focuses on the planning of and expansion of the infrastructure in the SLL as well as the integral participation from local community within the SLL, while still covering some necessary background information from our previous interventions. The paper starts by providing background on the SLL, describing the location and a brief history of the project. It then details the expansion of the footprint of the SLL, including discussions on technical, logistical and social considerations. The paper then finishes with some concluding remarks.

2   The Siyakhula Living Lab

2.1   Dwesa/Cwebe

The SLL includes several villages in the Mbashe municipality adjacent to the Dwesa-Cwebe nature reserve. The natural environment, consisting of the nature reserve and the adjacent coastline are assets for the communities. The unspoiled natural beauty and wild beaches have the potential to significantly promote eco-tourism in the region. Furthermore, the high levels of rainfall and rich soil in a typically dry area of the country, has potential for controlled agricultural intensification and commercial forestry [9].

Despite the distinctive features mentioned above, the Mbashe municipality is representative of many rural realities in South Africa and in other parts of Africa. It is characterised by a lack of electricity, telecommunication infrastructure and poor road conditions. Dwesa/Cwebe can be reached only via gravel roads (which vary between 40 and 50km in length and quality) and becomes inaccessible after heavy rain as a result of flooding in the Mbashe and Nqabara rivers. In many villages, schools and clinics are the only buildings connected to the electricity grid, although electrification efforts are underway to connect community members' homes (having begun in mid 2010). Fixed-line telecommunications are non-existent and members of the local communities rely mainly on mobile phones.

Service delivery in the area is poor and limited to basic education and health care. People have to travel to the nearest urban centre (approximately 40km away) to buy groceries and electricity, withdraw money at the ATM and reach the police station, hospital and local administrative offices. The cost of travelling to and from town adds to the burden of communities, which are characterised by endemic poverty and heavily reliant on government grants, subsistence farming and cattle-raising. The Mbashe municipality has recently been the site of various developmental projects. ICT can support rural development initiatives by enabling communication and access to relevant information and services over the Internet.

2.2   Project History

The Dwesa/Cwebe area has been the site of ethnographic research by the Anthropology Department at Rhodes University for a number of years [9]. Together with its potential for economic and social development and its representativeness of many African rural realities, this is one of the reasons why it was chosen for an ICT-for-development intervention. What is now known as the Siyakhula Living lab started as a joint venture of the Telkom Centres of Excellence (CoE) at Rhodes University and the University of Fort Hare to explore the potential of marginalised areas through the introduction of ICT. The collaboration provides the level of resources necessary to run an ICT project in a remote rural area. Other academic departments such as Anthropology, Education, Information Systems, Communication and African Languages have also joined the project.

Since 2005, a multi-disciplinary team of young researchers from the two universities has been visiting the Dwesa/Cwebe area for approximately one week of every month. The initial deployment of infrastructure was preceded by extensive consultation with the communities and the local power structures (e.g. headman, nature reserve trust etc.). Schools were chosen as the points of presence because of their role as centres of knowledge in community life, as well as for the availability of electricity and secure building infrastructure. The development of the project was based on the premise that the local communities would take responsibility for the safety and use of the equipment, and that the schools would become centres that provide access to computers and the Internet. Educators with an interest in the project identified themselves as ICT-champions [10], i.e. as the primary drivers of the implementation at the local level.

Informed by the principles of social informatics [11], our intervention has always coupled technological development with skills development and social integration. Following this holistic approach, the project has grown into the Siyakhula Living Lab, which currently connects five schools in the area and provides access and training for the respective communities. The living lab approach is defined as "an approach that deals with user driven innovation of products and services that are introduced, tested and validated in real life environments" [12. p8]. The community is an active participant in the project, and the impact of ICT in the area has been documented by a number of publications [7, 13] focusing on different (multidisciplinary), changing aspects within the project that has now been running for almost 6 years (November 2005 to November 2011). The SLL has attracted considerable interest by the media and by government officials at the local, provincial and national levels. An excellent collaboration with the local offices of the Department of Education resulted in the funding of an Advanced Certificate in Education (ACE) specialising in ICT. This is a part-time qualification for educators in the area and, as shown below, is instrumental to the expansion project. A wide array of Industry and Government parties are participating in funding the SLL. Funding by one such industry partner spear-headed the expansion described in this paper.

2.3   Current Network Configuration

From a technical point of view, the primary objective of the SLL is to develop and field-test a distributed, multifunctional community communication platform, using localization through innovation, to deploy in marginalized rural communities in South Africa. These communities, by sheer size and because of current political dynamics, represent a strategic emergent market. A reliable local loop access network was required; we decided to make use of wireless technologies as there was no fixed line infrastructure in the region onto which we could piggy-back. WiMAX technologies were chosen to build a wireless local access loop and more specifically the Alvarion BreezeMAX technology.

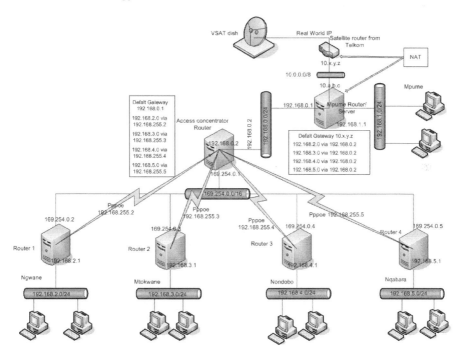

Fig. 1. Network diagram of the SLL

The communities access the SLL infrastructure and communications platform via the distributed access nodes (DANs) at the schools where the DANs are hosted. Currently five schools house DANs, namely, Mpume JSS, Ngwane School (both a primary and a secondary school), Mthokwane JSS, Nondobo JSS and Nqabara SS [see Figure 1]. Each DAN is equipped with a thin client computer lab running Edubuntu Linux and approximately 5 to 20 thin clients, depending on the size of the classroom made available and the level of security. At each DAN there is a community access point (CAP) which provides access to the local loop WiMAX network for all the clients at each site. The CAP is a FreeBSD router that is configured to manage and monitor the DAN through a number of services such as SMTP and Netflow to name a few.

The CAP acts as a gateway between the local area networks (LAN) within each school and the bigger local loop network. The CAP runs a Point-to-Point Protocol (PPP) client, specifically PPP over Ethernet (PPPoE), which contains the school's username and password for authenticating with the access concentrator housed at Mpume. Once authenticated and the link has been established the router will route all outgoing traffic, intended for one of the other schools (such as local VoIP traffic) or the Internet, onto the next hop which is the access concentrator.

The WiMAX micro base station is housed at the Ngwane School because of the schools currently involved it is situated at the highest point within the geographical area. WiMAX technologies do not require a clear line of sight (LOS) like WiFi, however large obstructions will still affect the signal path and either disrupt or prevent communication. Thus a high site is still required so that the best possible path is available for wireless communication between the micro base station and the customer premises equipment (CPE) at the various DANs. At Mpume, Mthokwane, Nondobo and Nqabara there is a CPE unit that connects back to the micro base station at Ngwane to allow network traffic to flow between the schools.

The local loop access network connects to the Internet via a Telkom VSAT connection. This equipment is however not housed at the Ngwane School (where the micro base station is installed). The VSAT unit was installed at the Mpume School. The reasons for this are both historical and strategic. The Mpume School was the first school to join the SLL project and so was the logical location (at the time) for VSAT installation. The Ngwane School only joined the project a year after the VSAT link had been installed and so its status as the geographically highest school in the SLL was only determined post VSAT installation. However, it was decided that the VSAT unit should not be moved retrospectively to the Ngwane School in order to ensure that no one school was responsible for all the network facilities. Rather, the schools and communities need to work together, pooling their resources and collective capacities to jointly run and operate the network for the benefit of all.

Mpume thus houses the Access Concentrator (AC) which terminates all incoming PPPoE connections from the DANs (school sites) in the SLL local loop network. Traffic from the other schools is switched at the micro base station and sent to the Mpume School where the AC terminates the PPPoE sessions; each router at each of the other schools runs a PPPoE client and authenticates with a PPPoE service running on the AC. These four schools (Ngwane, Mthokwane, Nondobo and Nqabara) are reliant on the AC in order to reach the Internet, while Mpume is reliant on access to the base station in order to make use of other local services such as VoIP and access to shared resources (off-line content) that are housed at the other schools. In the interest of collaboration and organic development, the principles informing the initial deployment will be maintained as far as possible during the expansion phase.

3   The Expansion

3.1   Technical/Logistic Aspects

There are three aspects to the network expansion project. These include: upgrading the existing networking infrastructure from the 802.16d (fixed WiMAX) technology to the 802.16e (mobile WiMAX) technology; adding five new clients to the new mobile WiMAX base station at Ngwane; and creating a new second "cell" (using the old 802.16d base station equipment) that peers with Ngwane. The upgrade of the WiMAX technology at Ngwane from a fixed wireless WiMAX base station to the mobile 802.16e WiMAX base station allows the SLL to experiment with the use of nomadic stations through the use of USB WiMAX dongles together with laptop computers or WiMAX enable mobile handsets that community members can use from their homes. Badi SSS is a secondary school which is approximately 10km from Ngwane. It was chosen as the host of the second cell because the school infrastructure has recently been renovated as part of the Dinaledi imitative to create centres of excellence in mathematics and Science Education and has a secure and fully furnished 30-seater computer lab. The school also has a water tower, which can be used to mount antennas onto in order to ensure links with remote schools. The second cell allows the network to expand to more sites.

In order to identify potential schools for inclusion in the expansion of the network, two methods were employed: a desktop survey and a site visit. The desktop survey produced visual representation of potential schools on a topographical map, using Radio Mobile and Google Earth, based on a comprehensive list of the possible schools in the area and their GPS coordinates. The set of potential schools had to be narrowed down to ten due to limitations in funding and prospective technical support.

Numerous factors played a role in selecting schools to be included in the newly expanded SLL. One of the key technical considerations was the location of the schools; we needed to connect schools that were within a 20km radius of Ngwane to firstly ensure that the Ngwane and the new base station host school would peer and secondly, because of logical constraints of moving around and supporting the numerous schools. Furthermore, the area around the Dwesa-Cwebe nature reserve is mountainous and there are many zones hidden in the shadows of higher mountain tops. We were able to make use of Radio Mobile to determine the likelihood of connecting schools to either Ngwane or Badi.

Even when considering schools within a 20km radius and not located in dead zones, we still needed to shorten the list further. At this point we considered the schools with at least one educator enrolled in the ACE ICT course mentioned in section 2.2. This yielded a list of nine schools: Badi Senior Secondary School (SSS); Lurwayizo SSS; Zwelidumile SSS; Lurwayizo Junior Secondary School (JSS); Ngoma JSS; Ntubeni JSS; Ngqeza JSS; Lower Nduku JSS; and Kunene Senior Primary School (SPS). While the desktop survey has its merits in narrowing down the list of possible schools, we still needed to conduct a physical site survey in order to confirm that the schools could in fact connect to the base stations at either of the two schools (Badi or Ngwane) and to ensure that the school had no physical constraints, such as a lack of power, preventing their inclusion in the expansion.

Our site survey revealed that one of the nine schools had no electricity with no time frame for connection. A further three schools (Lurwayizo SS, Lurwayizo JSS and Ngoma, JSS) were soon to be connected to the power grid (end of July 2011). In addition, the school principal of Ngwane, a key driver within the adoption of ICTs in the community, suggested a further three new schools (Mevana JSS, Nquba JSS and Hlabizulu JSS) all of which are connected to the power grid.

Another significant finding during the site survey was the need for a 12m mast at Ngwane in order to connect some of the new school sites and in order to peer with Badi. Furthermore, in order to support the link between Badi and Ngwane, we will need to make use of the water tower on the Badi school property to achieve enough ground clearance to facilitate the link between the two schools.

Combining the findings from the desktop and site surveys we found that the following five new schools could be connected to Ngwane: Lurwayizo JSS, Lurwayizo SS, Ngoma JSS, Ntubeni JSS and Ngqeza JSS. While, the following five schools can be connected to Badi: Kunene SPS, Zwelidumile SS, Nquba JSS, Hlabizulu JSS and Mevana JSS (see Figure 2 for a graphical representation of the expansion network, created using Radio Mobile). Within the group of new schools we have a combination of schools that are closer by to the original communities (expanding the facilities there) as well as some schools much further away, such as Zwelidumile and Lurwayizo, allowing new communities to have access to technologies. In addition, the schools that are further away allow the project to test to the capabilities of the equipment of greater distances (up to 16km hops).

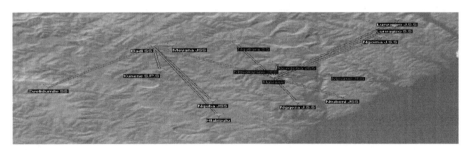

Fig. 2. SLL network's physical/geographical layout; original network sites in red and black with new sites in white and black

After the site visit, a meeting was organised by the researchers involved in the SLL to discuss which schools to prioritise and the nature of the intervention at each school. As mentioned previously there are three aspects to expansion, the network upgrade at the existing network sites, the creation of a new (second) cell within the network and the inclusion of the new distributed access nodes at the identified schools (of which there are 10 in total). Each aspect of the expansion and upgrade will be tackled at different stages:

- **Phase 1.** Upgrade existing network and deploy new cell. Ngwane: Install the mast and replace the base station with the new mobile WiMAX unit. Mpume, Mthokwane, Nondobo and Nqabara: Replace the CPEs for the new mobile

WiMAX units. Badi: Install the old base station; attach a pole to the water tower to house the omni-directional antenna.

- **Phase 2.** Connect seven new schools. Ntubeni and Ngqeza: Mobile WiMAX CPE. Zwelidumile: Old fixed wireless CPE. Kunene, Nquba, Hlabizulu and Mevana: Old fixed wireless CPE
- **Phase 3.** When electricity is available, connect remaining schools. Lurwayizo JSS, Lurwayizo SS and Ngoma: Mobile WiMAX CPE.

3.2   Social Aspects

The expansion of the SLL network was the topic of a session of the ACE ICT group (refer to Section 2.2. for details on this certificate). Twenty educators from the area discussed issues of inclusion/exclusion of schools, priority of connection and criteria to use. The purpose of this exercise was to make sure educators in the area are aware of the expansion and have a chance to contribute in shaping it. It was also an opportunity for us to gauge the opinions of informed stakeholders, many of whom work in the schools we intend to connect. The session was structured in three parts. The first part consisted of preparation. Educators were invited to work in groups on a list of schools in the Dwesa/Cwebe area they felt should be connected to the Internet and provide some motivation. No further details were provided, not to influence the educators' responses.

The second part consisted of an explanation of the rationale for expansion and of some of its constraints, such as number of schools, need for electricity and line of sight with either Ngwane or Badi. Educators were then invited to fill in a four-question questionnaire. Question 1 provided them with a list of schools (based on our proposed list, but with no particular order) and asked them to rank them in order of connection priority. The list excluded Badi which, as was explained, had to be connected as a matter of priority. Question 2 asked them to motivate their ranking. Questions 3 and 4 asked if there were any schools they felt should have been included or excluded from the list (respectively).

The third part consisted of a class discussion. Criteria were summarised, propositions were matched and reconciled with our proposed list and ranking, constraints to the inclusion were reiterated and clarified. This activity highlighted the need to prioritise: schools near the ones already connected; secondary schools; schools with identified ICT champions; new schools serving far-away communities; and schools of good quality and readiness. These are the same criteria which emerged from the analysis of the questionnaire responses and resulted in the following order: 1) Ntubeni, Mevana, Ngqeza (close to schools already connected); Zwelidumile (a faraway secondary school); 3) Lurwayizo (JSS and SSS) and Ngoma (faraway schools with identified ICT champions; and Kunene, Nquba and Hlabizulu (schools with identified ICT champions). The input of local educators also provided us with a list of additional candidates: Ngwane, Nqabara and Luvundu Primary School (close to more senior connected schools); Mpozolo and Dumalisile (secondary schools); and Lower Mbancolo and Lower Nduku (schools with identified ICT champions).

The first criterion was to connect schools near the ones already connected. This was often mentioned as a first or second criterion, together with the presence of ICT champions. It was mentioned by roughly half the class in relation to both ranking (10) and inclusion (12). Educators commented both on the technical advantages and on the possibility for collaboration (e.g. "Ntubeni, Ngoma and Lurwayizo are nearer to Mpume so connection may be easier and also ACE ICT teachers can help each other"). The use of proximity as a criterion clearly informed the proposed ranking, with Mevana and Ntubeni (close to Badi and Ngwane respectively in the first and third positions. Nqabara Primary School, which is close to Nqabara Secondary School which is already connected, was suggested by 8 as a strong candidate for inclusion. In similar cases (e.g. Nqabara and Ngwane Primary) schools will be connected in the foreseeable future to a school included in the expansion via WIFI.

The second criterion was the choice of secondary schools as a priority. This was mentioned by an equal number of educators in response to the ranking (7) and inclusion (6) questions. Making space for secondary schools was also mentioned by 2 educators as a reason to exclude some primary schools from the list (e.g. "Nquba and Kunene could be removed to give chance to two high schools"). The fact that some primary schools are feeder schools for secondary schools was mentioned as an explanation for high ranking (e.g. "Ngoma and Lurwayizo JSS are the feeder schools of Lurwayizo SS"). The only two secondary schools in the list (Lurwayizo and Zwelidumile) were in fifth and seventh position. Secondary schools like Mpozolo and Dumalisile were suggested by 4 for inclusion, while only 1 suggested primary schools (in combination with a secondary). These considerations suggest that prioritising secondary schools was more important for inclusion than ranking.

The third criterion was the presence of an ICT champion, often a participant in the ACE ICT course. This was mentioned as a criterion more often in relation to ranking (11, often after proximity to connected schools) than inclusion (4). Most schools in the list had educators who were part of the ACE ICT course. The presence of two educators from Ngoma is consistent with its second position, while the absence of educators from Nquba JSS and Hlabizulu JSS might explain why they were placed in the two lowest positions and were mentioned by two for exclusion. 5 educators mentioned the presence of ICT champions to motivate for the inclusion of schools not originally on the list, such as Lower Mbangcolo JSS and Lower Nduku JSS.

The fourth criteria was providing connectivity for schools and communities far away from the ones already connected in order to promote a sense of sharing of resources and social cohesion (e.g. "Connectivity should be spread evenly in order to sustain the project"). In terms of ranking, this was mentioned by 6 educators, invariably as the first criteria. The idea of forming a cluster with neighbouring schools and providing access for the surrounding community featured very strongly. In terms of inclusion, this criterion was mentioned by 10 educators. An educator indicated that some schools could be excluded because they were close to the ones already connected in order to "give a chance" to faraway schools (e.g. "I feel that Mevana should be excluded as is closer to Badi where it can access Internet easily"). On the one hand, the use of this criterion led to some interesting discoveries, such as Luvundu JSS which already has a computer lab and can be connected via

Zwelidumile SSS). On the other hand, two educators also suggested schools which are too far away to be considered because of technical constraints (e.g. Ngxunyana JSS, which is more than 40Km away in Willowvale). These unrealistic expectations had to be managed.

Educators also commented on the perceived quality and readiness of schools. Good performance seemed to have more bearing on inclusion (3) than ranking. Perceived readiness of the school management and neighbouring community were mentioned (e.g. "The principal is so interested for this project" and "There will be motivation in the community members"). Lack of electricity was mentioned by 6 educators as a reason not to connect some of the schools. In all cases, this referred to schools which, according to our site visit, have actually been connected to the electricity grid in recent times. Not surprisingly, the general consensus was that, if possible "All schools should benefit"). The presence of technical and logistic constraints gave some grounding to the exercise and teased out the most relevant criteria. These criteria will be probed at a meeting involving the whole community.

4   Conclusions

In this paper we discussed the framework for the extension of the Siyakhula Living Lab, an ICT4D project based in a rural area in South Africa. Consistent with the Living lab approach, we took both technical and social aspects into consideration. The framework we proposed in this paper relies on general principles, key dimensions and two sets of operational criteria (technical and social). General principles such as interdependence of the schools and system redundancy which had informed the initial deployment were upheld during the expansion.

The expansion presented two dimensions: inclusion and priority. With respect to inclusion, a decision had to be made on which schools it was possible and advisable to connect. The possibility of inclusion was dictated by technical and logistic constraints. The advisability was dictated by more social aspects, such as the presence of a potential ICT champion. A technical/logistic constrain was the creation of a second cell, required by the funder. Once this requirement was satisfied, the priority was dictated by social considerations.

Two sets of criteria emerged relating to technical and social aspects respectively. The criteria relating to technical and logistic aspects were proximity to the Dwesa/Cwebe area, presence of electricity and line of sight with one of the two proposed nodes. The criteria relating to social aspects were proximity and collaboration with schools already connected, level of school (i.e. secondary), presence of an ICT champion and providing access to new clusters of schools and communities. It is important to note that both sets of criteria were considered by both the technical survey team and the group of educators in the ACE ICT course.

The framework presented in this paper is by no means exhaustive and will be revised once the expansion is completed (September 2011). We also realise the limitations of our methodology due to possible bias and lack of knowledge of some of the participants. However, we believe this paper represents a meaningful contribution to modelling ICT penetration in Africa and a possible reference for similar experiences.

References

1. Goldstuck, A.: Internet Access in South Africa 2010: A Comprehensive Study of the Internet Access Market in South Africa 2010: World Wide Worx (2010)
2. Statistics South Africa. Census 2001: Investigation into appropriate definitions of urban and rural areas for South Africa. Discussion document. Report no. 03-03-20 (2001), http://www.statssa.gov.za/census01/html/UrbanRural.pdf (cited February 26, 2009)
3. South African Consulate General. Communications (2004), http://www.southafrica-newyork.net/consulate/telecom.htm (cited May 2004)
4. Siebörger, I., Terzoli, A.: WiMAX for rural SA: The experience of the Siyakhula Living Lab. In: Southern African Telecommunication Networks & Applications Conference: A society enabled by Innovation and Applications, Stellenbosch, South Africa (2010)
5. van Reijswoud, V.: Appropriate ICT as a Tool to Increase Effectiveness in ICT4D: Theoretical Considerations and Illustrating Cases. The Electronic Journal of Information Systems in Developing Countries 38(9), 1–18 (2009)
6. Wired. Internet a Human Right (2011), http://www.wired.com/threatlevel/2011/06/internet-a-human-right
7. Pade, C., Siebörger, I., Thinyane, H., Dalvit, L.: The Siyakhula living lab: a holistic approach to rural development through ICT in rural South Africa. In: ICTs and Sustainable Solutions for the Digital Divide: Practical Approaches - Development Informatics and Regional Information Technologies: Theory, Practice and the Digital Divide, IGI Global (2010)
8. Browne, D., Leitch, A.: Case Study of Telkom South Africa's Centre of Excellence Postgraduate Research Programme. In: IST-Africa 2009, Uganda (2009)
9. Palmer, R., Timmermans, H., Fay, D.: From Conflict to Negotiation Nature-based development on the South African Wild Coast. HSRC Press, Pretoria (2002)
10. Brandt, I., Terzoli, A., Hodgkinson-Williams, C.: Models of Internet Connectivity in Previously Disadvantaged Secondary Schools in the Eastern Cape. In: Southern African Telecommunication Networks & Applications Conference: A Future Fuelled by Communications 2004 (2004)
11. Kling, R.: Learning about information technologies and social change: The contribution of social informatics. The Information Society 16(3), 217–232 (2000)
12. Mulder, I., et al.: Real World Innovation in Rural South Africa. The Electronic Journal for Virtual Organisations and Networks 10, 8–20 (2008)
13. Kavhai, M., Osunkunle, O., Dalvit, L.: The impact of rural ICT Projects in South Africa – A Case Study of Dwesa, Transkei, Eastern Cape South Africa. In: Communication Department 2010, University of Fort Hare, Alice (2010)

Effect of Attitude towards SMS Technology and Its Applications on Blood Donation Behaviour

Harry H. Gombachika and Maganizo D. Monawe

The Polytechnic, University of Malawi
Private Bag 303, Chichiri, Blantyre 3, Malawi
{Hgombachika,mmonawe}@gmail.com

Abstract. This paper assesses the effect of attitude towards SMS technology and SMS based reminders on blood donation behaviour through a survey using a self-administered questionnaire. Specifically, the study assesses the attitude towards SMS technology and content of SMS based reminders among blood donors of the Malawi Blood Transfusion Service. Furthermore, the paper assesses the relationship between attitude towards SMS technology and SMS based reminders on one hand and blood donation behaviour on the other.

The paper has shown that blood donors at the Malawi Blood Transfusion Service have positive attitude towards the SMS technology and SMS message content on all dimensions. Although the results have shown that blood donors attitude towards SMS technology was positive irrespective demographic variations, the results have also shown that level of education of the donors moderates their attitude towards the content of SMS message with donors without formal education qualification exhibiting relatively negative attitude compared with those with formal qualification. However, the survey was limited to effects of overall attitude towards SMS technology on intention to donate blood. Since intention to donate blood is a socially accepted behaviour, the results may have been biased by respondents who may have given socially acceptable responses while their actual position may have been different. Furthermore, dimensions that significantly contribute to these relationships were not examined.

Keywords: Short Message Service (SMS), Attitude towards SMS Technology, Blood donation behaviour.

1   Introduction

The demand for blood in Malawian hospitals exceeds the available supply because of high prevalence of anaemic conditions such as HIV/AIDS, malaria, malnutrition and others. Although individuals can donate blood up to four times a year, trends have shown that most do not come back for a repeat donation [1]. Voice call reminders have been used to encourage repeated blood donations; however, they are expensive [2]. Although, there has been an increase in the use of mobile phone short message service [3], little or no effort has been made to use them to encourage repeated blood donations.

R. Popescu-Zeletin et al. (Eds.) AFRICOMM 2011, LNICST 92, pp. 239–247, 2012.
© Institute for Computer Sciences, Social Informatics and Telecommunications Engineering 2012

On the other hand, there has been an increase in the number of sectors that have deployed Short Message Service (SMS) function of a mobile phone. An SMS is GSM functionality that uses the signalling channel of the GSM network. The SMS started as a supplementary service to voice communication through transmission of simple text message limited to 160 characters by the mobile application part (MAP) protocol in GSM [4]. The technology has however been used to address an array of issues in recent years. Furthermore, several studies have been conducted to understand attitudes towards SMS in commercial activities such as advertising [2,5,6] and in activities that are of benefit to individuals [7-10].

In health sector, SMS applications have been used to improve the convenience, speed, and accuracy of diagnostic tests; monitoring chronic conditions, medication adherence, appointment keeping, medical test result delivery; and improving patient-provider communication, health information communication, remote diagnosis, data collection, disease and emergency tracking, and access to health records [11]. Specifically, research studies on the use of SMS technology to provide reminder service have received much attention mainly for health promotion and monitoring, and appointment keeping for patients [12]. Koshy et al., [13] investigated the effectiveness of mobile-phone short message service (SMS) reminders for ophthalmology outpatient appointments and they found that non-attendance rate was 38% lower for patients who received the SMS reminders than in those who did not receive. Similarly, Liew et al. [14] investigated if text messaging reminders can help reduce nonattendance of hospital appointments. They found that attendance was high in those who received SMS reminders than in those who did not. Furthermore, Armstrong et al. in [8] evaluated the effect of text messaging to sunscreen application adherence. They found that adherence was high in those who received SMS reminders than those who did not with a difference of 26.1%. These results however contradict research by Ollivier et al. [15] who found no difference in chemoprophylaxis compliance, partly due to respondents' negative attitude towards the chemoprophylaxis and not necessarily the SMS reminders. We can therefore conclude that SMS reminders can help change the behaviour of respondents. These studies were however limited to applications where the individuals had a direct benefit from the reminders. It could be interesting to find out if similar results are obtained in applications where individuals are not benefiting directly from the activity such as blood donation. In other words, little focus has been put on exploring attitudes and behaviour towards the use of SMS technology in voluntary activities where the individuals are not directly benefiting.

Although the cheaper SMS texting has been found to be as effective as the expensive voice call reminders [2] no further research has been conducted to assess the relationship between attitudes towards SMS reminders and behaviour towards blood donation. Therefore this study assessed the influence of attitude towards SMS technology and SMS based reminders on blood donation behaviour. Specifically the study assessed the attitude towards SMS technology and content of SMS based reminders among blood donors. Furthermore, the study assessed the relationship between attitude towards SMS technology and SMS based reminders on one hand and blood donation behaviour on the other.

The remainder of the paper is arranged as follows: Section 2 reviews the available literature while section 3 presents the methodology that was used in this study. Section 4 presents and discusses the results of the study. Finally, section 5 concludes the paper.

2   Theoretical Framework

Conceptually, attitude is used to understand and predict people's reaction to an object or change and how behaviour can be influenced [16] and is defined as a learned orientation, or disposition, toward an object or situation, which provides a tendency to respond favourably or unfavourably to the object or situation [17]. There are three models used to understand attitudes towards technology, however, only two models are applicable to SMS technology.

The first model focuses on the acceptance of the SMS technology based on Theory of Planned Behaviour (TPB) [18] and Theory of Reasoned Action (TRA) [19] resulting in Technology Acceptance Model (TAM). TAM represents the antecedents of technology usage through beliefs about two factors: the perceived usefulness (PU) and perceived ease of use (PEOU) of a technology. Perceived usefulness is defined as the degree to which a person believes that using a particular system would enhance his or her job performance while perceived ease of use refers to the degree to which a person believes that using a particular system would be free of effort. A comprehensive meta-analysis of TAM is presented in [20,21]. Recently, the perspective of subjective norms was included. Subjective norms refer to the extent to which an individual believes that people who are important or influential to him or her think he or she should perform the behaviour in question [22].

Several researchers have assessed the attitude towards SMS technology using TAM . Yan, et al. [23] used TAM to assess attitude towards SMS technology and usage and found that perceived usefulness, ease of use, and subjective norms lead to attitudinal changes towards text messaging and usage. Similarly, Aripin and Omar [24] found that attitude towards SMS usage is influenced by perception that SMS is easy to use, useful, fun, and expressive. However, Tang and Wong [25] investigated the role of permission towards the attitudes of SMS message recipients. They found that consumers had negative attitude towards mobile text messaging as a communication channel. These studies, however, focused on commercial applications.

The second model focuses on the attitude towards content of the SMS message. Differentiating between attitudes towards the technology itself and attitude towards usage is important because it is possible for people to hold positive attitudes towards the technology and negative attitude towards its usage [20]. Towards that end, Ducoffe [26] developed a model depicting the dimensions of entertainment, informativeness and irritation used to determine consumers' attitudes towards Internet advertising. Furthermore, Brackett and Carr [27] added a dimension to the model namely credibility and used the model to test consumer attitudes towards web advertising. Therefore the model that is used to assess attitude towards the content of the SMS message in this study has four dimensions: entertainment, informativeness, irritation and credibility which have been used widely to study attitudes towards SMS technology in advertising.

Tsang et al. [19] investigated consumer attitudes towards mobile advertising using Short Message Service. Similarly, Suher and Ispir [2] found that the respondents held negative attitudes towards receiving mobile ads because they found them irritating. However, they found out that respondents attitudes were however favourable for advertisements that were sent with permission. These findings agree with early researchers [28] although SMS advertising has been stated to be a more effective medium to generate consumer response [29].

The process of donating blood is a reasoned action requiring cognitive evaluation of available information before making the decision to donate. For a voluntary blood donor who has received an SMS reminder, the reminder becomes one input into the cognitive process of deciding the behaviour of either donating or not donating.

3   Methodology

The study took place at the Malawi Blood Transfusion Service (MBTS). MBTS is a Government of Malawi institution mandated to coordinate the process of blood supply to hospitals. Both the MBTS and the Ministry of Health in Malawi provided clearance for the study.

Data was collected through a self administered questionnaire that was developed based on models for assessing attitude towards SMS technology and attitude towards content of SMS messages. The questionnaire consisted four parts. Firstly, the questionnaire consisted of items that measure respondents' attitude towards SMS technology based on TAM's 3 dimensions. Secondly, it consisted of items that measure respondents' attitude towards the content of SMS message. Thirdly, the questionnaire had an item that measures the respondents' intention to donate blood after receiving an SMS based reminder. All items were measured on a five-point Likert scale (1=strongly disagree to 5=strongly agree). Finally, the instrument included questions related to demographic data.

The sample was randomly drawn from a population of blood donors who had previously received SMS based reminders to donate blood. A total of 120 questionnaires were distributed to a randomly selected sample from a population of 1137 blood donors. However, only 114 questionnaires were correctly completed and returned representing a response rate of 95%.

Both descriptive and inferential statistical analyses were carried out using SPSS. Descriptive statistical analysis was used to summarize the results while inferential statistics was used to test the relationships.

This research ensured that particulars of respondents were anonymous so that the data collected would not be traced back to them. Furthermore, permission was sought and granted from relevant authorities before conducting the research to ensure that all ethical issues were taken on board. The Malawi Blood Transfusion Service was requested to provide clearance to access blood donor data and the Ministry of Health was requested to provide ethical clearance.

4   Results

Demographic Characteristics of the Respondents

Table 1 summarizes the demographic characteristics of the respondents. The results show that the majority of the respondents (41.2%) were young (18-24 years) while some (8.7%) interestingly were in the senior (45years and above) age category. In addition, the results show that most of the respondents (38.9%) had a secondary school qualification (MSCE) while 9.8 % were primary school dropouts. Furthermore, the results showed that most of the respondents (72.8%) were male. Finally, the results showed that the majority were single (61.8%). Interestingly 1.8% of the respondents indicated that they were widowed.

Table 1. Characteristics of the Respondents

Variable	Attribute	Percent
Age (years)	55 and above	2.6
	45-54	6.1
	35-44	17.5
	25-34	32.5
	18-24	41.2
Academic Qualification	Postgraduate	8.8
	Bachelors	12.4
	Diploma	7.1
	MSCE	38.9
	JCE	16.8
	PLSCE	6.2
	Primary school dropouts	9.8
Gender	Female	27.2
	Male	72.8
Marital Status	Single	61.8
	Married	36.4
	Widowed	1.8

SMS Technology Acceptance

Table 2 presents the survey results on attitude towards SMS technology using technology acceptance model on three dimensions, namely, Ease of Use, Usefulness, and Subjective Norms.

Firstly, the results show the items used to measure respondents attitude towards SMS technology were reliable on all the three dimensions, with Cronbach's Alpha values above the conventional minimum of 0.70 [30]. This means that there was internal consistency among the items used for measurement scales for the three technology acceptance model dimensions. This supports meta-analysis results of the TAM model reported by Yousafzai et.al [20,21] that perceived usefulness and perceived ease of use are robust constructs with high predictive validity and they concluded that these constructs can be used in varying technological and organization context.

Secondly, the results show that the respondents had an overall positive attitude towards SMS technology ($M=4.200$, $SD=0.723$) on a five points scale. Furthermore, the results show that the respondents had a positive attitude towards SMS technology on all the three dimensions; ease of use ($M=4.414$, $SD=0.785$), usefulness ($M=4.194$, $SD=0.932$) and subjective norm ($M=3.994$, $SD=0.974$). This means that blood donors at the MBTS have a positive attitude towards SMS technology and can use SMS technology for various applications including receiving reminders for blood donation. This contradicts the results reported by Tang and Wong [25] who found that consumers had negative attitude towards SMS sent without prior permission. Furthermore, this contradicts Muk [31] who found that most of online consumers found receiving mobile adverts through their mobile phones irritating and intrusive.

Table 2. Attitude towards SMS technology

Dimension	Mean (standard Deviation)	Scale Reliability (Cronbach's Alpha)
Perceived Ease of Use	4.413 (0.785)	0.778
Perceived SMS Usefulness	4.194 (0.932)	0.865
Subjective Norms	3.994 (0.974)	0.778
Overall SMS Technology acceptance	4.200 (0.723)	

Finally, the difference in means of the overall attitude towards SMS technology based on respondents characteristics (age, education qualification, marital status and gender) were analysed using one-way analysis of variance (ANOVA). The results show that there was no significant statistical difference in means of the overall SMS technology acceptance based on age $F(4)=0.378$, $p>0.05$; qualification $F(7)=1.197$, $p>0.05$; marital status $F(2)=0.356$, $p>0.05$; and gender $t(112)=-0.508$, $p>0.05$. This means that these donors have positive attitude towards SMS technology irrespective of age, education level, marital status or gender. However, Yousafzai et. al [20,21] suggested that respondents or subjects characteristics accounted for the large size variances in the TAM variables.

Attitude towards SMS Message Content
Table 3 presents the survey results on attitude towards SMS message content on four dimensions, namely, entertainment, informativeness, irritation, and credibility.

Firstly, the results show the items used to measure respondents' attitude towards SMS message content were reliable on all the four dimensions, with Cronbach's Alpha values above the conventional minimum of 0.70 [30]. This means that there was internal consistency among the items used for measurement scales for the attitude towards SMS message content dimensions. As stated earlier on, this suggests that the four dimensions are robust and have high predictive validity. We can therefore conclude that the model can be used in various technological and organization context.

Secondly, the results show that the respondents had an overall positive attitude towards SMS message content $(M=4.265, SD=0.725)$ on a five points scale. Furthermore, the results show that the respondents had a positive attitude towards SMS message content on all the four dimensions; entertainment $(M=4.429, SD=0.913)$, informativeness $(M=4.496, SD=0.833)$, irritation $(M=3.903, SD=1.160)$ and credibility $(M=4.248, SD=1.007)$. This means that blood donors at the MBTS have an overall positive attitude towards SMS message content.

Table 3. Attitude towards SMS message content

Dimension	Mean (standard Deviation)	Scale Reliability (Cronbach's Alpha)
Entertainment	4.429 (0.913)	0.825
Informativeness	4.496 (0.833)	0.782
Irritation	3.903 (1.160)	0.769
Credibility	4.248 (1.007)	0.767
Overall attitude towards Content	**4.265 (0.725)**	

Finally, the difference in means of the overall attitude towards SMS message content based on respondents characteristics (age, education qualification, marital status and gender) were analysed using ANOVA. The results show that there was no significant statistical difference in means of the overall attitude towards SMS message content based on age $F(4)=0.669$, $p>0.05$; marital status $F(2)=0.022$, $p>0.05$; and gender $t(112)=0.616$, $p>0.05$. However there was a statistical significant difference in the overall attitude towards SMS message content based on education qualification $F(7)=2.397$, $p<0.05$. The attitude towards SMS message for primary school dropouts ($M=3.443$, $SD=0.705$) was lower than that for those with MSCE ($M=4.398$, $SD=0.593$). or JCE ($M=4.395$, $SD=0.788$) and the differences were statistically significant $p<0.05$,   and $p<0.05$, respectively. This suggests that education level moderates attitude towards SMS message content. Primary school dropout donors exhibited relatively negative attitude towards the content of the SMS message compared with those with higher educational qualification supporting the argument that there exists a differential capacity in terms of education, social skills, connection and language which exacerbates the digital gap [32].

Blood Donation Behaviour and Attitude towards SMS
Person correlation analysis between blood donation behaviour and attitude towards SMS were carried out. The results show that there was a positive and statistically significant relationship between blood donation behaviour on one hand and attitude towards SMS technology acceptance $r(112)=0.40$, $p<0.05$ and the content of SMS message $r(112)=0.30$, $p<0.05$, on the other. These results suggest that intention to donate blood after receiving an SMS message is positively influenced by donors' attitude towards SMS technology and SMS message content. However, the influence of the individuals' characteristics on the direct and strength of the relationship was not examined.

5   Conclusion

In this paper, we have assessed the effect of attitude towards SMS technology and SMS based reminders on blood donation behaviour through a survey using a self-administered questionnaire. Specifically, we have assessed the attitude towards SMS technology and content of SMS based reminders among blood donors. Furthermore, we have assessed the relationship between attitude towards SMS technology and SMS based reminders on one hand and blood donation behaviour on the other.

The paper has shown that blood donors at the Malawi Blood Transfusion Service have positive attitude towards the SMS technology and SMS message content on all dimensions. Furthermore, the results have shown that level of education of the donors moderates their attitude towards the content of SMS message with primary school drop outs exhibiting relatively negative attitude compared with those with formal qualification. However, the survey was limited to effects of overall attitude towards SMS technology on intention to donate blood. Since intention to donate blood is a socially accepted behaviour, the results may have been biased by respondents who may have given socially acceptable responses while their actual position may have been different. Furthermore, dimensions that significantly contribute to these relationships were not examined.

Acknowledgement. This study was conducted with funding from the University of Malawi – Polytechnic Research and Publication committee. We therefore accordingly acknowledge such financial support.

References

1. Manda, T.D.: Understanding Opportunities and Challenges in Using Mobile Phones as a Means for Health Information Access and Reporting: A Case Study from Malawi. Master of Science in Information Systems thesis, University of Oslo (2009)
2. Suher, H.K., Ispir, N.B.: SMS Advertising in Turkey: Factors Affecting Consumer Attitudes. Selçuk Üniversitesi Sosyal Bilimler Enstitüsü Dergisi 21, 447–458 (2009)
3. Scherr, D., Zweiker, R., Kollmann, A., Kastner, P., Schreier, G., Fruhwald, F.M.: Mobile phone-based surveillance of cardiac patients at home. Journal of Telemedicine and Telecare 12, 255–261 (2006)
4. Agarwal, N., Chandran-Wadia, L., Apte, V.: Capacity Analysis of the GSM Short Message Service. In: The Proceedings of the National Conference on Communications, Bangalore, India (2004), http://www.cse.iitb.ac.in/~varsha/allpapers/wireless/ncc03cam.pdf
5. Tsang, M.M., Ho, S.C., Liang, T.P.: Consumer Attitudes Toward Mobile Advertising: An Empirical Study. International Journal of Electronic Commerce 8(3), 65–78 (2004)
6. Haghirian, P., Madlberger, M.: Consumer Attitude toward Advertising via Mobile Devices - An Empirical Investigation among Austrian Users. In: Proceedings of European Conference of Information Systems, Regensburg, Germany (2005), http://aisel.aisnet.org/ecis2005/44/
7. Downer, S.R., Meara, J.G., Da Costa, A.C.: Use of SMS text messaging to improve outpatient attendance. Med. J. Aust. 183(7), 366–368 (2005)
8. Armstrong, A.W., et al.: Text-message reminders to improve sunscreen use: A randomized, controlled trial using electronic monitoring. Archives of Dermatology 145(11), 1230–1236 (2009)
9. Foley, J., O'Neill, M.: Use of mobile telephone short message service as a reminder: The effect on patient attendance. European Archives of Paediatric Dentistry (2009), http://www.thefreelibrary.com/
10. Mao, Y., Yantao, Z., Suodi, Z.: Mobile phone text messaging for pharmaceutical care in a hospital in China. Journal of Telemedicine and Telecare 14, 410–414 (2008)

11. Cole-Lewis, H., Kershaw, T.: Text Messaging as a Tool for Behavior Change in Disease Prevention and Management. Epidemiologic Reviews 32(1), 56–69 (2010)
12. Blake, H.: Innovation in practice: mobile phone technology in patient care. British Journal of Community Nursing 13(4), 160–165 (2008)
13. Koshy, E., Car, J., Majeed, A.: Effectiveness of mobile-phone short message service (SMS) reminders for ophthalmology outpatient appointments: Observational study. BMC Ophthalmology 8(9), 1471–2415 (2008)
14. Liew, S., et al.: Text messaging reminders to reduce non-attendance in chronic disease follow-up: a clinical trial. British Journal of general practice 59(569), 916–920 (2009)
15. Ollivier, L., et al.: Use of short message service (SMS) to improve malaria chemoprophylaxis compliance after returning from a malaria endemic area. Malaria Journal 8(236), 1475–2875 (2009)
16. Fishbein, M., Ajzen, I.: Belief, Attitude, Intention and Behaviour: An Introduction to Theory and Research. Addison-Wesley, Reading (1975)
17. Gross, R.: Psychology: The Science of Mind and Behaviour. Hodder and Stoughton, London (2001)
18. Ajzen, I.: The Theory of Planned Behavior. Organizational Behavior and Human Decision Processes 50(2), 179–211 (1991)
19. Tsang, M.M., Ho, S.C., Liang, T.P.: Consumer Attitudes Toward Mobile Advertising: An Empirical Study. International Journal of Electronic Commerce 8(3), 65–78 (2004)
20. Yousafzai, S.Y., Foxall, G.R., Pallister, J.G.: Technology acceptance: a meta-analysis of the TAM: Part 1. Journal of Modeling in Management 2(3), 251–280 (2007a)
21. Yousafzai, S.Y., Foxall, G.R., Pallister, J.G.: Technology acceptance: a meta-analysis of the TAM: Part 2. Journal of Modeling in Management 2(3), 281–304 (2007b)
22. Venkatesh, V., Davis, F.D.: A theoretical extension of the technology acceptance model: Four longitudinal field studies. Management Science 46(2), 186–205 (2000)
23. Yan, X., Gong, M.T., James, Y.L.: Two tales of one service: user acceptance of short message service (SMS) in Hong Kong and China. Journal of Policy, Regulation & Strategy for Telecommunication, Information & Media 8(1), 16–28 (2006)
24. Aripin, N., Omar, S.Z.: Perception and Attitude of Short Messaging Services (SMS) Among Students of Universiti Utara Malaysia. Paper presented at the International conference on Media, Culture and Society, Malaysia (2007)
25. Tang, E.P.Y., Wong, M.M.T.: Consumers' attitude towards mobile advertising: The role of permission. Review of Business Research 8(3), 181–185 (2008)
26. Ducoffe, R.H.: Advertising value and advertising on the web. Journal of Advertising Research 36(5), 21–35 (1996)
27. Brackett, L.K., Carr Jr., B.N.: Cyberspace advertising vs. other media: Consumer vs. mature student attitudes. Journal of Advertising Research 45(5), 23–32 (2001)
28. Zanot, E.: Public attitudes toward advertising: The American experience. International Journal of Advertising 13, 3–15 (1984)
29. Barnes, S.: Wireless digital advertising: Nature and implications. International Journal of Advertising 21(3), 399–420 (2002)
30. Nunnally, J.C., Bernstein, I.H.: Psychometric Theory, 3rd edn. McGraw-Hill, New York (1994)
31. Muk, A.: Consumers' intentions to opt in to SMS advertising. International Journal of Advertising 26(2), 177–198 (2007)
32. Toyoma, K.: Can technology eend poverty, Forum (November/December 2010)

The Intelligent City Operations Centre: An Integrated Platform for Crisis Management

Mweene Monze

IBM Software Group
IBM Park, 70 Rivonia Road, Sandhurst 2196, South Africa
mweenem@za.ibm.com

Abstract. Emergency and disaster management – collectively referred to here as crisis management – have traditionally been practised as distinct and separate disciplines. In recent years, however, it has been recognised that crisis management is a complex, multi-disciplinary problem that requires continuous collaboration among all stakeholders in order to be effective. At the same time, technologies have emerged that can support cross-disciplinary approaches to crisis management. This paper describes the essential components of the 'city crisis management problem', and then maps the people, process and technology requirements that emerge from this problem description. The intent is to identify the critical success factors by establishing clear linkages between the problem requirements, the solution space and crisis management best practices. The paper also describes an embodiment of the Intelligent City Operations Centre concept, an ICT platform that can be specifically configured to address these requirements in developing countries.

Keywords: crisis management, disaster management, emergency management, mobile applications, city management, collaboration.

1   Introduction

Instances abound of cities operating with relatively autonomous domains, where little or no collaboration exists in their day-to-day operational activities. Although the city is supposed to be a single entity, it generally delivers services through distributed means – for example, water, energy, public safety and housing services are typically delivered by different, and often independent, city agencies. The need exists for operational collaboration across these siloed domains, in order to facilitate more efficient service delivery. This is particularly true in the case of crisis management services, where it is recognised that collaborative, multi-disciplinary techniques often deliver the most effective interventions [1]. At the same time, technologies have emerged that enable Smarter Cities[1] to apply collaborative response approaches to

---

[1] Launched in 2005, Smarter Cities [2] is part of a multi-programme International Business Machines (IBM) corporate campaign known as Smarter Planet [3], whose goal is to develop and deploy technologies that promote more judicious use of our planet's scarce resources.

R. Popescu-Zeletin et al. (Eds.) AFRICOMM 2011, LNICST 92, pp. 248–257, 2012.
© Institute for Computer Sciences, Social Informatics and Telecommunications Engineering 2012

crisis management. The focus is on cities because of their increasingly important role as the social, economic and political hubs of a globally integrated world [2].

In line with the AFRICOMM 2011 goal to share perspectives and opportunities on technologies relevant to developing countries, this paper motivates the notion of the "Intelligent City Operations Centre" (iCOC) as an ICT tool to aid crisis management in cities. The rationale is that cities need to become smarter in the way that they manage hazardous events, and the iCOC supports this goal by providing an integrated and consistent view of resources across city domains, that inform critical decisions during a crisis. In a crisis event, the iCOC effectively defines a shared problem space where various city agencies can decompose problems in an orderly fashion, so that they can be understood and acted upon in a coordinated manner. The use of an integrated, collaborative, cross-domain platform to manage both day-to-day and crisis operations is an essential pre-cursor for effective disaster and emergency management. The paper also outlines the anatomy of the crisis management problem, and presents an IBM embodiment of the iCOC, explaining how some of its features can aid crisis resolution in cities.

2   Smarter Cities

Operationally, cities may be viewed as comprising six fundamental domains composed of different networks, infrastructures and environments related to their key functions: people, business, transport, communication, water and energy [1]. Each of these domains delivers services that are essential to sustain modern metropolitan environments. As an example, the people system includes public safety, health and education and is central to citizens' quality of life; water and energy are also core city services.

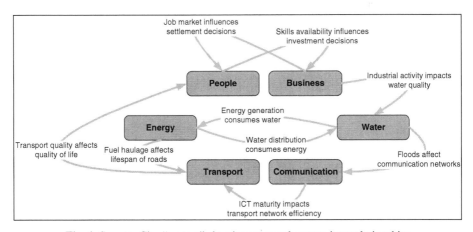

Fig. 1. Smarter City "system" showing some subsystem interrelationships

These domains effectively represent a "system of core subsystems" since they interconnect in a systemic fashion (Figure 1). These systems are characterised by multiple inter-dependencies among them, and the challenges they face interact in complex ways, with consequences that are sometimes difficult to predict and assess.

A Smarter City acts as a single entity with interconnected subsystems where city domains share significant event information to aid smart decision-making which, ideally, optimises the overall performance and efficiency. These operations are supported by Smarter City technology, which provides an integrated view of city-wide issues and enables coordinated decision-making. The technology delivers key capabilities such as holistic monitoring of city services and operations, effective management of planned and unexpected events, and predictive analytics to resolve problems earlier with optimized service delivery. These capabilities enable city executives to understand the inter-dependencies between the city's subsystems, empowering them to make informed decisions in a collaborative fashion in real time.

3   The Crisis Management Problem

Crisis management refers both to managing (hopefully) occasional disasters and as well as day-to-day emergency operations. In order to understand the role of the iCOC within a crisis management context, it is necessary to explain the essential components of the problem.

3.1   Crisis Management Continuum

The crisis management continuum shown in Figure 2 (based on [6]) provides a useful discussion framework that views the problem as a repeating cycle that consists of three distinct but overlapping phases.

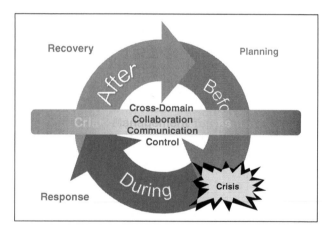

Fig. 2. The Crisis Management Continuum

- *Disaster Planning*: The collective term use to encompass all actions taken prior to the occurrence of a disaster in order to mitigate risk and impact. It includes preparedness, which consists of activities designed to minimize loss of life and damage, organize the temporary removal of people and property from a threatened location, and facilitate timely and effective rescue, relief and rehabilitation. It also includes measures put in place to mitigate long-term risks, such as early warning processes that monitor situations in communities or areas known to be vulnerable to slow onset hazards (e.g. famine early warning).

- *Emergency Response*: The period during which extraordinary measures have to be taken. Special emergency procedures and authorities may be applied to support human needs, sustain livelihoods, and protect property to avoid the onset of disaster. This phase can encompass pre-disaster, disaster alert, disaster relief and recovery periods. An emergency phase may be quite extensive, as in a slow onset disaster such as a famine. It can also be relatively short-lived, as after an earthquake.
- *Disaster Recovery*: Describes the post-disaster phase of a disaster. It includes rehabilitation, which consists of the operations and decisions taken after a disaster with a view to restoring a stricken community to its former living conditions, while encouraging and facilitating the necessary adjustments to the changes caused by the disaster. Disaster recovery also includes reconstruction, which comprises the actions taken to re-establish a community after a period of rehabilitation subsequent to a disaster. Actions would include construction of permanent housing, full restoration of all services, and complete resumption of the pre-disaster state.

The phases in the crisis continuum are distinct in the sense that they deliver services specific to each phase, but overlap in practice because they tend to occur concurrently, and not sequentially, in time. Different activities become more or less prominent and frequent, depending on the lifecycle stage of a crisis and the relationship between the hazardous event and the vulnerability of the affected communities and resources.

3.2   Team Collaboration, Communication and Control

Experiences from previous hazardous events in South Africa [3] have highlighted shortcomings in crisis management practice that frequently manifest themselves in other countries and regions [4], [5]:

- The lack of proactive disaster policy and strategy usually leading to haphazard and reactive responses to disasters.
- Uncoordinated responses to disaster due to unfamiliar and inadequate mechanisms for team collaboration communication and control.
- Incomplete and inconsistent data and knowledge related to disaster management and the local environment, which makes it difficult to identify those who need relief, and to determine how to deliver that relief.

A seminal understanding that has been gleaned from these events is that crisis management operations can involve a large number and variety of agencies (see panel below, as an example), and that collaboration between them needs to be continuous, although it typically peaks during the response phase. These participants need to be managed as one team during a crisis, using four main team management functions:

Johannesburg City Crisis Management Team

- Head: Emergency Services
- Head of the Disaster Management Centre
- Director of Metro Police
- Regional Directors: 11 Regions
- Regional Managers: Health and Social Services
- Regional Manager: Environmental Health
- Regional Managers: Housing and Urbanization
- Regional Managers: Sport & Recreation

- Managers: People Centres
- Director: City Power
- Director: Joburg Water
- Director: Pikitup (waste management)
- Director: Roads Agency
- Director: City Parks
- Ward councillors and/or committees
- Community leader(s)

Extract from the City of Johannesburg Disaster Management Plan [**Error! Reference source not found.**]: the city crisis management team will comprise any of the above agencies or entities, depending on the nature of the event. In practice the team will often include agencies external to the city, such as national and provincial units, and external Non-Governmental Organisations.

- *Locate*: In preparation for, during, or in response to an event, rapidly identify and assemble a team across agency boundaries.
- *Invite*: Using information provided during the location of those individuals or roles, invite them to collaborate.
- *Authenticate*: Using authentication information previously available or now provided, authenticate those individuals or roles.
- *Collaborate*: Work together, synchronously or asynchronously, to solve a problem or set of problems.

Collaborative, multi-disciplinary approaches are also useful in planning activities, such as hazard identification and mitigation, and recovery tasks that ensure continuity and restoration of service. Thus, best practice mandates mechanisms that support inter-agency collaboration, communication and control at all times, and not just during a response phase.

4   The Intelligent City Operations Centre

The Intelligent City Operations Centre (iCOC) is a concept that draws on the requirements of city day-to-day and crisis management operations, and melds them with commonly available ICTs and best practices to create an intelligent crisis management platform. The iCOC offers a relatively new perspective, even though emergency command or operations centres already exist in many cities to provide security (police), fire, rescue and medical emergency services. These centres generally focus on delivering time-sensitive emergency response services that are aimed at protecting lives and property. On the other hand, planning and recovery have traditionally been viewed as separate disaster management functions, and conducted by different teams with little or no collaboration with emergency response teams. The systems that support these functions are typically implemented as islands, disconnected from any 'line-of-business' systems containing information that is vital for crisis management.

Furthermore, and critically so, experience informs that other city domains, such as water, energy and transportation, do not participate actively in crisis management planning efforts, even though they are obliged to respond during a crisis. Hence the view [3], that "disasters are often managed haphazardly" and therefore "the approach taken to disasters may thus be as costly (or even more costly) than the [hazardous] event itself". This outcome could be due, in part, to the fact that city domains typically implement focused centres to support domain-specific operations only.

The Intelligent City Operations Centre approach differs significantly in several areas:

- It provides greater width and depth of coverage because it is a cross-domain operations centre that encompasses many more domains. Furthermore, it provides capabilities that coordinate crisis management activities across them, by integrating with the 'line-of-business' systems that support these domains.
- It encourages a collaborative approach to all activities, especially decision-making and problem decomposition, by providing pervasive collaborative tools delivered through Web technologies.
- It is architected to address the full range of events from minor (e.g. day-to-day emergency response events) to major (e.g. large scale city disasters).
- It supports several deployment configurations, which make it fit for the operations in developing countries.

The next sections outline the key features of the iCOC from the perspectives of relevance to stakeholders, architecture and intelligent processing.

4.1   Relevance

The Intelligent City Operations Centre provides cross-domain awareness and important status information on city services. Realising this technique requires collaborative involvement from many stakeholders, throughout the lifecycle of the system, including city executives such as mayors or council representatives, citizens, business, and the city domains, amongst others. Each of these individuals or entities has a different role to play in crisis management and requires specific capabilities to collaborate via the iCOC. As examples:

- City executives need summary information that can hep them understand event dynamics and make informed decisions around their resolution;
- Citizens may be consulted when decisions are contemplated that affect their well being; they can also provide early warnings, and may need to be notified, about significant incidents or hazard events.
- City domains must collaborate continuously and provide information that supports executive decision-decision making; to do this they must understand the detailed event dynamics and the impact of certain courses of action both within and across their spheres of jurisdiction.

The implication is that an iCOC must provide capabilities that are relevant to each role – a blanket approach will not succeed here. The IBM iCOC provides its capabilities in personalised views that are structured in a hierarchy, from high-level summary views for city executives to detailed issue decomposition views for operational domain specialists.

4.2   Architecture

- The architecture overview (Figure 3) shows the high-level functional components that comprise the IBM Intelligent City Operations Centre. These include gateways for accessing domain-specific information, analytics to support advanced early problem resolution, and visualisation services that enable visualisation of events, alerts, KPIs, directives and impact assessments, with geospatial representation on maps.

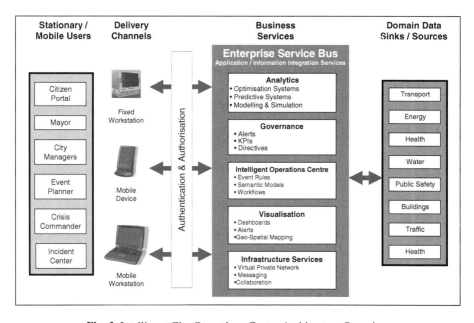

Fig. 3. Intelligent City Operations Centre Architecture Overview

The complementary software infrastructure provisions essential security (authentication and authorisation), collaboration, mobility, infrastructure management and messaging services, amongst others. In addition, the iCOC must also maintain and provide data for historical reporting as well as accounting and audit purposes. Please refer to [10] for a detailed description of the functions and architecture of the IBM Intelligent City Operations Centre.

4.3   Intelligence

So why is the iCOC said to be "intelligent"? With reference to Figure 1, let us suppose a flood event occurs in a part of a city with potentially undesirable consequences. In deciding a course of action, some of the key questions that city executives may need to answer include:

- What is the current extent of water coverage?
- How will the water coverage change in the next hour, day, month and/or year?
- What communities and assets (buildings, roads, communication/energy networks, etc) are affected and how?
- What are consequences of shutting down segments of affected energy and transport networks?

The different components of the iCOC would interact with each other and people to generate the required information. As examples in such a scenario:

- Modelling capabilities could be used estimate the extent of the affected area, and simulation could be used to project dynamic situational changes by hour or day.
- If combined with community and property vulnerability data in the city domain systems, as defined by the disaster management discipline, an impact assessment could begin to be built.
- Predictive systems could be used to evaluate the impact of shutting down portions of the energy network, and optimisation systems invoked to select the 'least cost' alternatives.
- Should decision-makers need unknown domain specifics, then they have the option to acquire such information by collaborating with city domain specialists.

The purpose of this rather simplistic scenario is to illustrate how the intelligence in different components of the iCOC can be brought to play in a crisis. We must note that the concept of the iCOC is wide ranging in scope and in the timescales involved; it is about managing predicted incidents that might or might not happen now or far into the future, as well as incidents happening now in real time. These intelligent capabilities can all make a vital contribution to managing such crisis scenarios in real time. By modelling patterns of subsystem behaviours and interactions, this intelligence allows iCOC users to explore, and thereby predict and assess, the implications of their decisions.

4.4   Fit for Purpose

A key characteristic of any viable solution is that it must meet the requirements of the operational environment in which it will be deployed. The iCOC incorporates features that are designed to leverage the exponential uptake of mobile technologies in developing countries, as well as to address some of their unique challenges, including:

- *Communications infrastructure*: Much of the data ingested by the iCOC will likely be captured on mobile devices in remote areas where communications are patchy; an optional iCOC capability enables IP-based connectivity over multiple protocols including analogue an digital mobile, wireline, radio and satellite networks.

- *Disconnected operations*: For the same reason, the iCOC is designed to support disconnected operations, which allow mobile workers to continue working in areas which have no connectivity. It also supports traditional browser-based technologies, but it should be noted that they are useless in such situations, and that this may change with the emergence of the HTML5 standard which might support disconnected operations in the future [9].
- *Efficient power management*: Rural areas will typically not be connected to the national power grid and will rely, instead, on solar power, especially for mobile devices. Unlike traditional mobile applications, the iCOC mobile platform is based on technologies that only utilise resources on-demand (e.g. network, memory, etc), thereby keeping power consumption extremely low.
- *Skills availability and cost*: The iCOC can be delivered as a near black-box within a cloud infrastructure: the black-box approach reduces 'build-run-operate' expertise requirements, and there is increasing evidence that shared deployments on cloud architectures can reduce costs [11].

5   Conclusion

This paper has introduced the notion of the Intelligent City Operations Centre and showed how it can be deployed to enhance crisis management practice, by providing an integrated, collaborative, cross-domain platform to manage both day-to-day and crisis operations in Smarter Cities. Given that it takes time for teams to start using new collaboration platforms productively, especially in a crisis situation, an important feature of the iCOC concept is that it is designed to also support normal city operations. The paper has also illustrated the relevance, architecture and intelligence embedded within the IBM realisation of the Intelligent City Operations Centre, and highlighted how it addresses some of the key deployment considerations in developing countries.

The motivation for this paper was to stimulate discussion around the role of cross-domain approaches and ICT platforms in the practice of the disaster and emergency management disciplines in developing cities. Future work will focus on reporting the results of iCOC implementations around the world, including projects that are already underway in Gauteng Province, South Africa [12] and Rio de Janeiro, Brazil [13].

References

1. Kristensen, M., Kyng, M., Palen, L.: Participatory Design in Emergency Medical Service: Designing for Future Practice. In: Proceedings of the ACM Conference on Human Factors in Computing Systems CHI 2006, pp. 161–170 (2006)
2. Dirks, S., Keeling, M.: A vision of smarter cities - How cities can lead the way into a prosperous and sustainable future, IBM Institute of Business Value (2009)

3. International Business Machines Corporation,
   http://www.ibm.com/smarterplanet/
4. Government of India, Ministry of Home Affairs, National Disaster Management Division,
   http://www.ndmindia.nic.in/GoIUNDP/ReportPub/
   DM-Statu-%20Report.pdf
5. Association of Caribbean States, http://www.acs-aec.org/
   Documents/Disasters/Projects/ACS_ND_000/
   NDProjectsEval_Williams_eng.pdf
6. United Nations Development Programme: An Overview of Disaster Management, 2nd
   edn. (1992)
7. City of Johannesburg Metropolitan Municipality: Corporate Disaster Management Plan
   (April 4, 2003)
8. South African National Disaster Management Centre: Disaster Management Guidelines for
   Municipalities (2006)
9. The w3 Consortium, http://dev.w3.org/html5/spec/Overview.html
10. Cosgrove, M., Harthoorn, W., Hogan, J., Jabbar, R., Kehoe, M., Meegan, J., Nesbitt, P.:
    Smarter Cities Series: Introducing the IBM City Operations and Management Solution,
    IBM Corporation (2011)
11. The Brooking Institution, http://www.brookings.edu/papers/2010/
    0407_cloud_computing_west.aspx
12. IBM Corporation, http://www-03.ibm.com/press/uk/en/
    pressrelease/24507.wss
13. IBM Corporation,
    http://www-03.ibm.com/press/us/en/pressrelease/33303.wss

Enabling New Interaction Forms and Applications through Next Generation Mobile Platforms for Urban and Rural Africa

Kasper Løvborg Jensen[1] and Gary Marsden[2]

[1] Polytechnic of Namibia
Windhoek, Namibia
leafcastle@acm.org
[2] University of Cape Town
Cape Town, South Africa
gaz@acm.org

Abstract. Mobile phones constitute the most ubiquitous computing platform across Africa and in many rural areas it is the only computer available. Through rapid technological development a new wave of "low-end smartphones" are becoming available and affordable, and in this work we investigate how to use the new features of these devices to enable more natural interaction forms that lower the technical and knowledge threshold for people to access and use mobile ICT solutions in urban and rural African contexts. Specifically we investigate how new sensor-based interactions can be designed for mobile applications and how to implement a software platform for facilitating the development of such applications.

Keywords: HCI4D, ICT4D, mobile, context-aware, sensor-based interaction, NUI.

1 Introduction

While it is well established that people in both urban and rural areas can benefit from information and services provided through ICTs, it is still unclear how to design and deploy such systems in an effective, efficient and sustainable way in the developing world context [1]. Mobile phones constitute the most ubiquitous computing platform across Africa and in many rural areas it is the only computer available. This makes it the optimal platform for ICT solutions, even though it comes with a range of limitations and challenges; not least from the perspective of human-computer interaction [2][3].

Through rapid technological advances a new wave of "low-end smartphones" are becoming available and affordable. In this work we focus on this emerging wave of devices and acknowledge the fact that such technology will eventually reach even the remote areas of Africa. The questions are then: how can this next generation of mobile devices be utilized to enable new interaction forms to lower the technical and knowledge threshold for users to access the benefits of deployed mobile ICT solutions, and how can this pave the way for new information and services for people in both urban and rural areas in Africa?

R. Popescu-Zeletin et al. (Eds.) AFRICOMM 2011, LNICST 92, pp. 258–259, 2012.
© Institute for Computer Sciences, Social Informatics and Telecommunications Engineering 2012

1.1   Towards New Interaction Forms and Applications

Besides the increasing processing power, memory, storage, and data networks, the most interesting features of these new devices come from their range of built-in sensors. These allow application developers to access information about the current environment and situation of device and users such as orientation, acceleration, light intensity, location and proximity to objects and people. It is possible to leverage such information to create more advanced computer systems, and by combining these sensors it is possible to create systems with more natural user interfaces that are e.g. location-based, proximity-based or gesture-based.

Solutions for implementing such interaction forms are already available from the body of research and development within mobile technology and novel interaction paradigms such as ubiquitous, pervasive and context-aware computing. Another branch of research, often referred to as HCI4D (Human Computer Interaction for Development) [3], is concerned with HCI and interaction design methods focused on ICT for developing countries. With the emerging mobile platforms the combined results from both of these endeavors can now find their way into the African context.

The goal of our research is to design, implement and study new interaction forms and investigate how they lower the technical and knowledge thresholds for users to access the benefits of deployed mobile ICT solutions. This can be used to empower semi-literate handset owners to use their technology more effectively. By lowering the barriers to technology usage it will be possible to create and deploy new applications and services for a large target group that were not previously possible or feasible and thus help bringing sustainable ICT solutions to people and communities in developing regions.

As part of this work we also focus on the development and study of a software platform for facilitating easier development and deployment of applications using these new interaction forms. Based on experiences from the development of a previous sensor-enabled context capture tool [4], we aim to provide a generic platform that allows for rapid prototyping and large-scale field testing of mobile applications in both urban and rural Africa.

References

1. Heeks, R.: ICT4D 2.0: The Next Phase of Applying ICT for International Development. Computer 41(6), 26–33 (2008)
2. Marsden, G., Maunder, A., Parker, M.: People are people, but technology is not technology. Phil. Trans. R. Soc. A (366), 3795–3804 (2008)
3. Ho, M.R., Smyth, T.N., Kam, M., Dearden, A.: Human-Computer Interaction for Development: The Past, Present and Future. Information Technologies and International Development 5(4), 1–18 (2009)
4. Jensen, K.L.: Remote and autonomous studies of mobile and ubiquitous applications in real contexts. International Journal of Mobile Human Computer Interaction 3(2), 1–19 (2011)

Author Index

Printed by Publishers' Graphics LLC
BT20130311.19.21.61